T0285639

A MURDER ON THE HILL

THE SECRET LIFE
AND MYSTERIOUS DEATH
OF RUTH MUNSON

ROGER BARR

MINNESOTA
HISTORICAL
SOCIETY PRESS

mnhspress.org

The Minnesota Historical Society Press is a member of the Association of University Presses.

Manufactured in the United States of America

10 9 8 7 6 5 4 3 2 1

♾ The paper used in this publication meets the minimum requirements of the American National Standard for Information Sciences—Permanence for Printed Library Materials, ANSI Z39.48–1984.

International Standard Book Number
ISBN: 978-1-68134-289-4 (paper)
ISBN: 978-1-68134-290-0 (e-book)

Library of Congress Control Number: 2023950042

To Ruth Margaret Munson, a woman made vulnerable by her circumstances, and in memory of all women whose murders remain unsolved.

Contents

On the morning of December 9, 1937, St. Paul firefighters discovered a charred body in the burned-out hallway on the second floor of the long-vacant Aberdeen Hotel. Police detectives quickly identified the body as that of Ruth Munson, a "small-town girl" who had moved to the big city in search of a new opportunity. In Depression-ridden St. Paul, the Ruth Munson murder case was a sensation, grabbing headlines in the daily newspapers for weeks on end.

Everyone knows the arc of a murder mystery: a body is discovered; a sleuth steps forward and searches for clues associated with motive, means, and opportunity. Examining a plethora of clues and casting off the red herrings, the sleuth eventually identifies the murderer, who is brought to justice, providing the reader with a happy ending.

I was attracted to the Ruth Munson murder case because there was no happy ending. Despite an investigation that stretched out over many years, the case was never solved. More than eighty-five years later, many blank spots remain in the narrative that police investigators constructed.

Why wasn't the Ruth Munson murder case ever solved? *That* is the question I set out to answer. And what better place to start than with the police reports themselves? Police records hold all kinds of unproven allegations, and it is important to keep that in mind. But because the case is old and everyone involved is deceased, the St. Paul Police Department allowed me access to the case files, which filled a cardboard bankers box. It contained hundreds of "Miscellaneous Reports" filed by detectives over the course of the investigation, photographs of the crime scene and other important locations, as well as photographs of evidence collected by detectives. It also held several letters written by Ruth Munson and her five-year diary, as well as dozens of tips sent in by citizens—most of which were anonymous. I supplemented these resources by reading hundreds of articles culled from the six daily newspapers that served St. Paul and Minneapolis at the time the case broke, as well as issues of the *St. Paul Recorder* and the *Minneapolis Spokesman*, which served the Black community.

This account is not a traditional murder mystery that follows the familiar arc. It is not a so-called "nonfiction novel," which fills in the blanks to complete, in effect, the arc of a story. This is a book of history, blanks and all.

In "Part 1. The Investigation," the reader steps back into 1937 St. Paul and follows the investigation in real time, hour by hour, then day by day, and later, month by month and year by year. The narrative is confined to what was known in 1937 and in the succeeding years. The reader will be able to follow the clues, discover the red herrings, and, just like the detectives who worked the case, experience frustration when a promising clue leads to a dead end.

The reader should keep in mind that the world was different in 1937. Men and women were usually addressed formally. In polite company, sex was talked about in formal, often awkward terms and couched in euphemisms. Black Americans were commonly referred to as "colored" or "Negro," and on occasion something even worse. Other racial slurs were common. The prejudices of the day were, I believe, a factor in why the case was never solved. The direct quotes from police reports, newspaper articles, letters, and other documents of the period shared here retain almost all of the inappropriate language people used. When not quoting someone directly, I use today's more culturally appropriate words. This shift in language does not minimize the racism that pervaded American culture at the time of the murder and how racism influenced the public discourse and policy making.

In "Part 2. "Autopsy," the reader jumps to the present day. In the same way that a coroner's autopsy seeks to establish the cause of death of a murder victim, this section seeks to discover why this case was never solved. What were the circumstances that made the case difficult? Did the investigation get off track, and if so, how? What opportunities were missed? Were there cultural reasons why a solution to the case was never found? With the benefit of hindsight or the use of current forensics, can this case be solved today?

Back in 1937, the murder of Ruth Munson caused a sensation. But what makes this long-forgotten case worthy of our attention today? This case involves the vulnerability of women, economic insecurity, mistrust of the police, police reform, race, and racism. Unfortunately, many of these issues plague today's culture. Perhaps by studying this case and understanding the complex reasons why it remained unsolved, we can apply the lessons learned to mitigate the impact of these destructive issues in today's culture. To do so would not only benefit our lives today; it would also bestow a measure of meaning and dignity to Ruth Munson, whose life was senselessly taken so many years ago.

Part 1

The Investigation:
December 9, 1937–September 4, 1953

1   "There's a Body Here!"

Thursday, December 9, 1937

St. Paul's Ramsey Hill neighborhood, December 9, 1937, 4:45 A.M. Darkness. To save money during these tough Depression years, the city shut off the streetlights at 2:30 A.M., and they would not come on again until 5:00. On the southwest corner of Dayton Avenue and Virginia Street, right next to the vacant Aberdeen Hotel, several paperboys gathered under the unlit streetlight and shivered in the near-zero temperatures. The boys waited with growing impatience for the arrival of the *St. Paul Pioneer Press*'s route driver, Harold Lewis, who always delivered their copies to this corner by 4:45. On this frigid morning, Lewis was running late. Once they received their papers, the paperboys would fan out into the dark streets to deliver the latest news to their faithful subscribers.[1]

The Aberdeen Hotel, about 1900. *MNHS*

At this early hour, the streets of Minnesota's capital city were quiet. Only the paperboys and the hardiest of souls were out. The men and women who had dressed up and gone out the night before to forget their troubles through a night of drinking, dancing, and (hopefully) romance had either met with good fortune or straggled home during the night's wee, dark hours and crawled into bed. Those men and women facing a new day's work were still tucked warmly in their beds.

Much to the boys' annoyance, Lewis did not arrive with their papers until almost 5:30 A.M. There had been a problem with the presses, he explained. The boys quickly loaded their papers into their shoulder bags and set out. Paperboy Herman Koroschetz on his route passed by the hulking shadow of the Aberdeen Hotel twice—once by the hotel's front entrance at 350 Dayton Avenue and later past the rear of the building, which faced Selby Avenue. In his haste to deliver his papers, return home, and get ready for school at Mechanic Arts High School, the seventeen-year-old paperboy noticed nothing out of the ordinary.[2]

Stephen Westbrook on his delivery route passed by the east side of the Aberdeen on Virginia Street twice, once at the beginning of his route and once at the end. On his second trip by the hotel, he noticed something odd about the iron gates in the hotel's backyard garden that opened onto Virginia Street. "If I'm not mistaken," the eighteen-year-old Westbrook recalled, "other mornings when I come by, they are wired shut, but this particular morning, it seems they were open when I went by. I cannot say positively."[3]

The open gates were noticed by another resident out at this early hour. Mrs. L. Bradbury left her apartment at 207 Virginia every morning at precisely 5:40 A.M. and walked south, crossing Dayton on her way toward Selby where she caught the streetcar to work. This morning, when she passed the hotel, she also noticed that the iron gates were open.[4]

As the paperboys finished up their deliveries, lights began to wink on in the houses and apartment buildings. Early risers beginning the workday.

Among the winking lights were those of Mrs. Nellie McKernan in the Dacotah Apartments, Number 5, at 370 Selby Avenue. Mrs. McKernan's daughter, Margaret, was also up at this early hour because she had to go to work. At 6:45 A.M., when Margaret McKernan started to lower the shade so she could dress for work, she noticed what appeared to be a fire burning in the windows of the Aberdeen Hotel. The eight-story structure towered above the buildings lining the north side of their street. It took several minutes for mother and daughter to convince themselves that the vacant hotel was really on fire. Mrs. McKernan then called the fire department.[5]

A dozen blocks to the north, the fire alarm rang at Station 9 at 6:59 A.M. The station stood on the corner of Edmund Avenue and Marion Street in the heart of Frogtown, one of the city's working-class neighborhoods. In a swirl of well-practiced maneuvers, the firemen quickly donned their fire gear and took their positions on Engine 9 and Truck 1. The two rigs rolled out into the darkness, racing south, crossing University Avenue, Rondo Avenue, and Marshall Avenue, then reaching the Aberdeen. Someone turned in a second alarm, bringing three additional engine companies and three hook-and-ladder companies to the scene.[6]

That the Aberdeen was on fire came as no great surprise to anyone familiar with the building. The once luxurious hotel had stood empty and forlorn for eleven years, making it a likely destination for vagrants seeking shelter or scavengers scrounging for materials they could strip from the rooms and resell.

The Aberdeen was shaped like the letter U, its broad base facing Dayton Avenue. Two wings extended to the south, one bordering Virginia Street on the east side, the other on the Western Avenue side of

Firemen from Station 18, at St. Albans Street and University Avenue, shown here in about 1920, answered the call to the Aberdeen. *MNHS*

The southwest corner of the Aberdeen, December 1937. This is the wing in which the body was found. The boiler room is at right, with a fire escape going up from its roof; the annex, which held the laundry, is at left. *Courtesy SPPD*

the building. A single-story brick areaway connected the two wings. Adjoining the west wing, an annex that served as the hotel's laundry shared its west wall with Dayton Avenue Garage. On the south end of the west wing, a one-story brick boiler room jutted out into the neglected gardens at the rear of the property.

The fire crews quickly determined that the fire was burning on the second floor of the Aberdeen's west wing. Simultaneously, several crews broke into the building at its various entrances with axes and pikes. Firemen used a door ram to break in the front doors that faced Dayton Avenue. Though locked securely with a padlock, the doors were not closed tightly. The firemen made their way to the second floor and raised several windows by hand. Elsewhere, a crew from Hook and Ladder Company Number 1 raised ladders against the outside wall of the boiler room, on the building's south side. Once on its flat roof, Ladder 1's Captain J. Giles took the iron fire escape up to the first landing, where he broke a glass window with an ax to gain entry onto the second floor. Captain Bickel of Ladder 9 raised a ladder to the roof of the areaway between the east and west wings and entered a second-floor room through a raised window.[7]

1. "THERE'S A BODY HERE!" | 9

The only light inside the hotel came from the orange flames, which had already engulfed the second-floor hallway and were spreading through doorways into adjoining rooms. Ladder 1's G. Morgan helped firemen from Engines 8 and 3 feed lines into the hallway to pour water on the intense flames as they consumed the flooring and licked at the wainscoting. The water gushing from the firehoses onto the intense flames added steam to the hot, smoky air. It was hard to see and hard to hear the firemen's shouts.

Other lines were brought in to help beat down the flames, and the firemen soon began to gain the upper hand, tearing the smoldering wood apart with axes and pikes. Engine 9's Captain William Davenport and firefighter Joseph Harris attempted to enter a large room off the hall to help extinguish the flames. In the dim light, amidst all the smoke and commotion, Harris made a startling discovery on the hallway's wet, debris-strewn floor.

"There's a body here!"[8]

Harris's shout no doubt sent a shiver through everyone who could hear it. The Aberdeen was no longer just the scene of a fire. It was now the scene of at least one fatality. Who was it? What happened? Were there more victims in the debris? Along with the smoke and soot, the possibility that a crime had been committed suddenly permeated the air. This was beyond the fire department's boundaries. The discovery of a body required an immediate police presence.

Outside, Patrolmen Thomas McMahon and James Fahey were on traffic duty, managing the customary knot of cars and trucks that formed at the site of a fire. They were immediately called up to the second floor, where they confronted a most gruesome sight. "It appeared to be the body of a child," they wrote in their report later that morning, "the lower part of its legs were missing; its sex could not be determined."[9]

Knowing a full-scale investigation was forthcoming, McMahon and Fahey reported the discovery to the department's detective division. Their call initiated a series of administrative steps. Detectives Boyd Carrier and Frank Kennedy were dispatched to the Aberdeen to secure the scene and begin the investigation. The Ramsey County coroner was also summoned.

Detectives Carrier and Kennedy arrived at 7:47 A.M. and made their way to the southwest corner of the building's second floor. "The fire was put out when we arrived," the detectives wrote in the first of many reports they would forward to Police Chief Clinton Hackert, Assistant

Chief Charles J. Tierney, and others. "There was a number of news-paper photographers, news reporters, and spectators walking around the body. We ordered everyone who had no business there to leave and told [the] officer at door to let no one in [the] building but police and firemen."[10]

With the scene cleared, the detectives were able to get down to business. The "body lay on a pile of debris in a hall at the head of steps leading from rear main floor. The body was lying on its back, the head to the east and feet to west toward [the] steps."[11]

The body was covered with "a canvas used by firemen for carrying bodies." At some point, Carrier and Kennedy used the phone in the garage next door to notify Dr. John B. Dalton, head of the department's crime lab. They kept the body covered until he arrived. "He examined [the] body and took pictures of it as it lay on the floor." While Dr. Dalton was setting up his camera, a fire investigator worked nearby, examining the floor to see if he could determine what had been used to start the fire. His movements visited another indignity on the victim. "He was using a fire ax and when he hit [the] floor the plaster on [the] ceiling . . . fell on [the] uncovered body."[12]

The incident exacerbated a brewing controversy between the fire and police departments. The fire itself had seriously compromised—if not destroyed—the crime scene, making it all but impossible for the police department to conduct a full and proper investigation. The actions of the firemen around the body as they continued to work the fire scene only made the situation worse. "The firemen were shoveling debris from room adjoining hall; they had cleared all debris to where body was lying when we arrived," the detectives observed, "and we told them not to move any more debris until [the] coroner arrives. They had been walking back and forth around this body and everything was tramped down quite a bit." In the days to come, an investigator would interview many members of the fire crews in an effort to determine their roles, their entry points into the building, and their proximity to the body as they fought the fire or assisted in the cleanup, all in an effort to determine the condition of the building prior to the fire, which, the policemen hoped, might provide them with clues. For the moment, however, Dr. Dalton "picked some of this plaster off before [the] picture was taken and this is the only plaster that was on body," the detectives recalled. "There was no plaster on [the] body when canvas was first removed."[13]

The detectives and Dr. Dalton made a careful examination of the victim. "The legs from the knees down were missing and part of the lower

Scenes from inside the
Aberdeen, after the fire.
Courtesy SPPD

left arm," the detectives later wrote. "The skull had a crack in it between [the] nose and right eye, running back about three inches and some substance oozing out. There was a hole in right chest caused by someone either kicking or stepping on body; part of the fingers on the right hand were burned off."[14]

Assistant Coroner Otto Bunde arrived. After a preliminary examination, the charred body was transferred to a metal basket stretcher. The detectives felt the winter chill creeping into the hallway as the heat generated by the fire dissipated. They began to sift through the debris "that lay alongside and under the body" for anything that would help their investigation. Dutifully, they recorded the grim contents of their search in the report they filed later that morning.

> The first article picked up was a woman's girdle and a woman's garter or abdominal belt. These things seemed to be alongside upper part of body just under left shoulder and arm. We later found that these two articles were complete but burned in several places. These were evidently taken off body before fire was started. We also found part of a dress, part of a coat and pieces of underwear and these were under body but were up near shoulders. We also found a small compact, a large compact, a key ring with five keys and the metal part of purse. These articles were on right side of body near waistline.[15]

A later report filed by the detectives noted that the dress fragment was "a dark green." Additionally, the detectives "found part of the bones to lower legs" among the ashes, which were added to the metal basket along with the victim's personal effects.[16]

The assistant coroner and Dr. Dalton would accompany the body to the morgue, leaving Detectives Carrier and Kennedy at the scene to take stock of the circumstances that would form the foundation for the murder investigation that loomed before the St. Paul Police Department.[17]

The circumstances were indeed grim: a charred body with severe head and chest wounds that may have been inflicted by an unknown assailant or assailants—or inadvertently caused postmortem by a firefighter working with an ax or a pike—and a crime scene that had been badly compromised, not just where the victim was found but in other parts of the building. Firemen had broken into the building at various entrances, poured water on the flames, and tromped through the hallways, disturbing whatever dust may have caught incriminating footprints. The fragments of clothing suggested the victim was a woman. The purposeful removal of her clothing from her body suggested that she had been sexually assaulted. Her personal effects were all but destroyed by the fire. The fire was most likely intentionally set to conceal . . . what? If the fire had not been discovered so quickly, the victim's body most certainly would have burned to ashes, and the woman would at best have been forever listed as a missing person, leaving loved ones to grieve in a vacuum.

It was not much to go on, but investigators needed to make a positive identification and start solving what appeared to be a murder perpetrated in the Aberdeen. Or perhaps the woman had been slain elsewhere, late at night, and the body brought here, and the hotel set on fire to cover up the crime.

The key ring with its five keys was on its way to the morgue with the body and other personal effects. Seeking out the locks that those keys fit seemed like the most productive place to begin.

In confronting these circumstances, Detectives Carrier and Kennedy were addressing what they could see before them and how what they saw might impact the standard procedures of the pending investigation. But other circumstances that would complicate the investigation extended far beyond what lay before the detectives' eyes, encompassing both the city's history and that of the Ramsey Hill neighborhood where the Aberdeen Hotel stood. These complicating circumstances included a near decade-long financial depression and, indeed, the St. Paul Police Department's own dark legacy of corruption.

2   Complicating Circumstances

On the day the murder was discovered, St. Paul was a maturing city whose roots dated back nearly a century. The city grew up on a bend in the Mississippi River in the ancestral homelands of the Dakota people, who called the area Imniza Ska—White Cliffs. The Dakota lived along the banks of the Mississippi, and throughout what is now Minnesota, around the time the first Europeans explored the area in the late 1600s. By the early 1800s, European and American fur traders, along with the US military, were living in the area. As the American agricultural frontier moved west, the federal government forced the Dakota to sign treaties relinquishing the land.

By the late 1840s, white people were flooding into the area. From its beginning, St. Paul was a transportation hub, the head of navigation on the Mississippi. It was close to the military post of Fort Snelling and to the factories powered by the falls of St. Anthony, which gave birth to Minneapolis. Steamboats docked at two landings to discharge goods and take on freight for the return trip downriver. St. Paul was also the southern terminus of several overland oxcart trails, trade routes that linked the city to Canadian settlements.

The city's future as the region's transportation hub was secured with the completion of the Northern Pacific Railway in 1883 and the Great Northern Railway a decade later. The Great Northern and Northern Pacific were just two of a dozen railroads headquartered in or serving the city. During the late nineteenth and early twentieth centuries, these railroads fueled business growth in the city. Thousands of immigrants and residents of eastern states seeking work opportunities stepped off the trains at the St. Paul Union Depot.[1]

In the late 1850s, the first residential neighborhoods were platted on the outskirts of the business district, among them the Ramsey Hill neighborhood. Early Hill residents included US senator Henry M. Rice, Minnesota governor William R. Marshall, and Reverend Edward Duffield Neill, founder of Macalester College.[2]

The bluffs along Summit Avenue soon became a premiere location for the city's wealthiest residents. Railroad baron James J. Hill and businessman Amherst Wilder built mammoth mansions on spacious lots that showcased their immense wealth and position. Throughout the neighborhood, prominent business leaders, merchants, and politicians built elegant, if somewhat smaller, homes. By the middle of the 1880s, Ramsey Hill had become one of the most influential neighborhoods in St. Paul.[3]

The Aberdeen was a crown jewel of the neighborhood. Designed as a luxury apartment hotel by the architectural team of Minnesota-born Clarence H. Johnston Sr. and nationally known William H. Wilcox, the Aberdeen was completed in 1889 at a cost of $250,000. The eight-story, stone-and-brick hotel offered passersby a stunning visual symbol of the capital city's growing prosperity and the accumulating wealth of the neighborhood's residents. Most of the new hotel's 200 rooms were part of seventy-eight luxury apartment units ranging in size from two to eight rooms. Even the fourteen rooms available for single-night occupancy included private baths. The rent for a single room was five dollars a night, almost double the going rate in nearby hotels. Residents of the Aberdeen included Minnesota governor John A. Johnson and architect Emmanuel Masqueray, designer of the mammoth Cathedral of St. Paul just down the street.[4]

General improvements in inner city transportation helped attract people of more modest means to the Hill neighborhood. The completion of the Selby Avenue streetcar line in 1888 made the neighborhood easily accessible from downtown. The route received further improvement in 1907 with the construction of the Selby Tunnel, which began at Nina Street, went under Summit Avenue, and proceeded down the hill to downtown. Along Selby Avenue and on adjoining streets, multiunit apartment buildings began to replace single-family homes, which put the once exclusive neighborhood within economic reach of citizens of modest economic means, including grocers, druggists, tailors, unskilled laborers, and household servants.[5]

As the new century began its second decade, the growing popularity of automobiles brought further changes to the neighborhood's demographics. Wealthy residents, the mainstay of the neighborhood, began to move out of the Hill to nearby communities. By the late 1920s, Ramsey Hill had evolved from an exclusive neighborhood into one populated by residents of modest means.

The stock market crash on October 29, 1929, touched off the greatest financial depression the nation had endured in its more than 150-year history. Across the country, banks failed, financial credit disappeared, businesses closed, and unemployment rates rose dramatically. Everywhere, people experienced hard times. They bought less, did without, and looked for ways to save money.

Passengers board the streetcar at the mouth of the Selby Tunnel, about 1929. The row of apartment buildings sits directly through the block from where Ruth Munson lived. *MNHS*

Farm foreclosures and the scarcity of jobs in small towns and cities brought many people to larger cities in search of opportunity. St. Paul's population was estimated at 271,606 in 1930. In 1935, the city's estimated population was 290,061, an increase of 6.7 percent.[6]

By 1937, hard times had brought more changes to Ramsey Hill. The Depression began at a time when the neighborhood's housing was aging. Throughout the Depression years, many homeowners deferred maintenance and repairs, hoping times would improve. In some cases, houses stood vacant because their owners were unable to pay the taxes. Elsewhere in the neighborhood, residences were subdivided into apartments, and many apartment buildings were converted into rooming houses, where single rooms could be rented.[7]

Despite visible signs of physical deterioration, the Ramsey Hill neighborhood retained enough of its original visual grandeur to catch the eye of renters in search of something they could not necessarily put into words. To men and women uprooted by the Depression, the neighborhood's wide streets lined with substantial houses and stately apartment buildings must have presented an attractive alternative to the city's working-class neighborhoods or the small towns and farms many had left behind. The look and feel of the neighborhood offered the illusion of prosperity, if not actual wealth, to those who rented one of the apartments carved out of the expansive houses, or even a single room, on the Hill.

As a result, the neighborhood's population increased. In 1930, 34,594 residents lived in Ward 7, which included the Ramsey Hill neighborhood. How much the Hill area's population increased between 1930 and 1935 is unclear, but anecdotal information indicates that it saw substantial increases. At the time of the murder, for example, at 280–282 Dayton Avenue, five people lived in Apartment 4, five in Apartment 5, and seven in Apartment 6. The units were each originally intended to serve a single family.[8]

Like the neighborhood itself, the Aberdeen was a victim of changing demographics and hard times. In 1920, the hotel was sold and its new owner leased the building to the US Veterans Bureau, which used it as a hospital. The hospital was relocated to new facilities at Fort Snelling in 1927, leaving the building empty for the next eleven years. At one point, the hotel was sold for the pitiful sum of $750, plus unpaid taxes. On the morning of the murder, the derelict hotel was one more blemish in a once-grand neighborhood suffering from more than a decade of decline.[9]

This was the city and the neighborhood that detectives would work as they searched for clues that would lead them to a murderer. But as they canvassed the neighborhood's streets and followed clues to other parts of the city, St. Paul police officers also had to reckon with the circumstances created by the department's own dark legacy of decades of corruption.

The problems in the department involved many of the men who would lead the investigation into the murder at the Aberdeen, including Public Safety Commissioner Gustave H. Barfuss, Police Chief Clinton A. Hackert, and Assistant Chief Charles J. Tierney. Just two years earlier, they had survived the collapse of the O'Connor system, and they carried that heavy history.

No individual exercised more influence over the St. Paul Police Department or did more to shape its legacy than John J. O'Connor. After almost two decades working as a detective, O'Connor became chief of police in 1900. As chief, he instituted an informal arrangement in which St. Paul police granted criminals immunity from arrest and prosecution in return for their good behavior within St. Paul's city limits. Known as the O'Connor layover agreement, or simply the O'Connor system, the arrangement was simple: upon arrival in town, a criminal was expected to check in with a "go-between," who then notified police of his presence. As long as said criminal committed no crimes in the city, he would not be targeted for arrest by the police.[10]

During his tenure, O'Connor was credited with keeping crime rates down in St. Paul. But the layover agreement also blurred the legal line between criminals and the police and encouraged police corruption. O'Connor retired in 1920, shortly after the 1919 ratification of the Eighteenth Amendment to the US Constitution, which prohibited the production, transportation, and sale of alcoholic beverages. Prohibition did little to curb Americans' appetite for alcoholic beverages or reduce crime. Organized crime—gangsters—quickly developed an illegal and highly profitable industry to provide alcohol to thirsty Americans. In St. Paul, bootlegger Leon Gleckmann was said to have secured annual profits of $1 million from illegal liquor sales.[11]

Throughout the 1920s, O'Connor's system flourished under his successors, even as its effectiveness deteriorated. Bootleggers bribed officers. Officers tipped off bootleggers and bar owners before police raids. Other sworn officers were cut in for a share of the profits. In the early 1920s, St. Paul police chief Frank Sommers was believed to have received one dollar for every gallon of illegal liquor sold through Gleckmann's syndicate.[12]

The repeal of Prohibition in late 1933 put gangsters and bootleggers out of the illegal liquor business. Rather than pursue legitimate employment, some gangsters turned to robbery and kidnapping to make money. Thanks to the O'Connor system, St. Paul had gained a national reputation in the criminal world as a safe haven. The system that had once protected the city now attracted gangsters who made national headlines for their crimes. The Barker-Karpis Gang, bank robber John Dillinger, Machine Gun Kelly, and Babyface Nelson, among others, migrated to St. Paul in search of safety. Unfortunately, they ignored the O'Connor system's rules about not committing crimes within the city.

For years, St. Paulites shrugged their shoulders at bootlegging operations, gambling establishments, and houses of prostitution under the O'Connor system. But beginning in 1932, just five years before the murder at the Aberdeen, a spectacular series of local robberies, kidnappings, and other crimes terrorized the city. In separate incidents, the Barker-Karpis Gang kidnapped businessman William Hamm and banker Adolph Bremer and demanded six-figure ransoms for their

The St. Paul Police Department with new "radio cars" built at St. Paul's Ford Plant, 1932. The cars were equipped with one-way radio transmitters. Left to right: Captain Charles W. Coulter, a man identified as "Insp. DMS," Deputy Commissioner Gustave H. Barfuss, Commander Ned Warren, Chief M. J. Culligan, Inspector of Detectives Charles J. Tierney. *Norton & Peel and Hibbard Studio, MNHS*

release. The gang stole the payroll for Swift and Company in South St. Paul. Gang members shot and seriously wounded airline employee Roy McCord, who they thought was a policeman. Community leaders suddenly saw their own safety at risk. A reform effort was mounted, and in the wake of the Bremer kidnapping in January 1934, a Ramsey County grand jury was convened to investigate the police.

Primary among the reformers was *St. Paul Daily News* editor Howard Kahn, whose biting editorials attacked police corruption. He predicted that the grand jury investigation would result in a "whitewash" of the police, and he was right. The grand jury's report, released on the morning of March 31, 1934, asserted that "Charges of official incompetence and neglect" and "Charges of collusion between police and underworld" had not "been sustained by evidence." The report also assured St. Paulites that "Your police department is essentially honest."[13]

At almost the same moment the report was being released, two FBI agents and a St. Paul detective cornered fugitive bank robber John Dillinger in an apartment building. During a five-minute gun battle,

Dillinger and his girlfriend, Evelyn "Billie" Frechette, escaped down the back stairs into the alley, where they retrieved their car from a nearby garage and fled.[14]

That afternoon, the *Daily News* ran a double-decker headline proclaiming MACHINE GUNS BLAZE AS JURY WHITEWASHES POLICE. In side-by-side stories, the *Daily News* announced the grand jury's findings and recounted the gun battle between the police and Dillinger. Enraged, Kahn published an editorial promising to produce evidence documenting police corruption. Acting with permission of Public Service Commissioner H. E. Warren, he privately convinced ten businessmen to establish a $100,000 fund to expose police corruption and hired criminologist Wallace Ness Jamie to tap the telephones within police headquarters. In the spring of 1935, Jamie recorded 2,500 telephone conversations that produced 3,000 pages of damaging evidence.[15]

On June 24, 1935, the *Daily News* broke the story with several front-page articles gathered under another double-decker headline: TRAP NINE IN POLICE SIFT; FOUR OUSTED, CHIEF SUSPENDED. One article reprinted a letter from Commissioner Warren to Mayor Mark E. Gehan describing the corruption. "Conservatively at least 50 per cent of the conversations were damaging," the letter declared, noting that "we have surprising evidence of police ownership of slot machines, a tip off system on raids, police connection with prostitution, police political activities, police efforts to block proper management of the department, a sensational and illicit connection between police and criminal lawyers, and many other activities."[16]

Warren's letter demanded the resignations of James Crumley, inspector; Fred Raasch, lieutenant; Ray Flanagan, patrolman; and Michael McGinnis, detective, "or they will be discharged within 24 hours." It also announced that "M[ichael] J. Culligan, chief of police, Thomas Dahill, lieutenant, and C. T. [sic] Tierney, detective inspector, are suspended for 30 days pending further developments." If Dahill and Tierney were to be reinstated after a review, it would be at a lower rank.[17]

Displayed across the front page were photographs and biographies of the same nine men identified in Warren's letter. There, for all to see, were the faces and names of some of St. Paul's finest—men who had occupied the desks where leadership decisions were made, or walked the city streets to maintain law and order and protect the public. For the first time, the public began to learn the true depth of corruption within the St. Paul Police Department.

The Ramsey County attorney called a new grand jury, which handed

Public Safety Commissioner Gustave H. Barfuss. *MNHS*

down twenty-one indictments against the police. Thirteen of those indicted were later discharged or suspended. Police Chief Culligan resigned under pressure, and department veteran Barfuss was appointed acting chief of police. His tenure as acting chief was short. Upon the appointment of Charles W. Coulter as the new chief, Barfuss was reassigned to assistant chief of police in charge of personnel. On June 2, 1936, he was elected to the city council and became the new public service commissioner, replacing Warren. (At that time, St. Paul's commission system of city government gave council members charge of individual departments.) Barfuss quickly ousted Coulter and appointed the reform-minded Clinton Hackert as acting chief.[18]

On September 30, 1936, fourteen months before the murder at the Aberdeen, Hackert was confirmed as chief of police under a new amendment to the city charter that removed political favoritism from the appointment process. He began serving a six-year term; he could only be dismissed for cause. Hackert immediately pledged to create "a

Police Chief Clinton A. Hackert. *MNHS*

Charles J. Tierney, photographed on his first day as chief of police in 1943. *Courtesy St. Paul Police Historical Society*

permanent police school to be operated as part of the department."
Charles J. Tierney, who had weathered the indignity of suspension for
"flagrant neglect of duty" during the big cleanup a year earlier, was
appointed assistant chief of police.[19]

Hackert's first significant act was to dismiss former police chief
Thomas A. "Big Tom" Brown from the force. No other police officer
had done more to soil the department's reputation. Brown had been
appointed chief of police on June 3, 1930. Two years later he was
demoted to detective on suspicion that he had tipped off the Barker-
Karpis Gang of an impending raid on their hideout. He was also head of
the kidnap squad when the Hamm and Bremer kidnappings occurred.
Those investigations again produced evidence that Brown had leaked
information to the Barker-Karpis Gang that helped them avoid capture.
One gangster claimed that Brown received $25,000 from the $100,000
Hamm ransom for his support. In short, Brown had betrayed the very
people he had sworn to protect.[20]

The year 1937 began with the hope that the St. Paul Police Department's
days of graft and corruption were a thing of the past. Per Hackert's
pledge, new officers were required to attend a police training school run
by the assistant chief of police. They studied laws and ordinances, rules
and regulations of the department, first aid, handling unruly prison-
ers, physical instruction, use of arms and tear gas, and courtesy, among
other subjects. Before the year was out, Hackert also would require
veteran officers to undergo the training.[21]

The training school complemented the forward step taken in November 1935, when a crime laboratory was completed just three years after
the FBI established its own laboratory. The crime lab was directed by
a professional criminologist and was "equipped for chemical analysis,
firearms examination, handwriting comparison, and photographic
work."[22]

At the start of the year, there were 361 officers on the force to police
the city's 867 miles of streets and serve and protect the citizens. The
city was patrolled by ten radio-equipped cars, each carrying two officers
armed with shotguns and a first aid kit for emergencies. Four separate
radio-equipped cruiser cars carried two detectives who would handle
all investigations in their district and answer other police calls when
necessary.[23]

Any hopes Hackert had that his department had indeed turned
the page on its past were quickly dashed. On February 15, readers of
the *St. Paul Dispatch* opened their evening paper to a front-page story

about a new police department scandal. Officers Peter Barrett and Michael McGinnis were under suspension "as investigation has begun of alleged 'protection' of a raided disorderly house"—a house of prostitution. The situation was made all the more scandalous by the fact that McGinnis was one of the officers suspended during the big cleanup of the department in June 1935.[24]

Two days earlier, the department's morals squad had raided an apartment at 170 West Summit Avenue, on the eastern edge of the Ramsey Hill neighborhood. Officers arrested Paul Johnson, his common-law wife Irene Kingston, and three other women. The police confiscated business cards that read "Patsy and Buddy, Photographers," bearing the address and phone number of the apartment. According to the *Dispatch*, authorities believed that "if a wife found [a card] in her husband's pocket he could explain it was a business card." The police also confiscated an "Index file of patrons [that] consisted of preferred customers, former customers and others admitted on recommendation of a friend."[25]

Under questioning by Assistant Police Chief Tierney, Johnson, also known as Paul Larson, said he had told taxi drivers and patrons that he received police protection to "inspire confidence and encourage business," as the newspaper phrased it. Johnson claimed to have paid out $50, but later admitted he had not paid any money to police.[26]

The investigators determined that McGinnis and Barrett had visited Johnson's apartment on February 6 after receiving a complaint. "We had no reason to make any arrest at his flat as we saw nothing illegal going on," Barrett told investigators. "We understood it was Larson's home and his wife was there. Also it was [Winter] Carnival Week."

Tierney, it must be noted, had been suspended along with McGinnis less than two years earlier and was now involved in an investigation that would no doubt impact McGinnis's career.

But what was at stake included more than just the reputations of the two officers and the entire police department. If Johnson and Kingston pleaded not guilty, County Attorney M. F. Kinkead told the *Dispatch*, customers whose names appeared in the index file and the cabdrivers who drove them could be called as witnesses. Among the "customers" were "men prominent in the Twin Cities."[27]

The criminal case against Johnson and Kingston continued, but the department resolved its issues quickly. Chief Hackert suspended McGinnis and Barrett for thirty days for failure to note on their log sheets their activities at the apartment on February 6 and the fact that they had given Johnson a ride in a police car. But Hackert concluded "that the investigation by his department had satisfied him there was no foundation for the protection charges."[28]

From the police department's perspective, the issue had been resolved. Hackert had taken quick action to discipline two of his officers, but he had dismissed the more serious protection charge. The resolution left citizens to ponder whether they should take the officers' exoneration at face value or wonder if the department leadership had, as in the past, quietly swept the scandal under the rug.

In the Aberdeen, as Detectives Carrier and Kennedy watched Assistant Coroner Bunde and Dr. Dalton prepare to transport the body, it is unlikely they were thinking about the character of their city, the recent changes in the Ramsey Hill neighborhood, or the legacy of the O'Connor system. But as they worked the Hill and the surrounding neighborhoods, the past was not behind them. Anyone they interviewed could look back just a few months at the protection scandal and legitimately wonder: was this officer honest, or secretly on the take?

3 | The Key to Identification

As the general workday got underway across the city, Dr. John B. Dalton, the police criminologist, and Otto Bunde, assistant to Ramsey County Coroner Dr. C. A. Ingerson, accompanied the victim's burned body from the Aberdeen Hotel to the Ramsey County Morgue at 164 Hill Street, just down the hill from the St. Paul Public Library.[1]

Like the police, the coroner was responsible for investigating a death, especially an unnatural one. Part of the job was to work with the police to identify the victim. The coroner also would conduct an autopsy to determine the cause of death. Due to various tests, the full autopsy report would not be completed for days, perhaps even weeks. In the meantime, the coroner would issue a death certificate, which would indicate the preliminary cause of death.

Identifying the body was going to be difficult. There were no remaining facial features to aid identification. If the victim was carrying any form of identification in her purse, it had been burned to ashes. Only a few metal fragments of the purse and its contents remained. The remains of a green dress and a sealskin coat that had lain under the body and out of the flames' reach might be recognized by a friend if a description of them was publicized. In this instance, whatever information the reporters had gleaned before Detectives Boyd Carrier and Frank Kennedy shooed them out of the Aberdeen might actually be helpful if published.

While the coroner's office began its work, the murder investigation kicked into gear under the direct supervision of Assistant Chief of Police Charles J. Tierney at police headquarters in the Public Safety Building. Tierney was from a law enforcement family. He had joined the department in March 1921 as an operator and had been promoted to detective five years later. He held several positions within the detective division until, just eleven months earlier, as part of the reform effort, he was appointed assistant chief of police in charge of the detective division.[2]

The new case was assigned the identification number 33436. Any report connected to it would carry this number to distinguish it from the other reports police personnel filed daily. It was standard procedure for detectives and patrol officers to handwrite their reports. These were given to a typist, who typed an original along with multiple carbon copies. For the Munson case, at least, copies of the reports usually went to Chief Hackert, Assistant Chief Tierney, and Public Safety Commissioner Barfuss. As necessary, copies were distributed to the county coroner, to Dr. Dalton, and to various division heads.

Several lieutenants under Tierney's command doled out assignments to detectives and patrolmen on the streets. Some assignments were responses to new complaints; others followed up on information the department generated during its investigations. As the new investigation progressed, the department would be flooded with calls offering new information, which would require an immediate response—and generate a host of follow-up calls.

At 10:00 A.M., Detective Lieutenant Ray McCarthy assigned Detective Lieutenant Bertram Talbot and Detectives Alfred Jakobson and Ralph Merrill to conduct a roof-to-basement search of the Aberdeen for possible evidence. On the top floor in Room 825, dust on the floor showed promising marks of tennis shoes and women's shoes. Nothing of interest caught the detectives' attention as they worked their way down, floor by floor. On the second floor, fire and water damage made their task all but fruitless. By the time the detectives filed their report later that day, another officer had informed them that the footprints in Room 825 had been observed by other officers inspecting the building the previous summer.[3]

In the end, "The only evidence which might be of value," Detective Merrill wrote in a later report, "was found in the barber shop in the basement where we found someone had peeled some potatoes and apparently had some lunch some time ago. A tomato can, a pea can, some milk bottle tops and some pieces of paper with writing on [them] were brought to headquarters and turned over to Dr. Dalton for examination. We could not tell if this was fresh or not. There also was a mattress on a settee in the barber shop [which] very recently had been cut with a knife or scissors. About ¾ths of this mattress is still on the settee and the other ¼th which was cut off is on the first floor frozen in the ice from the fire. This was not disturbed."[4]

News of the fire had traveled quickly throughout the Ramsey Hill neighborhood. At 12:58 P.M., Detectives Donald Kampmann and Raymond Schmidt were dispatched to follow up on a citizen's call. The detectives had been on the case since early that morning, when they traced the origin of the call to the fire department to Mrs. McKernan and her daughter and took the former's statement. Now, they followed another

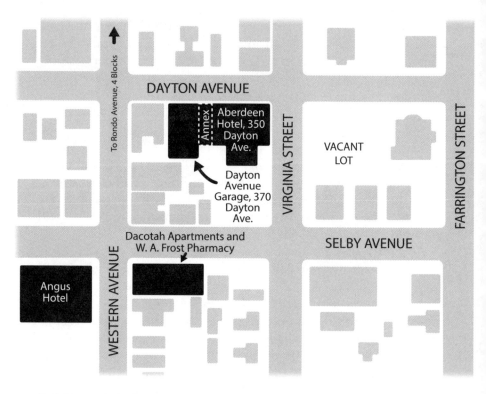

Ruth Munson's St. Paul neighborhood, 1937. *Map by Elliot Butzow*

lead to 276 Dayton Avenue, a three-story red brick Pullman-style apartment building just two blocks east of the Aberdeen. The sturdy structure was one in a complex of seven nearly identical buildings, four of which faced north on Dayton Avenue. The other three faced south on Selby Avenue. All the buildings were conveniently located on or near the Selby streetcar line.[5]

The detectives made their way to Apartment 17 on the third floor, where Clara Broughton answered their knock. The seven-room apartment was originally designed for a single household, but to generate income, Broughton rented out three of the rooms. She told the detectives that "a roomer by the name of Ruth Munson had not reported for work this morning." Presumably, the woman's employer had called Broughton's phone number to ask Ruth's whereabouts. Broughton told police she "had heard a woman's body had been found in the fire. She thought it might possibly be her."[6]

Thinking of the keys found near the victim's body, the detectives took Broughton to the Ramsey County Morgue to see if her house keys

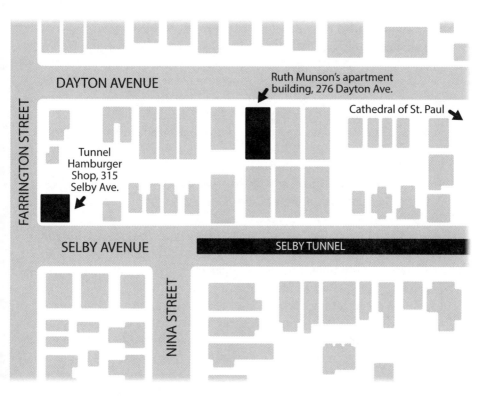

matched any of the keys found with the victim. The landlady's house key matched one of the blackened keys, which tentatively identified the victim as Ruth Munson.

No doubt the detectives felt they had caught a lucky break in making this tentative identification so early and so easily in the investigation. From the morgue, they drove the landlady to Assistant Chief Tierney's office in the Public Safety Building. Exactly what information Broughton first shared with Tierney, Kampmann, and Schmidt was not recorded. The focus of subsequent assignments handed out to several teams of detectives, however, suggested that Broughton told them that Ruth Munson was originally from Grantsburg, Wisconsin, that she worked as a waitress at the St. Paul Union Depot, and that she had a gentleman friend named Derrick Das.[7]

In additional conversation with Broughton, Detectives Kampmann and Schmidt learned that while Ruth Munson was out the previous afternoon, between 3:00 and 4:00 P.M., a woman had called for her two or three times. Shortly after Ruth returned to the apartment, the phone rang again, and Ruth answered it. "Yes, I would just as soon come and stay with you," Broughton remembered Ruth saying, but that was all she recalled of the conversation. Ruth had left the apartment again at about 7:00 P.M. A man called on the phone for her, and when he learned she had gone out, he left no name or message. His voice was unfamiliar, Broughton said. Ruth Munson received many calls from men, the landlady told the detectives, but she only had one man come to see her at a time, and it might be several months before a different one called to see her. As for her personal habits, Ruth usually ate at the Tunnel Hamburger Shop. She had a sister, Helen, who was a teacher in Amery, Wisconsin, who often came to visit her.[8]

Chief Hackert and Assistant Chief Tierney, accompanied by Det. Lt. McCarthy, drove to 276 Dayton Avenue and searched Ruth Munson's room. According to McCarthy's report, they gathered up "letters and other articles" as well as "$16 in currency, $11 in bills and $5 in nickels"— handy change for the ten-cent streetcar fare. The money was turned over to staff at the Bureau of Records.[9]

Among the letters and articles they retrieved was an unframed black and white portrait, approximately three by five inches in size. The photograph gave the detectives their first look at the woman whose life they were about to reconstruct in order to find her killer. She was posed with her body turned slightly to her right, her faced turned just to the left to directly face the camera. Her dark hair was cut fashionably short and loosely parted on the left side, gently flipping out just below her ears. Intense, searching eyes and tight lips with a fresh application of lipstick gave her a somewhat solemn expression. In this portrait at least, she appeared attractive in the manner of Barbara Stanwyck or Bette Davis.

The three policemen also retrieved a four-and-a-half-by-five-inch volume with a dark blue cover. In the upper left-hand corner, gold-embossed lettering labeled it a five-year diary. The lower right-hand corner bore the name Ruth Munson in gold capital letters. A leather flap with a metal tip extended from the back cover over the pages and clicked into a lock on the front, secured with a small key.

On the inside of the front cover, in the upper left-hand corner, was an ink notation in a neat, precise hand: "Gift from Mother & Dad Dec. 25, 1935." The right-hand title page read "Five Year Diary," printed in stately capital letters. Near the bottom of the page, an italicized phrase noted this was a volume "In which should be recorded important events most worthy of remembrance." On the next page, left blank by the printer, was a three-line notation in neat penmanship:

Ruth Margaret Munson
Born March 13, 1906
(Mon?) Between 5 & 9 A.M.

The volume contained several pages showing calendar dates for holidays, both Christian and public. In the margin perpendicular to "Mother's Day—(2nd Sunday in May)" Ruth had written "Lucky date 9th." Ditto marks appeared under the word lucky, followed by "No. 6."

Today, ironically, was December 9.

Tucked in the margins on a page featuring gift themes for wedding anniversaries, Ruth had written anniversary dates for nine couples, including "Dad & Mother Jan 29, 1913." Across the page spread, under the headline "Birthdays," Ruth had recorded a full page of names and dates. Some entries were only first names, other entries included a surname. The birthday entries continued on the next page.

Each of the people listed here would need to be contacted and interviewed for what information they could offer.

Police officers found this photo of Ruth in her papers. *Courtesy SPPD*

The diary entries began on the opposing right-hand page. Under January 1, there were five sections of four lines each on which to summarize events of that day over a five-year period. Although Ruth's note suggested that the diary had been a Christmas gift in 1935, she had filled in the four-line spaces allotted for the year 1935 from January through December, suggesting that the date of her note was off by a year. That meant detectives would have the opportunity to study nearly three years of her life, as she chose to record it. Ruth appeared to be regular in making her entries, commenting about the weather, summarizing an activity or two. Names and places popped up in many entries. The last entry was made on December 8, 1937. Yesterday. It read "Day off."[10]

The last entry Ruth Munson made in her diary. *Courtesy SPPD*

Another item the detectives retrieved was a small green address book. In Ruth's penmanship, several dozen names and addresses were listed in alphabetical order on its pages. More legwork for the detectives working the case.[11]

It was now early afternoon. A theory about the murder had emerged. Perhaps the victim, now identified as Ruth Munson, had been hit by a car, and the driver had covered up the accident. Under orders from the dispatcher, Emergency Squad 5, consisting of V. Michel and Arthur Curran, began checking neighborhood garages to see if any of their trucks had towed a "suspected hit and run car." Through the course of the afternoon, the duo would check nine garages without success.[12]

By this time, Talbot and Detectives Jakobson and Merrill had finished their roof-to-basement search inside the Aberdeen. At 1:40 P.M. Jakobson joined Detectives Kennedy and Carrier and Lieutenant Ray Doenges outside the hotel on the Virginia Street side. The four men went through the contents of a rubbish container standing near the back of the Aberdeen property. "We found a bundle containing a suit of mens underwear and a black straw ladys hat, partly ripped," Carrier and Kennedy later wrote in their report. The men went back inside the hotel, where they drew "a diagram of the southwest corner of the 2nd floor." The bundle, a torn-up note they found with it, and the diagram were turned over to Dr. Dalton.[13]

Detectives Carrier and Kennedy interviewed C. J. Warren, janitor at the Dacotah Apartments, located a short block south of the Aberdeen on the southeast corner of Selby and Western Avenues. Warren had noticed the fire at the vacant hotel about the same time that the fire rigs were rolling to a stop. Always an early riser, he had not seen anything unusual around the neighborhood that morning. But, he told the detectives, he had noted that the windows near the fire escapes on different floors of the Aberdeen had been open for some time.[14]

Talbot and Jakobson expanded their review of the grounds to the back side of the hotel. They removed a small padlock from the back basement door, which "was hanging open on the staple." Inside the door they picked up "part of a white handkerchief found on a pile of sawdust on the floor of the second room to the left as one comes up the back stairway (west side) to the main floor." These items were turned in to Dr. Dalton at the crime lab.[15]

Detectives Kampmann and Schmidt had completed their conversation with Clara Broughton. They were sent down to the St. Paul Union Depot to bring two of Ruth Munson's coworkers, Bertha Hopland and

Streetscape near St. Paul's Union Depot, about 1925. *MNHS*

Joan Pivoran, to Assistant Chief Tierney's office. In Tierney's office, the detectives took statements from both women.[16]

If the detectives had had time to study Ruth's diary, they would have seen both women's names in the long list of birthdays. Their names were also in her green address book.[17]

There was a general procedure for taking a subject's statement. Following preliminary questions to determine if a formal statement was beneficial to the investigation, a stenographer was called in. The stenographer's notations were later typed, establishing a permanent transcript of the session, and the interviewee was asked to read, then sign the statement, attesting to its accuracy. The statement was not sworn testimony.[18]

The detectives interviewed Joan Pivoran first, at 2:15 P.M. She had worked with Ruth Munson since August of 1936.

"Have you been intimate with her or gone out with her?" the detectives asked.

"Just shopping together," Pivoran replied.

"You never kept company with her when she was out with her boy friends?"

"No."

"You don't know her boy friend?"

"No, I don't."

"When did you last see Ruth?"

"Monday, because Tuesday was my day off." Wednesday had been Ruth's day off. It was now Thursday.

"When you left her what did you say to her?"

"I said, take care of yourself and she said the same to me."

"Do you know when Ruth was supposed to go to work today?"

"She was supposed to be to work at 6:30 until 2:30."

"Did she come to work this morning?"

"No."

"Is there anything else that you could add to this statement?"

"No, except if I could see her purse because I would know it."

The detectives ended the interview with a standard pair of questions designed to secure the subject's agreement that the statement correctly recorded what she said.

"This statement is the truth to the best of your knowledge and belief?"

"Yes."

"After it is typewritten and you read it, are you willing to sign it?"

"Yes, I am."[19]

The detectives interviewed Bertha Hopland at 2:20 P.M. Rather than repeat the questions they had asked Pivoran, they focused on other issues, picking up helpful information about Ruth's family background.

"Do you know if Ruth Munson has any relations here in St. Paul?"

"She has none here—her folks live in Grantsburg, Wisconsin, and she has a sister that is a teacher in Amery, Wisconsin, and another sister that's a nurse in Austin, Minnesota."[20]

While Kampmann and Schmidt were interviewing Pivoran and Hopland, Det. Lt. McCarthy dispatched Detectives Herman Schlichting and Edward Harkness to 2368 Territorial Road in the city's Midway district to pick up Derrick Das, believed to be Ruth Munson's boyfriend, and bring him to the Public Safety Building for questioning.[21]

Kampmann and Schmidt next located Mrs. Raymond Nelson, identified as an acquaintance of Ruth's, brought her to the Public Safety Building, and interviewed her at 4:27 P.M. She had known Ruth since September of the previous year. Despite the fact that Ruth "visited me quite often," the last time being "before Thanksgiving," Nelson knew little about Ruth's life.

"Do you know of any of her friends or acquaintances?"

"I know of two, but I don't know their names; one is named Ann she is a maid on Summit Avenue but I couldn't say where. It may be C. W. Gordon. Another woman by the name of Ethel. She lives now I think on the west side; she did live on Jackson about a year ago, about a block from the end of the car line."

"Do you know any of Ruth Munson's boy friends?"

"No."

"Do you know anything about her personal life?"

"No. She was a very good girl and friendly but I don't know anything of her personal life."

"Is there anything that you know of that would help us in our investigation of her death?"

"No, she didn't tell anyone of her personal affairs. Very quiet and reserved."[22]

By 3:45 P.M., Schlichting and Harkness had returned to the Public Safety Building with Derrick Das. He was questioned by Detective Lieutenant Frank R. Cullen. The boyfriend was always a suspect when a woman was murdered. Cullen faced the delicate task of asking questions without exposing what meager information they had already learned about St. Paul's most recent murder victim. While some questions confirmed information they had in hand, Cullen was on a fishing expedition.

Das, Cullen learned, was from Minneapolis and generally went by the name Dick. He was a truck driver for Furnell & Webb Transfer Company, headquartered in St. Paul's Midway district, where Schlichting and Harkness had picked him up. His wife had died October 1, leaving him with two young girls, one aged three and the other age six.

"Do you know a girl named Ruth Munson?" Cullen asked.

"Yes. I do."

"How long have you known her?"

"Since October 7, 1937."

"Where did you meet her?'

"I met her at the Friendship Club in Minneapolis."

"What kind of club is that?" Cullen asked.

"It is a dancing club."

"Were you introduced to her?"

"I met her at a dance."

Das said he had been seeing Ruth a couple of times a week since then. The last time was Tuesday night, when she had been at his house. She had caught the Bloomington Avenue streetcar at 12:30 A.M. to begin her trek home. He had called her at her home early the previous night (Wednesday) between 5:30 and 6:00. She had offered to come and take care of the children for him on Thursday, while he attended a union meeting. Cullen zeroed in on the nature of their relationship.[23]

"Have you had intercourse with her?"

"No sir, I haven't."

"At no time?"

"No sir."

Cullen asked about Ruth's relationships with others. Das revealed that Ruth had once been engaged, though he didn't know to whom or how long ago the relationship had ended. Ruth had told him that the man lived in the Grantsburg area and had written her recently, wanting to go out with her again. He did not know any of Ruth's other friends.

Throughout the questioning, Das had been kept in the dark about the murder.

"Is there anything else that I haven't asked you that you care to add to this statement at this time?" Cullen asked.

"I realize or I have a hunch what happened," Das answered, adding "if there is anything that I know of I would be glad to tell you but at the present time I don't know of anything that I could say for sure. I don't know what happened, but from the way you have questioned me, I have an idea."

"What is your idea?"

"That something must have happened. I don't know what else to think—that's my idea from the way you questioned me."

"Whatever happened to her, are you responsible for?"

"No sir."

Das agreed to sign his typed statement once he had read it.[24]

Sometime during the late afternoon or early evening, perhaps while Dick Das was still being questioned, Detectives Kampmann and Schmidt were sent with Detective Merrill to Minneapolis to "make an investigation on 9th Ave South." According to Ruth's green address book, Das lived at 1509 Ninth Street South in Minneapolis. What the detectives found there was not recorded in their reports. A later interview with Das's housekeeper, Nellie Johnson, would confirm the accuracy of Das's statement. He was never considered a suspect in the murder. (At a later, unknown time, Das would give detectives letters Ruth had written to him on November 3 and 5, 1937, in which she dodged his marriage proposal. In the letters, Ruth spoke of her "love" for Das, but felt she couldn't measure up to his wife, Martha, who had died on October 1: "She lead [sic] such a beautiful Christian life that I am sure she must have been an ideal wife and mother and you being the type of person you are deserve one equally as good." Das continued to pursue her.)[25]

The *St. Paul Dispatch*'s presses started rolling by late morning, and the first edition of the paper reached newsstands by early afternoon. Paperboys across the city picked up their issues on street corners by late afternoon and made their deliveries so subscribers had the latest news on their doorsteps when they arrived home from work.

Dispatch readers opened their newspapers to a banner headline splashed across the entire front page: HOTEL FIRE HERE DISCLOSES MURDER. The sensational headline was augmented by a two-column-wide subheading: WOMAN'S BODY FOUND CHARRED. Below that, a "kicker" in smaller type identified the location of the crime: VACANT ABERDEEN HOSTELRY YIELDS MYSTERY CRIME AS CREWS COMPLETE BATTLE WITH FLAMES AT HISTORIC SITE.[26]

Readers' eyes were drawn to a photograph that grimly displayed the burned-out hallway on the second floor where the body of the victim had been discovered. Below it, a second photograph showed the fire escapes on the back of the hotel, a white dotted line added by an editor to highlight the fire escape that led to the second-floor hallway. Next to this photograph was a hand-drawn diagram of the floor plan of the west wing, including a representation of the body itself, head pointing east, feet pointing west.

"Murdered and burned beyond recognition," the unnamed reporter began, "the charred body of a woman was found shortly after 7 A.M. today in the vacant Aberdeen hotel, Dayton and Virginia avenues. Police believe the murder may have been committed by a sex crimi-nal who fractured the woman's skull, possibly attacked her and then poured inflammable material over the body, igniting it to destroy the evidence." The reporter described the condition of the body, the burned clothing, and the personal effects with the same gruesome details out-lined by Detectives Carrier and Kennedy in their reports.[27]

In random order that no doubt was influenced by the rush to make the press deadline, the reporter briefly described the search of the hotel's 200 rooms for possible evidence, documented how the fire was discovered, and mentioned a "greasy gallon measure such as those used for oil and sometimes for gasoline" that had been found by firemen.

If the sense of mystery wasn't already apparent to readers, the reporter drove the point home with prose more appropriate for a pulp novel: "The crime was committed in surroundings as eerie as in any mystery thriller. Once the scene of glamorous social events, where gay throngs gathered, the eight-story hotel has been vacant the past eleven years. Its empty halls and hollow rooms echo every footfall, but its thick walls and dusty windows effectively hide what goes on within." The article announced that Assistant Chief Tierney had taken charge of the investigation and concluded with a brief history of the hotel.[28]

A later edition of the paper added new reporting that the police had released: a "30 year old waitress whose description tallies generally with that of the victim, had been missing since 7 P.M. Wednesday" and that "She did not report for work this morning for the first time in the two years she had been employed." These details suggested that the newspaper had learned the identity of the victim, but in a rare display of decorum had withheld the name until the next of kin had been notified. The updated story included the possibility that the victim may have been struck by a hit-and-run motorist who dragged the body into the hotel, gaining entry by way of a rear fire escape.

The update also noted that a triple investigation was underway by "police, the coroner's staff and fire marshals," suggesting many more stories to come.[29]

Across the Mississippi River, the afternoon *Minneapolis Journal* also covered the crime on the front page. The reporter relayed the same grim details about the condition of the body, taking special note of the victim's fractured skull and quoting Coroner Ingerson saying that the severe injury was "definitely indicating murder." Further, the reporter noted that the fragments of clothing and personal effects found near the body "might help to establish the identity of the victim."[30]

The dinner hour had come and gone. Det. Lt. Cullen was still working the case. At 8:05 P.M., he questioned Belle Luke, a waitress who frequently worked the 6:30 A.M. to 2:30 P.M. shift with Ruth Munson at the restaurant in the Union Depot.

"Had you noticed any person in particular who has been there on a number of occasions?" Cullen asked.

"Yes," Luke replied.

"When was that?"

"I don't know what the days were. There was one man in there about three days ago. I've seen him in there several times. She has talked to him for quite a little bit."

"Do you know his name or did you ever hear it?"

"No."

"Did you ever have any conversation with her about this man, or any of the others?"

"No." She described Ruth's friend as "in the late thirties, ruddy complexion, wore glasses, quite tall, dark hair. Very neatly dressed, always."

Asked if she had anything else to add, Belle Luke opened the doorway to another line of investigation.

"Well, I do know that she always went out an awful lot [of] evenings. She went to Minneapolis more than over here."

"Did she ever talk to you about a young man that she was going with just recently?" Cullen asked.

"No. She never did confide with me very much. She was much more friendly with the other two girls you had up here this afternoon." Pressed further, Luke admitted that Ruth had once invited her to go to Minneapolis with her, and when she declined, "she didn't bother asking" again.

"Did she mention places that she went?"

"One place was the Friendship Club in Minneapolis."

The name must have made Cullen's pulse quicken. Derrick Das had met Ruth Munson at the Friendship Club.[31]

Already news of the murder was having an impact on St. Paul's residents. At 8:30 P.M. Detectives Kennedy, Carrier, and Robert Murnane drove to 280 Dayton Avenue, an apartment building just two doors west of where Ruth Munson lived, to investigate a report that a woman who lived there was "afraid to go out nights for fear of being molested by a degenerate living in the neighborhood." There was general talk in the building, the detectives learned, about one Mark Fitzpatrick, who lived alone across the street and had many young girls come to the house where he lived. Following up on a tip, the three detectives then drove to 1628 Thomas, where they picked up Carl Gash and brought him to the Public Services Building for questioning.[32]

At 8:40 P.M., Cullen began a series of interviews with women who knew Ruth Munson in one way or another. Alma Hill, whose name was in Ruth's green address book, had worked with her at an earlier job: in the cafeteria at Miller Hospital, which sat in the tangled streets between the cathedral and the capitol. She hadn't seen Ruth in six months and had last talked to her on the Sunday after Thanksgiving, when Ruth had spoken vaguely about Dick Das.

"Did you ever hear her express fear of anybody?" Cullen asked.

"No. Never," Hill answered.

"Did she ever tell you that she had been followed or bothered, annoyed at any time?"

"No. She never mentioned anything."[33]

Miller Hospital, about 1925. *MNHS*

Fifteen minutes later, Cullen interviewed Sue Schaffer, thirty-one years old, who worked the Union Depot's evening shift, which began at 4:00. She sometimes saw Ruth on those days when Ruth worked until 4:00, the last such day being Tuesday. That day, Ruth had told Schaffer she had just missed seeing her boyfriend, who had left a few minutes earlier. Schaffer had seen the boyfriend only once before and could only describe him as tall, dark-haired, and neatly dressed.

"Did she ever express any fear to you?" Cullen enquired.

"No, she didn't," Schaffer answered. "She never told me anything of her private life or her comings or goings or anything."[34]

At 9:15 P.M., Cullen interviewed Marie Miller, twenty-eight years old, another Miller Hospital employee who had worked with Ruth several years before. Marie Miller had last seen Ruth six months earlier.

"Do you know anybody that she has kept company with recently?" Cullen asked.

"No, I don't. I couldn't tell you anything about that at all." They never went out together, Miller admitted; they just didn't know each other that way. She had never talked to Ruth on the telephone.[35]

Marion Gavin, thirty years old, sat down with Cullen at 9:30 P.M. She was a former tenant at 276 Dayton Avenue, and it is likely the landlady,

Clara Broughton, had given her name to the police earlier in the day. Though they had lived in the same apartment, Gavin knew Ruth Munson only slightly. "During our acquaintance there we would meet in the hall and that was all," she told Cullen. She had last seen Ruth a week and a half earlier, when she visited Broughton.

"Did she ever tell you of being followed by anyone?" Cullen asked.

"No."

"Have you ever been followed?"

"No."[36]

If Cullen needed a break, he didn't get one. At 9:35, he sat down with Olaf Anderson. Exactly how Anderson's name had surfaced during the day's relentless pace is unclear. Anderson's birthday, February 5, was included in the list of birthdays at the front of Ruth's diary. Mr. and Mrs. Olaf Anderson were listed in her green address book, though the address was different from the one he now gave Cullen.

In answer to Cullen's questions, Anderson said he was a painting contractor by trade.

"Do you know Miss Ruth Munson?" Cullen asked.

"Yes, I do."

"How long have you known her?"

"Known her for the last—about 7-1/2 years."

"Where did you first become acquainted with her?"

"In a dance hall was the first time I met her."

"Where at?"

"71 West Seventh. (The Old Central Hall)."

"Did you keep company with her?"

"Yes, for about five years."

"Were you engaged during that time?"

"No."

"When did you stop keeping company with her?"

"Two years ago this Fall."

Like current boyfriends, former boyfriends were viewed as suspects in murder investigations. Cullen's questions immediately shifted toward searching out any potential conflict between Ruth Munson and Olaf Anderson.

"Did you just disagree, or what?"

"Well, I met another girl and started going with her, and we got engaged." Anderson had not had any contact with Ruth for the past two years, with the exception of his sending her a Christmas card the previous year.

Cullen shifted to Ruth's background. Anderson told him that Ruth was from Grantsburg, that she had worked for B. W. Harris at his home and Miller Hospital before she started at the Union Depot. In Wisconsin, she had taught school, either in Rice Lake or Luck. Yes, she had told him that she had been engaged once, to a mail carrier, but she didn't say much about him.

"You are positive you haven't seen her since two years ago?"

"Yes, I'm positive."

"Haven't met her in the Depot Lunch at the lunch counter?"

"I saw her there once a year ago last summer. I just saw her but she didn't see me. It was quite a distance."

"You didn't talk to her."

"No, I didn't."

"You're sure of that?"

"Positive."

"Did you have a disagreement when you separated?"

"She felt kind of bad about it when I told her. She cried a little bit but there was no argument of any kind."

"Had you had intercourse with her at any time during the time you had gone with her."

"Yes, a few times."

"How long before you and she broke up did you have intercourse with her?"

"Oh! A couple months, I would say."

"And quite often in a period of five years that you kept company with her?"

"Well, just a few times toward the last. The last year or so."

"Was she ever pregnant as a result of this?"

"No. I never asked her."

Once again, Cullen switched his line of questioning, this time zeroing in on Anderson's activities over the past couple of days. Anderson said he had not worked on Wednesday. He had spent time with a coworker, Conrad Swanson, and run some errands. On Tuesday, he had worked a small job at an apartment house on Randolph Avenue, finishing about 2:30 in the afternoon. He was home by 3:30 and remained there all evening with his wife.

"Is there anything else I haven't asked you that you care to add to this statement at this time?"

"Not that I can remember, except that she used to call me Bob."

If in the future a need developed to investigate Anderson further, Cullen had at least two names to contact to verify his statements about his activities on Tuesday and Wednesday. Learning that Ruth Munson had called him Bob gave an additional name to ask others about.

Cullen asked if there was anything else that could help them in this case.

"Not that I can think of right now," Anderson replied. "I would like to help you fellows as much as possible as I feel it's a terrible thing. She was a nice girl—a respectable girl."[37]

At this late hour, others were still engaged with the case. Det. Lt. Talbot and Detective Jakobson were working the neighborhood close to the Aberdeen. Willard (Bill) Wolf was the proprietor of the Dayton Avenue Garage at 370 Dayton Avenue, next door to the Aberdeen. (He was usually referred to as William or Bill in police reports—and his last name was often spelled Wolfe.) He told them that the previous night (Wednesday) a man came in seeking to purchase a gallon of gas, saying his car had run out. He had come from the west, and Wolf directed the man to a service station to the west of the garage, but the man had left walking east, toward the Aberdeen. He described the man as about fifty years old, five feet eight inches in height, about 170 pounds. He had gray hair, a dark hat, and an overcoat.

Wolf also told them about a neighbor who had heard noises in the night. The detectives located Mrs. Adams at 208 Western Avenue. She told them that the window at the back of her apartment faced the hotel. During the night, as Wednesday turned into Thursday, she had heard four shots fired at short intervals, preceded by the sound of breaking glass. She was so alarmed, she said, that she fastened her window, which she usually left unfastened.[38]

Cullen's long day was still not finished. At 10:20 P.M. he questioned Theodore Thompson. How Thompson came to be sitting in front of Cullen is not known, but the murdered woman's green address book listed a Ted H. Thompson, suggesting that detectives were going through the little volume and targeting men for questioning. Thompson admitted that he had met Ruth two years earlier at a place called the Bowl, but they had never gone out. They bumped into each other occasionally.

"At the time of your first meeting, did you give her your name and address?" Cullen asked.

"Well, I was introduced to her."

"By whom?"

He had been introduced to Ruth by a friend, Ludwig Nicholson. How long Nicholson had known her, Thompson didn't know.

"Did you see her Tuesday of this week?" Cullen asked.

"No."

"Did you see her Wednesday?"

"No."

Under further questioning, Thompson went through his activities for Tuesday and Wednesday nights in detail.

"Do you know of anything that will assist us in any way in this case?"

"No. To be frank, I don't know how I can assist you because it's probably over a month since the last time I saw her and I don't know her friends."[39]

Cullen had been on the job since the discovery of the body at 7:45 A.M., some fifteen hours earlier. At 10:45 P.M. he sat down with Carl Gash, who had been cooling his heels since 8:30 when Kennedy, Carrier, and Murnane had brought him to headquarters. Through the usual line of questions, Cullen determined that Gash was a decorator. On Wednesday, he had worked for a Mrs. Lee. The Aberdeen had come up during their conversation earlier in the day, and Mrs. Lee had quickly called the police to report her suspicions of him.

"I think I mentioned to her that a bunch of us had gone through there one time," Gash explained, "but I don't remember if there was any conversation that led up to that or not."

"Do you know anything about the fire and the finding of the woman's body in the hotel?" Cullen asked.

"Nothing whatsoever except she mentioned that there was a body found there," Gash said, referring to Mrs. Lee. "That was after the paper come out."[40]

Cullen released him and called it a day. As he headed home, he had much to think about. A burned body had been found in the vacant Aberdeen Hotel by firemen this morning. Through a stroke of good fortune, the victim had been identified. Many people questioned today seemed to know Ruth Munson, but no one seemed to know her very well. No significant clues had emerged, but it was still early in the investigation. Already the murder had put the city on edge. Case in point: Mrs. Lee, unnerved by the mere mention of the Aberdeen. Her calling the police about Gash was probably the first of many such calls the police operators would field.

Tomorrow would be another long day.

4 | Gathering Facts

Friday, December 10, 1937

Under the direction of Assistant Chief of Police Charles J. Tierney, the investigation began its second day. The investigation had established few facts beyond the tentative identity of the murder victim as Ruth Munson, who had left her room at 7:00 P.M. on Wednesday, destination unknown. Twelve hours later, Ruth's charred remains were found in the debris of a fire at the Aberdeen.

Detectives would continue gathering information in an effort to close the twelve-hour gap. They would seek out the young woman's favorite haunts, follow her through her daily routine, and dig deeply into her personal relationships and social activities. They would study her diary for leads, check out the names in her address book, and contact the intended recipients of the sixty-two Christmas cards they had found in her room, addressed and ready to mail.

In filling out their reports, detectives stuck to facts. Rarely did they express an opinion or propose a theory about the case on paper. Knowing that her killer or killers probably read the newspapers, detectives were equally sparing in sharing their theories of the case with the press.

The newspapers, however, were more than happy to speculate. The *St. Paul Daily News* printed her picture and reeled off a succession of questions that detectives were most likely asking themselves:

Where did Ruth Munson spend Wednesday night?

What was the exact time of the killing?

Was she seized nearby and dragged into the hotel?

Was she killed immediately?

Was she held prisoner in the hotel and killed later?

Did she spend the night with some friend? If so, was she walking back to her apartment Thursday morning when she was waylaid and killed?[1]

Tierney himself seemed uncertain about where she was slain. The *St. Paul Dispatch* noted that Tierney "expressed the opinion that the murder was committed where the body was found." But according to the *Minneapolis Journal*, Tierney thought "it was still undetermined

This photo of Ruth Munson was published in the *St. Paul Daily News* and many other newspapers. *MNHS*

whether Miss Munson was murdered and then carried into the building, or lured or forced into the structure and then slain."[2]

Detectives also had to investigate *why* Ruth Munson had been killed. The fact that her clothing had been removed before the fire was set suggested a sex crime. Or perhaps the disrobing was a ruse by the killer to misdirect the investigation. For every theory posed, its opposite remained a possibility.

The scant scientific evidence established thus far shed little light on the case. In preliminary findings, Ramsey County Coroner Dr. C. A. Ingerson had concluded that microscopic evidence proved that Ruth Munson had been criminally assaulted before or after she was killed. Paraphrasing the coroner's findings, the *Minneapolis Journal* reported that "her skull was fractured by a terrific blow from a blunt instrument which forced portions of the skull as deep as an inch and a half into the brain," adding that other abrasions on her skull suggested "at least a few other blows had been struck."[3]

The coroner's findings are typically accepted without question. Ingerson's conclusions, however, were disputed by Dr. John B. Dalton, police criminologist, and Dr. John Schoberg, city chemist. From their own examination, the two men concluded that they were unable to state positively that the murdered woman had been raped.[4]

Nevertheless, the investigation proceeded under the assumption that Ruth Munson had been sexually assaulted when she was killed. On the orders of Police Chief Clinton Hackert, "known degenerates" who had been arrested for or convicted of sex crimes would be systematically checked out. "We will bring in and question everyone who might by even the wildest stretch of the imagination have had anything to do with this case," Hackert declared.[5]

It would be a lengthy process. Detectives were working off a couple of lists compiled over time by the department. One list, labeled "St. Paul Sex Cases," contained forty-two names. A second list of "persons arrested for various sex crimes for the year 1937" contained 176 names.

The brutal murder had unnerved the city, focusing attention on women's vulnerability on the streets of St. Paul. Throughout the day, officers and detectives responded to calls from nervous citizens. Detectives Oscar Enebak and Axel Soderberg were sent to the Riverview Hotel, just down the hill from the Ramsey Hill neighborhood, where Ethel Baldyga, proprietor, told them that at 4:00 on the morning of the Aberdeen fire, a man requested a room where he "just wanted to rest for a couple hours." Baldyga rented a room to him for a dollar, and he tried to get her to go to bed with him. She refused and he left.[6]

In response to a complaint filed the night before, Tierney ordered Detective Lieutenant Bertram Talbot and Detective Alfred Jakobson to bring in Lee Len, forty-three years old, aka Charles or Charley Lee, a Chinese immigrant who operated a laundry at 187 North Western, around the corner from the Aberdeen. (Mrs. Bernard Knorr told detectives that he had "annoyed her on at least a dozen occasions. . . . He did not touch her but spoke to her and grinned.") Questioned with the assistance of an interpreter, Lee denied he molested any women, though he sometimes delivered laundry to the address of the complainant. Lee had a good reputation among business owners in the neighborhood, the detectives noted. He was "released with a warning not to annoy" women.[7]

Meanwhile, the press connected Ruth's murder to a string of recent attacks involving women. The front page of the *St. Paul Daily News* featured a map of the Ramsey Hill neighborhood labeled as a "crime center." Of the fourteen rapes and attempted rapes marked with an "X" on the map, twelve had occurred within a mile of the Aberdeen Hotel. Police labeled seven of those twelve cases rapes.[8]

At police headquarters, the name of Mrs. Milton Otto, a friend of Ruth's, crossed the desk of Detective Lieutenant Ray McCarthy. He dispatched Detective Paul Hanft and Detective Lieutenant Thomas Jansen to the Otto home at 521 West Lynnhurst Avenue, in the city's Midway district. Mrs. Otto, the officers learned, had worked with Ruth Munson "seven or eight years ago" at the William Harris home on Summit Avenue, but she hadn't seen Ruth in four or five years. Ruth was "very quiet about her affairs and [kept] very much to herself," Mrs. Otto recalled.[9]

McCarthy sent Detectives Donald Kampmann and Raymond Schmidt to the Harris home at 2029 Summit Avenue. A spacious Spanish Colonial mansion on a corner lot, the Harris place was a stark contrast to the single room Ruth Munson called home. Mrs. Harris told the detectives that Ruth had worked for her from 1926 until August 31, 1928, and until 1934 occasionally took care of their daughter. The previous May, Ruth had turned down the opportunity to return to the Harris household because she was "going to marry a carpenter" who had a Swedish accent. Harris described Ruth as "one of the finest girls that ever worked for her."[10]

Sometime during the morning, police headquarters received a call from Gus Gavanda, who gave detectives one of their first significant clues. Gavanda was a bartender at the Ace Box Lunch, a bar and café at 2360 University Avenue, near St. Paul's border with Minneapolis. He and his colleague, bartender Fred Meyer, had seen the large photograph of a smiling Ruth Munson printed on the front page of Friday's *Pioneer Press*, and they agreed that she was a customer. He told police that she

Ace Box Lunch, 1937. *MNHS*

had been at the bar on Wednesday evening, the day before her body was found. She was accompanied by two girlfriends, one a brunette and the other a redhead. They came on nights that the Happy Hollow Gang played so they could dance.[11]

Detectives Boyd Carrier and Frank Kennedy drove to Minneapolis to connect with members of the Happy Hollow Gang. Band members told the detectives that because they were often asked to play dance numbers, they knew many women by sight but not by name. The Happy Hollow Gang would play at the Ace the following Wednesday night, the detectives learned. Gavanda would point out the two women who came in with Ruth Munson on the night before her death—if they came in.[12]

While officers were scattered across the city in search of clues, Chief Hackert prepared himself for the sad duty of meeting with the bereaved Munson family. Around noon, Ruth's older sister, Selma Munson, arrived at police headquarters from Austin, Minnesota, where she worked as a hospital administrator. While waiting for the arrival of her father, Nels Munson, from Grantsburg, Wisconsin, and sister Helen, a schoolteacher from Amery, Wisconsin, Selma was cornered by a reporter for the *St. Paul Daily News*. "She was a good girl and nothing anyone can say or do will bring her back," Selma tearfully told the reporter. "I don't know why this horrible thing had to happen to us. Why is it that everyone takes advantage of girls whose folks live out of town? It always happens that way. It's terrible. Terrible. I just wish everyone would leave us alone so we can forget how awful it is. Nothing we can do will help her now." The trio met with Hackert to receive information about the investigation and make arrangements to claim Ruth's remains.[13]

While Hackert was meeting with the family, detectives received another significant lead. Patrolman Harold Harrington was grabbing a meal in a Ramsey Hill neighborhood restaurant when he struck up a conversation with Julius Loberg, who lived at 292 Dayton Avenue, Apartment 10. The conversation turned to the Munson case, and Loberg told Harrington that his brother Oscar had heard a woman scream on the morning of the murder. Harrington and his partner Patrolman Walter Grun went to Apartment 10 and asked Oscar Loberg to come to the station and make a statement. He consented, and another brother, Clarence, who had information of his own, accompanied him.[14]

Under questioning by Det. Lt. Jansen, Oscar described what he had heard. "Sometime between 2:00 and 4:00 in the morning I heard an awful scream and all of a sudden it was all over." Asked where the scream came from, he added, "It was on Dayton Av. Just what direction

I don't know because it was echoed between the walls of the buildings but it was on Dayton Ave., that I know because it come from that direction but on the [exact] spot, I don't know."[15]

Clarence Loberg told Jansen that he had been to a dance with a friend and was on his way home between 2:00 and 3:00 A.M. "I was going up Dayton, there. I see this car parked just about in front of 276 Dayton. I seen the [head]lights were on and the motor was running and there was two persons sitting there as close as I could see." Pressed for details, Clarence said he thought the occupants were a man and a woman sitting in a normal posture in the front seat. He described the car as "a Chev. or a Plymouth either a 1936 or a 1937 as close as I could see and it was either a dark blue or a black; I think it was a sedan but I wouldn't say for sure."[16]

The Lobergs' apartment at 292 Dayton was between the Aberdeen to the west and Ruth's apartment at 276 Dayton to the east. Conceivably, the scream could have come from either location. Was the car Clarence saw connected to the scream, or was it separate? Such tantalizing information, but what did it mean?

At 1:20 P.M. Det. Lt. McCarthy took a long-distance call from Arlington, Minnesota. The caller, Elmer Unglamb, said he had received a letter from Ruth Munson dated December 7 in which she stated that a few days earlier she had been out to "Louie's place" at Hugo, Minnesota; on Thursday evening she was at the Midway Amusement Company, and on Saturday she was at the Wagon Wheel, both St. Paul establishments. McCarthy noted in his report, "This is the same party who goes by the name of 'Whitey' from Arlington, Minnesota." McCarthy had probably picked up this information from Ruth's address book, or from numerous recent mentions of him in her diary.[17]

After the long day of interviews on Thursday, Detective Lieutenant Frank Cullen was back at the task. At 3:00 P.M. he offered a chair to Ella Wormley. Wormley, twenty-seven years old, was also known as Bertha. She worked as a cook for the Towle family in the fashionable Crocus Hill neighborhood just south of Summit Avenue. She told Cullen that she had known Ruth for about a year and a half, after getting acquainted with her at the Friendship Club in Minneapolis. The last time she had seen Ruth was on Thanksgiving evening at the Friendship Club, a fact confirmed in Ruth's diary entry for that date.

"We were what I call very close friends," Wormley said.

"Do you know any of her associates or boyfriends?" Cullen asked.

She knew Dick Das and Whitey.

"This Whitey that you speak of, did Ruth used to go with him?"

Yes, was the answer, but Wormley did not know Whitey's last name, where he lived, or where he was employed.

"Did Ruth and Whitey have any dispute when they stopped going with one another that you know of?"

"Nothing Ruth ever mentioned to me."

"Are there any other boyfriends of Ruth's that you know of?"

There was a fellow named Lawrence, from Minneapolis, before she met Whitey. Lawrence had a nice house and lived with his mother.

"Did she ever mention any travelling salesman from Nebraska?"

"By the name of Wally." She didn't know his last name, but Wally had once driven Ruth home, and she had ridden with them.

"Do you know a fellow by the name of John from Chicago, a salesman?" How police learned about these two traveling salesmen is unknown.

"No."

"Did Ruth ever tell you that she had been bothered or annoyed by anyone, or followed at any time?"

"No."

Asked if there was anything else that she could add to this statement, Wormley named Art Miller as another man Ruth used to go out with. They were just friends, she thought.[18]

Dick, Lawrence, Whitey, Wally, John, Art. It was apparent Ruth Munson had a lot of male friends if not quite boyfriends. The detectives would have to figure out what each of Ruth's male friends meant to her and, just as importantly, what she meant to each of them.

Detectives Carrier and Kennedy had returned from their trip to Minneapolis. They talked to Ruth Munson's landlady, Clara Broughton, hoping for leads that would help identify the two women who were with Ruth at the Ace the previous Wednesday. The landlady said that about a year and a half before, she saw Ruth Munson with a redheaded woman whom she thought lived nearby at 280 Dayton. At that address, the detectives talked to Catherine Conroy, who said she had seen "Miss Munson and a redheaded girl together around Selby and Nina." She also saw this redheaded woman at Tunnel Drug on different occasions but had never learned her name. The detectives inquired at several different places along Selby Avenue, but no one seemed to know the redheaded woman.[19]

The detectives were dispatched to 762 Case Street on the city's East Side to interview Mrs. C. E. Hanson in regards to Marion Peterson, a friend of Ruth's. Marion Peterson had moved back to Lindstrom, Minnesota, and was living on her father's farm; her sister, Singheld, worked as a maid in Minneapolis. The detectives were given photographs of both women to show to employees at the Ace for possible identification as the two women who accompanied Ruth on Wednesday night.[20]

At 7:40 P.M., Cullen sat down with William Nelson, who, detectives had learned, was Ruth's former fiancé. Nelson had driven voluntarily to St. Paul from Frederic, Wisconsin, where he worked as a bartender and substitute mail carrier. Due to his past romantic relationship, Nelson was an obvious suspect, and Cullen questioned him like one.

In answer to Cullen's opening questions, Nelson described his employment history, stated that he had never been arrested, and confirmed that he had known Ruth Munson for nine years.

"Were you engaged to be married to her?"

"At one time."

"What year?"

"Probably about 1929." They had been engaged for about a year and a half.

"How did you happen to break with her?"

"Well, I would say it was the depression caused it. We could not afford to be married and she didn't feel like waiting."

"Did you ever have intercourse with her?"

"No."

"Never in your life?"

"Well, I had years ago."

"When did you have intercourse with her?"

"Well it was only once, during the time we were engaged. . . . The reason I was reticent about saying it was that I did not want it made public."

"We are not in the habit of making these things public."

Mindful of Detective Jansen's interview of Clarence Loberg earlier in the day, Cullen asked what kind of car Nelson drove.

"Ford, 1937, 60-coach, a black one."

Cullen established that after some years of estrangement, Nelson had been in touch with Ruth again, exchanging letters on occasion. He sometimes visited her in St. Paul. They had talked about renewing their relationship, though not recently. Nelson had driven to St. Paul on November 30 and taken her to dinner in Hugo the next day, which she had recorded in her diary. Cullen asked Nelson about his activities on December 8 and 9. He asked how Nelson had learned of Ruth Munson's death, then doubled back to his trips to St. Paul.

"Have you been in St. Paul since that last Wednesday you told us about?"

"No."

"Is there anything that I have not asked you that you know about this case? Anything you care to add to this statement at this time?"

"I cannot think of anything else."

"Do you know how Ruth Munson met her death?"

"No, I don't. I cannot read the whole story, when I looked at the pictures it turned my stomach."

"What do you mean?"

"She and I were pretty good friends, you know."

"Have you any idea who may be responsible for her death?"

"No, I haven't."

Nelson agreed to sign his statement if "it is written as I say," and the interview ended.[21]

At 8:30 P.M. Detectives Carrier and Kennedy went to the state capitol, where they checked "about one hundred different combinations of license numbers to place a 1936 or 1937 Plymouth coupe seen at the Tunnel Tavern, 293 Selby Avenue." They would later learn that this car belonged to a *Pioneer Press* reporter.

Their next stop was a visit with Mary McNeely, a maid at 2057 Portland. McNeely told them she had known Ruth for the past four and a half years, sometimes seeing her with Olaf Anderson at the Strand Ball Room. She had been at the Ace on Wednesday night between 8:00 and 9:30 P.M., but did not see Ruth during this time. "She was sure," the detectives reported, "that if Ruth come that she would have noticed her as there was not a very large crowd at the Ace that night."[22]

Perhaps it was Mary McNeely's contradictory report about Ruth's presence at the Ace Box Lunch on Wednesday evening that inspired the detectives to drive over to the café themselves. Located on the southeast corner of University and Raymond Avenues, the Ace was casually known by a variety of names: the Ace, the Ace Box, the Ace Café, or the Ace Bar. Tucked into the ground floor on the east end of the Specialty Building, its Streamline Moderne storefront of curved windows and smooth beige stone stood out in sharp architectural contrast to the functional red bricks that characterized the rest of the three-story building. The interior housed a long bar, a dance floor, and tables covered with checkered tablecloths, flanked by round-backed wooden chairs. The dance bands that regularly played at the Ace attracted men and women from around town who mingled peacefully with the neighborhood regulars.

During their visit, Detectives Carrier and Kennedy talked to bartenders Meyer and Gavanda and confirmed that both had seen Ruth Munson with two women standing at the bar on Wednesday night. Gavanda knew them only by sight. He noted that the trio came every night the Happy Hollow Gang played. One of the band members, Vernon (Ole) Hanson, knew them well. Gavanda said he had never noticed the women in the company of any men and that two of the "girls" always danced together.[23]

The Ace was fast becoming a focal point of the investigation. At 10:00 P.M., Detectives Kampmann and Schmidt stepped into the bar. Gavanda told them the same thing he had told Carrier and Kennedy earlier that evening—that Ruth Munson had been there with two other women until about 11:30 P.M. on the night before she was found murdered. The detectives called Tierney and made arrangements to bring Gavanda to the station for a statement the following morning. While at the Ace, Kampmann and Schmidt connected with a man who had gone out with Ruth on several occasions. They drove him to headquarters, where he was questioned by Det. Lt. Cullen, who was still working.

Vincent Nels Sorg, twenty-eight years old, told Cullen he was a shipping clerk and worked next door to the Ace. He often went there for supper. He had known Ruth Munson casually for about two and a half years. He had gone out with her "in company" two or three times, including evenings at the Ace. He had even danced with her.

Cullen got right to the point. "Have you ever had intercourse with her?"

"No, I never tried it."

"When was the last time you saw her?"

"Last Wednesday night was the last time."

Sorg explained that he was at a table eating supper and Ruth and her party were standing at the bar. He'd planned to go up and speak to her after completing his meal, but by the time he finished, she was no longer standing at the bar.

"Who was she with?"

"Two girls but I could not identify them. Never saw them before. One looked like a brunette, maybe not as tall as Ruth. I could not tell how she was dressed."

"What did the other girl look like?"

"She had kind of sandy hair or reddish hair as far as I noticed. I was sitting pretty far back."

"How was Ruth dressed?"

"She had a green dress on, seal skin coat, and black hat." He could not describe how the others were dressed.

"Do you think you could identify the girls [who] were with her?"

"I don't think so. Never saw them before and I didn't get a good look at them."[24]

It was late. Through the course of the day, detectives had filed forty-one reports on different aspects of the case, most of which were about leads that would take them nowhere. But two important pieces of information had been established. The informal statements by the Ace bartenders Gavanda and Meyer had reduced the twelve-hour gap to about seven hours, between midnight Wednesday and 7:00 Thursday morning. Further, the bartenders had described possible witnesses—two women who were with Ruth at the Ace and had left with her.

Oscar and Clarence Loberg had identified a time window of 2:00 to 4:00 A.M. in which a scream had been heard somewhere on Dayton Avenue and a car had been spotted in front of 276 Dayton, Ruth's building. The next day's work would focus on these two leads.

Whether detectives realized it or not, one more piece of new information that would figure prominently in the investigation was collected that day. In the midafternoon, J. E. Brooks, a driver for the Blue and White Cab Company, filed a report at the police department's front desk. Brooks said that on December 2 at 1:15 A.M., he had driven two Black men from the Lowry Hotel in downtown St. Paul up to 276 Dayton Avenue. According to the police report, after talking together, the two passengers concluded "that this was not the right place, that it must be the other street." Brooks drove the two men back to the Lowry.[25]

At this point in the investigation, detectives were recording every detail they uncovered about the building where Ruth Munson lived. But this incident stood out to those who knew the city. Most of St. Paul's Black residents lived in the Rondo neighborhood, a couple of blocks north of the Ramsey Hill neighborhood. Rondo Avenue, often incorrectly referred to as Rondo Street in police reports, extended west from Rice Street approximately two miles to Lexington Parkway. From the backbone of Rondo Avenue, the neighborhood roughly extended north four blocks to Aurora Avenue and south two blocks to Marshall Avenue—which was one block north of Dayton. The neighborhood was bisected by Dale Street, running north to south. Poorer residents lived east of Dale in "Cornmeal Valley," characterized by older homes, apartment buildings, and commercial structures. The more affluent residents lived on "Oatmeal Hill," which lay west of Dale in a slightly newer portion of the city. The neighborhood boasted forty-seven Black-owned businesses, and approximately half of its Black residents owned or were buying their homes.[26]

Nonresidents had their own terminology for the Rondo neighborhood. A 1935 map of St. Paul labeled the Rondo neighborhood as the "Largest Negro Section in the City." As blunt as the label was, it bore some accuracy. Within the Rondo neighborhood, approximately 83 percent of the city's Black population lived in geographic, social, and economic isolation. The majority of the neighborhood's workers were porters, unskilled laborers, or domestic servants. Nearly half of those employed worked for the railroad; about one in five worked in one of the area's meat-packing plants.[27]

Veterans on the police force understood it was unusual for an automobile carrying Black folks to stop in the Ramsey Hill neighborhood and in front of Ruth's apartment building, to boot. Cabdriver Brooks's account marked the first time the investigation was linked to members of St. Paul's Black community. It would not be the last.

5   "Mighty Near the Perfect Murder"

Saturday, December 11, 1937

Saturday morning. The temperature hovered around zero. There would be no weekend off for detectives. In the forty-eight hours since Ruth Munson's body was discovered, Assistant Chief of Police Charles J. Tierney had worked continuously on the case. Detectives had questioned a hundred people, and no solution was in sight.

Clues considered important in the early hours of the investigation had turned into dead ends. When firemen discovered the "oil can" or "coffee can," detectives initially thought the killer used it to carry the accelerant. But recognition that the container had been found some distance from the body now made detectives doubt it belonged to the killer (Indeed, detectives would receive a confirming report later that boys exploring the empty hotel the previous summer had seen the vessel there.)[1]

The mysterious person Ruth Munson spoke to on the telephone Wednesday afternoon had been identified. Eavesdropping, Ruth's landlady had overheard her tenant say that she would prefer to come over and stay for the night. The detectives had learned that Ruth was talking not to her killer, but to her boyfriend, Dick Das. The two were simply making plans for her to babysit his two children.[2]

A lack of helpful clues lent a sense of urgency to the investigation. Detectives knew the more days that went by without a solution, the less likely a solution would ever be found. The press took notice of the lack of significant clues. An obviously frustrated Tierney told the *St. Paul Pioneer Press*, "the investigation is greatly hampered by lack of clues and background." Further, "old time detectives" who remained unnamed told the paper the crime was "mighty near the perfect murder," noting that as of Friday evening there was "no definite clue nor a tenable theory."[3]

While the *St. Paul Daily News* was satisfied the police were "making every effort," its editorial page warned the force not to "slow down" its search. "The thought that such a fiend may be in St. Paul inspires fear and horror. He must be apprehended."[4]

Tips from an alarmed public were piling up at police headquarters—

documenting past assaults on women, registering complaints about window peepers, and telling police where to find suspicious-looking men who should be investigated. Concerns about public safety kept people off the streets. "It has been noticeable," the *Pioneer Press* reported, "that very few girls are on the streets of the district after dark unescorted."[5]

As detectives turned to follow leads from Ruth's evening at the Ace, new details from the coroner's autopsy report proved more puzzling than helpful in determining what occurred after Ruth and her friends left that nightspot. According to the *Pioneer Press*, the coroner had concluded "the murdered girl had not eaten food nor consumed any alcoholic beverages Wednesday night." Not only did this contradict statements from bartenders who had served the three women, it defied common sense to say the trio would not eat or drink while at a bar. But if there was no evidence of food or alcohol in her system, perhaps Ruth remained alive long enough to absorb traces of the alcohol in the beer.[6]

Detectives also hoped to track down more information about the scream Oscar Loberg heard during the dark hours of the night somewhere along Dayton Avenue. They would also be on the lookout for automobiles matching the description given by Clarence Loberg. As the day got underway, a new tip came into headquarters about strange sounds in the night. After taking a call from the fire department, Detective Lieutenant Ray McCarthy sent Detective Lieutenant Bertram Talbot and Detective Alfred Jakobson to talk to the man who drove Fire Chief Peterson's car on the day of the fire. The driver sent them to the caretaker of an apartment building across the street from the Aberdeen. The caretaker, Phil Lukenheimer, told the detectives he had heard several shots or a car backfiring and the crash of breaking glass at about midnight on Wednesday night. The two detectives spent the morning checking the neighborhood for broken windows, but in the end, they found nothing significant.[7]

Meanwhile, at 8:35 A.M., Walter Lucci, a "chauffeur" for the Blue and White Cab Company, walked into police headquarters on his own initiative. Det. Lt. McCarthy met with him in Tierney's office.

"I hear this Wilbur," Lucci began, "he drives Blue [and] White #40 at night and he said 'that's the girl I took two n - - - - - s up to call for her.' He said that was the place at 276 Dayton Ave. He also said my boss said that she goes out of her way to talk to the porters in the Union Depot . . . n - - - - - s in other words."

Perhaps mindful of J. E. Brook's earlier report, McCarthy pressed Lucci a bit to determine if he was referring to the same incident. "Was there something said to you sometime ago about some cabdriver that took two negroes to 276 Dayton Ave. and you understood that they went up to 276 Dayton Ave. to pick up Ruth Munson?"

"I wouldn't say," Lucci said. "Wilber says that he thinks this is the girl they went to pick up."

"And he drives Cab #40?"

"Yes."

"You mentioned something to me about the Keystone Hotel at Carrol and Western Aves." The Keystone was a hotel in the Rondo neighborhood.

"I have none about that, but I figured out that it could have been two men or 1 man that had her around—find out where these fellows live[—]he could have this all fixed up as the door was opened."

"What door?"

"At the Aberdeen Hotel."

In so many words, Lucci had just accused the two men of participating in the murder of Ruth Munson.

"Do you know from your own knowledge that it has been opened for some time?" McCarthy asked, referring to the Aberdeen's door.

"No just what I heard in the Beer Parlor that the children run in and out and play—the children from the grocery store at Western [and] Selby Aves. play on the fire escape."

"Walter, do you know Ruth Munson?"

"No, I don't, never seen her or anything."[8]

Lucci's pejorative language, attitudes, and accusations notwithstanding, the police needed to check out the possibility that a second cabdriver had driven two men, be they Black or white, to Ruth Munson's home. By 10:00 A.M. the cabdriver, Darrell Wilber, had been brought to police headquarters, and Detective Lieutenant Frank R. Cullen questioned him.

"Have you had occasion to make a trip to 276 Dayton?" Cullen asked.

"Yes, the last one was about two weeks ago or a week and a half ago."

"Where did you pick up your fare?"

"Across the street from Thompson's Restaurant on Wabasha St. [in downtown]. They came out of the restaurant and hailed me, two colored men about the same height, 5′ 6–7,″ and one of them asked me to take them to 276 Dayton."

During the short trip, the two men talked together, mostly about money and who was paying the fare. At one point, Wilber recalled, "one of them asked the other fellow how he got broads like that and he said he'd be damned if he could. I don't know what the other fellow said."

At their destination, a woman, evidently white, came out when the cab stopped. Wilber estimated the time to be between 2:00 and 2:30 A.M.

"What conversation did she have?"

"She told one fellow to get out, that he wouldn't need a cab where they were going . . . I took the second one to Arundel and Rondo."

"Did you get a good look at the woman when you drove up there?"

"She stayed in the shadows," Wilber admitted. But about two nights later, when he saw her a second time, "I recognized her enough so [that when] she came up 5th St. to St. Peter and the fellow that was sitting with me asked if she wanted a cab and she looked around. I said I didn't think so cause I thought she had some colored boy friend coming to meet her."

That second time Wilber had seen her, the woman stepped inside a drugstore and waited about ten minutes. At about 2:00 A.M. a sedan with three men drove up and she got in the back seat.

"Were they white or colored?" Cullen asked.

"Colored."

Cullen asked what kind of car the men drove. Wilber described the car as a 1933 or 1934 Buick, tan or olive in color.

"Have you ever hauled any other colored people to 276 Dayton Ave.?" Cullen asked.

"No."

"Have you ever hauled this girl at any occasion?"

"No, I don't remember that I ever drove her any place."

"Can you be positive that Miss Ruth Munson is the girl that you seen that morning?"

"No, the only thing that made the connection was that Miss Munson was a little too overly friendly with the porters at the depot. We were talking and somebody mentioned '276 Dayton.' I had read the article but I never noticed the address especially. As soon as somebody mentioned '276 Dayton,' I recalled that a week before I had taken two colored fellows up there to get a girl."

"Is it quite unusual for you to haul colored people to that locality?"

"I don't remember that I ever hauled colored people anywhere along there."

Under further questioning, Wilber said the woman at 276 Dayton wore "a black sealskin, or imitation sealskin coat, small dark hat, dark shoes, dark stockings." He added a curious detail: "She was standing inside the hallway there. There was about two or three people walking by just as she got out on the Boulevard and she hesitated and turned her back to them and then she came over."

Asked to describe the fares he had driven from downtown to 276 Dayton, Wilber described the man who got out of the car as "5′ 6–7,"; about 150 lbs. I think he had a dark coat, either gray or black, and a hat, fairly well dressed." The man he drove to Arundel and Rondo was about the same age and height and weighed about 165 pounds. His coat was brown. Wilber didn't think he would recognize either man if he saw them again.[9]

A later check of Blue and White's trip sheets confirmed the reports of drivers Brooks and Wilber on their trips the night of December 2.[10]

Two different pairs of African American men had been driven from downtown St. Paul to 276 Dayton, where Ruth Munson lived, on the same date at approximately the same late hour. It looked as though people were searching for a party of some kind.

Ace bartender Gus Gavanda came in to give his statement, as arranged. He sat down with Cullen at 11:00 A.M. and told much the same story he told reporters, with a bit more detail. Gavanda, thirty years old, had been bartending at the Ace for nine months. He knew Ruth Munson only by sight, as a bar customer, and he had never gone out with her. He was positive she had been at the Ace on Wednesday, December 8. Ruth and her two girlfriends had stood at his bar for fifteen to twenty minutes before moving to a table next to the dance floor.

"Can you describe them?" Cullen asked of Ruth's companions.

"One was short, about 25 years old, about 5 feet tall, 125 lbs."

"Light or dark complected?"

"Light."

"Blonde or reddish or anything?"

"Medium light."

"Now the other girl."

"She was about 5 feet–4½ inches, about 26 years old or 27 years old."

"Was she light or dark?"

"Auburn hair—fiery red." A natural color, Gavanda added. As for Ruth, she "had on a green dress, I would say it was a satin shiny silk with a low neck and a white collar."

He had seen the three women there on other nights. They usually came about 8:30 P.M. They always drank 3.2 beer. On Wednesday night they had consumed maybe four or five beers. He had never seen Ruth Munson intoxicated. The trio had left between 11:30 and 12:00, going out the front door. They were always together, never with men.[11]

At 1:15 P.M., another individual connected to the Ace arrived at police headquarters to make a statement. H. A. Nielsen managed the

Arions, billed as "America's only blind road orchestra," which played frequently at the Ace. He was questioned by Detective Lieutenant Nate Smith. Although the newspapers made it sound like the Happy Hollow Gang played on Wednesday, December 9, it was Arions that played that night, Nielsen insisted. But he had heard that the Happy Hollow Gang's accordion player, Ole Olson, knew Ruth Munson.

"Do you know of any of Miss Munson's acquaintances?" Smith asked.

Nielsen noted that Ruth Munson always came with two other "girls," one with brownish hair, the other with reddish hair. Usually, they came on Thursday nights.

"The girl with the reddish hair and Miss Munson were standing in front where they take pictures," Nielsen recalled. "They had their coats on then. That was in the neighborhood of 10:15 or 10:20."[12]

At the same time that Smith was interviewing Nielsen, Det. Lt. McCarthy was meeting with John Comerford, night auditor and clerk at the once-palatial Ryan Hotel in downtown St. Paul. Comerford had contacted his close friend Detective Harry O'Keefe the previous night with a tip on the Munson case, and O'Keefe had talked him into coming to headquarters to make a confidential statement. Comerford told McCarthy that at about midnight on Tuesday, December 7, a couple came into the hotel lobby. The woman sat in the corner and looked at a magazine. The man roamed about the lobby, periodically talking to the woman. After forty-five minutes, the man requested a room, registering as J. R. Miller, 1137 Blair Street. After more negotiation, the couple agreed to have the bellboy show them to the room. About 2:00 A.M. they both left the hotel. Wednesday night, December 8, at approximately the same hour, the couple returned and went through the same lengthy negotiation, but in the end did not engage a room. They left at approximately 1:30 A.M. The woman, Comerford said, resembled the "girl" whose picture appeared in the *Pioneer Press* on Friday morning. She was, McCarthy noted in his report, "about 30; very calm type; not intoxicated; had a coat with high collar, which was turned up, (unable to tell kind of fur) and had either a green coat or else her dress was green as it showed." According to the city directory, McCarthy noted, the address the man gave was fictitious.[13]

Ruth's diary made no mention of her activities on the evening of December 7. On December 8, she was at the Ace, leaving as late as midnight, making it theoretically possible for her to be the woman in this couple.

In the middle of the afternoon, detectives received a new tip about the scream in the night. At 3:15 P.M., Mr. A. Russell came to the station and talked to Det. Lt. Cullen, who was between interviews of Ace employees. Russell told Cullen that he got up at 4:45 A.M. every morning and then woke up his daughter Genevieve. On the morning of the fire, she told him that in the night she had heard "wailing like a person in agony and pain" about four times "and the wail kept up approximately a minute or so each time." She felt bad, she told her father, that she didn't get up to investigate, "as she felt sure it was a human being in distress." Russell lived on Marshall Avenue, about two blocks northwest of the Aberdeen.[14]

Having questioned Gus Gavanda earlier in the day, Cullen questioned Ace waitress Dorothy Lolly at 5:38 P.M. Married and twenty-six years old, she had been a waitress at the Ace for about three months. She didn't know Ruth Munson personally, but had waited on her "several times," the last time being Monday. She didn't recall seeing Ruth and her friends on Wednesday, but said they could have been there and she didn't see them.

"Can you describe, say the shortest one of the two?"

"She is about medium height," Lolly said, "must weigh about 128 pounds, brown hair, medium complexion, wore a cloth coat, I think tan color; plain collar; I don't remember the dress she wore."

"How about the other girl's appearance?"

"I imagine the tallest one would be at least 25, about 5 ft 3½ or 4; weight about 130; sort of auburn hair, reddish tint, more light complected, usually wore a skirt and sweater."

"What did they usually drink when they came in?"

"Miss Munson always drank a Schmitz, and the short one did, too, and the other one would start with one beer then ordered a shot of gin with lime rickey and that was about all she drank; Miss Munson and the other girl might order one more beer." They never seemed intoxicated.[15]

Cullen next interviewed Ace bartender Fred Meyer, who had been the first to make the connection by recognizing Ruth's picture in the newspaper. Meyer was certain that Ruth and her companions were "at my bar; oh I would say roughly, they were at my bar half an hour." Beyond that, he offered little in the way of new information. He didn't know any of the three women by name. He could not recall how they were dressed, other than one of them had a fur coat, "a Hudson seal." They never seemed to be with men, never appeared to be intoxicated. He did not know what time they left.[16]

Over the course of the day, detectives had interviewed four individuals associated with the Ace. Their statements had been variations on a theme. Ruth Munson and two women were at the Ace on Wednesday night, avoided men, and left sometime between 11:30 P.M. and midnight. One of Ruth's companions was a redhead, the other had brown hair. No one knew their names. That was it.

In the early evening hours, Detectives Oran Stutzman and Fred Nielsen filed a report on an investigation that had consumed much of their afternoon. Earlier in the day, Albert Ramsell had come to the police station on his own initiative with information about Ruth Munson. Det. Lt. McCarthy had interviewed him. Ramsell, a carpenter who lived in a basement apartment at 438 Portland, had been at the Union Depot on the evening of March 15, 1937, to get a cup of coffee. He claimed to have overheard another waitress say to Ruth Munson, "You dam [sic] bitch you I ought to cut your head off, and you'll get it someday too." Later, the waitress had addressed Ramsell, saying "well she sure is a bad devil," referring to Ruth. The waitress, Ramsell said, was still working at the Union Depot and he could point her out.[17]

Any threat made against a murder victim needed to be investigated. McCarthy had dispatched Detectives Stutzman and Nielsen to follow up on Ramsell's story. They picked up Ramsell and drove him to the Union Depot. Looking at the waitresses on duty at that afternoon hour, Ramsell could not make an identification. The waitresses on duty mentioned another server, Joan Pivoran, who had been interviewed the day the murder was discovered. They drove Ramsell to her residence in the city's North End. Ramsell said she wasn't the one who made the threat. Back at the Union Depot, the officers met with the restaurant manager, C. E. Blackburn. He checked his time book and noted that Ruth Gruenwald and Eliza Kovarik were the only waitresses who worked the night of March 15, 1937. Ruth Munson, Blackburn said, had never worked at night since she began her employment. Nevertheless, Stutzman and Nielsen interviewed Gruenwald, who lived on the East Side, and Kovarik, who lived in downtown. When Stutzman and Nielsen filed their report at 6:45 P.M., they concluded that Ramsell's story "does not involve" Ruth Munson.[18]

Another day winding down. Detective Herman Schlichting was working up a report of his conversation with a Miss B. Spink. The woman told him that some time ago, on the evening that "the Sheep Barns [sic] burned in So. St. Paul," she was parking her car in front of 276 Dayton when a green coupe stopped alongside. "Two colored men and a colored lady were in this car," she reported; the men got out of their car and one of them opened the door of Spink's car. Spink was frightened and quickly ran into her apartment. The men got into their coupe and drove away.[19]

For the third time, the police had received information about men of color stopping at 276 Dayton Avenue. What was to be made of it? Was it coincidence, or was there something to it? The information was kept within the department and not shared with the press.

At 9:40 P.M., while Detective Schlichting was completing his report, Detectives McGowan and Lannon were dispatched to the Globe Building in downtown to talk to Mrs. M. S. Martin. Mrs. Martin and her husband lived approximately two blocks west of the Aberdeen at 450–452 Dayton Avenue on the south side of the street. Mrs. Martin gave the detectives a broken bracelet that her husband had found in front of their building about 11:00 on Friday morning. The bracelet was lying in the snow against the curb, about a foot from an old-fashioned curb step from the horse-and-carriage days.

There was something else, she told the detectives. Before she went to bed Wednesday night—actually, after midnight, making it early Thursday morning—she heard a woman "utter two loud screams." She estimated the time as being about half or three-quarters of an hour before the streetlights were shut off for the night at 2:30 A.M.

There was one other thing. At about 6:00 P.M. on Wednesday night, the last night Ruth Munson was alive, Martin got off the streetcar at Virginia Street on her way home from work to go to the grocery store down on Selby Avenue. On the Selby side of the Aberdeen, on the building's second floor, she noticed "a light on."[20]

6 Contrasts

The investigation was a twenty-four-hour-a-day effort. Around 1:00 A.M. Detectives Oscar Enebak, Donald Kampmann, Raymond Schmidt, and Axel Soderberg returned to police headquarters to write up a report for an evening's work that had begun hours ago. The detectives had driven over to Minneapolis to visit the Friendship Club, just off Lake Street at 2935 Nicollet Avenue. Though not an actual club with membership dues, the Friendship Club did require its guests to be at least twenty-eight years of age. Admission was twenty-five cents until 8:30 P.M., thirty-five cents thereafter. Club patrons could enjoy old-time and modern dancing, play cards, and win prizes. "Yes, we play Scandinavian and modern music," proclaimed the advertisement for its grand opening. "If you miss our good time, it's your own fault. Just imagine dancing with those of your own age." The advertisement promised "Trained hostesses to help you meet new friends."[1]

The detectives had spent four hours at the club. They talked to Linda Best, Euphrosine (Babe) Hadish, and Ella (Bertha) Wormley, all St. Paul friends of Ruth's. Hadish, according to the detectives, observed "that Ruth was very quiet and conservative and was attempting to break up with Derrick Das by letter as she did not want to face him." Wormley had already given a statement to Detective Lieutenant Frank R. Cullen on Friday. Friendship Club manager Frank Kenny informed the detectives that he and the cashier had noticed Ruth Munson and Ella Wormley recently "came to the club rather late and appeared to have been drinking on several occasions."

Kenny also noted that Ruth had been escorted by "a man by the name of Whitey" and once by another man, name unknown, about "34 years, 6 ft. 2 in. good looking, brown eyes, dark hair, slender build." During the past two months, Kenny noted, Ruth Munson had "divulged very little information to her girl friends," an observation detectives were to encounter time and again.[2]

The detectives returned to police headquarters about 1:00 A.M. on Sunday to write up their report. Almost immediately, Detective Schmidt partnered with Detective Ernest Woodhouse on another assignment. They picked up Blue and White Cab driver J. E. Brooks and took him to the Lowry Hotel to see if, among the employees, he could identify the two Black men he had driven to Ruth Munson's building on December 2. At some point, the detectives also called Darrell Wilber from Blue and White to come and identify these men. Brooks positively identified Merton Ewing, a waiter from Minneapolis, as one of the two men. With less certainty, he tentatively identified Lawrence Louis as the second man. In their report, the detectives neglected to mention any attempt by Wilber to identify the men. The detectives then took the Lowry employees and the cabdrivers to see Assistant Chief Charles J. Tierney, who was still working at that late hour. They left Ewing and Louis with Tierney and drove the cabbies back to the Lowry. At the Lowry, the cabdrivers attempted to identify another man for the detectives, but they were unsuccessful. Tierney later released both Ewing and Louis without any charges.[3]

Readers opened their Sunday edition of the *St. Paul Pioneer Press* to learn that the city's mayor, Mark H. Gehan, planned to request that the Ramsey County Board of Commissioners offer a $500 reward for information leading to the capture and conviction of Ruth Munson's slayer. "Witnesses apparently are backward about volunteering information toward solution of this brutal crime," Mayor Gehan explained. "I hope the reward may bring in information leading to the capture and conviction of the killer. Undoubtedly there is much information that has not been given police."

Specifically, the authorities hoped the reward would inspire someone to identify the two women who accompanied Ruth Munson to the Ace on the last night of her life. For Tierney, their identification was "his main hope for solving the murder." Although newspapers reported that police had "partially identified" the two women, at this point they had nothing more than general descriptions of them—descriptions that fit many women.[4]

The investigation was struggling in other areas. So far, 126 miscellaneous reports and statements were stacked on Tierney's desk. No progress had been made in tracing the screams heard along Dayton Avenue during the night, or in finding the car that had been seen about the same time. But experienced detectives knew this was the way investigations went. A promising lead would come in, and it could take days to nail it down. Too often, the lead proved to be a dead end, or even worse, it would be left dangling without an answer.

Yesterday, out of the blue, the bracelet found on Dayton Avenue had been turned in, adding yet another facet to the investigation. That was also the way investigations went. Who knew what new leads or clues would surface during the day, or at what hour?

At 8:30 A.M., Chief Clinton Hackert dispatched Detectives Kampmann and Schmidt to investigate a new report that a James Lyttle had "stepped out" with Ruth Munson the previous March or April. The term "stepped out" added yet another dimension to the investigation. Married men "stepped out" on their wives when they engaged in sexual relationships outside their marriage. Women who engaged in such activities with men were known as "steppers." In some circles, "stepping out" was vaguely associated with prostitution.

The detectives traced Lyttle through two addresses before locating him at 270 Dayton Avenue, an apartment building close to Ruth's. The recently divorced Lyttle was not home. The detectives escorted his roommate, Joseph J. Rhiner, to headquarters, where he was interviewed by Detective Lieutenant Nate Smith at 11:00 A.M.[5]

Rhiner said he didn't know Ruth Munson. Prior to the murder, he and Lyttle had never talked about her. On Wednesday, December 8, the two of them had spent most of the evening at De Courcy's, a bar on Wabasha Street. Lyttle had left the bar briefly to get something to eat. He left again at midnight, saying he was going home. At 1:00 A.M. when Rhiner returned home, Lyttle was asleep.

"You are positive in your conversations with Lyttle you never heard him speak of Ruth Munson?"

"Absolutely. That is, of course, before this murder happened." Rhiner was equally positive that James Lyttle had never mentioned that he knew Ruth Munson. When Det. Lt. Smith interviewed James Lyttle the next day, he denied knowing Ruth Munson, though he admitted knowing a different Munson family in St. Paul.[6]

Sex outside of marriage was frowned upon culturally, and it was illegal in some cases. James Lyttle had every reason to lie about any sexual relationship he might have had with Ruth Munson with little concern about being disproven. After all, Ruth was not there to contradict him. The investigation of James Lyttle went no further.

By midmorning, Detectives Robert Vick and Ernest Woodhouse were detailed to follow up on a letter found among Ruth's possessions. Dated December 1, 1937, the form letter announced the December meeting of Union Lodge #82 of the Scandinavian American Fraternity. According to the letter, at this "very important meeting" changes to the bylaws would be discussed, along with the possibility of future cuts in benefits paid out from the sick fund. The letter included a monthly dues assessment made out to Ruth Munson for $3.42, due by the end of the month.

Vick and Woodhouse arrived at Union Lodge #82 headquarters at 10:15. The lodge's financial secretary, H. H. Elmquist, informed the detectives that the lodge would pay out a $500 death benefit to the father and mother of the deceased. Unfortunately, Elmquist knew nothing of Ruth's personal life, other than she never attended the lodge's business meetings, but often attended dances it sponsored. He did not know any of her acquaintances. (The next day, December 13, Ruth's sister Helen mailed a letter to Tierney asking that he "kindly look among Ruth's letters for the insurance policy with the Scandinavian American Fraternity and please send it to me." She also asked Tierney to "please keep all the letters until we call for them.")[7]

Contrasts were starting to emerge in the information being compiled about Ruth Munson. Ruth visited the Ace accompanied only by her two girlfriends. They stood at the bar or sat together, ignoring men in the establishment, and danced only with each other. On occasion, Ruth had been escorted to the Friendship Club by men. At the Ace, she was never intoxicated, but lately at the Friendship Club she had exhibited signs of drinking. What did these contrasts mean? Was Ruth content with her life? Who really knew her well? Did anyone?

Perhaps Detective Schmidt had these contrasts in mind when he and Woodhouse retraced some early steps in the investigation by making a return visit to Ruth's friend and coworker Joan Pivoran. Pivoran had given a statement on the afternoon her friend's body was discovered. Now the detectives asked if she had "noticed any change in the actions or in the behavior of Ruth in the past five months." Was she "More friendly or more distant?" Pivoran, the detectives wrote, claimed "that Ruth has seemed happier during the past month than ever before."[8]

Around noon, Hiram Miller approached Patrolmen Harold Harrington and Walter Grun, telling them he had overheard two women talking about the Munson case the previous night when he was out buying a paper. The officers drove Miller to police headquarters, where Detective Lieutenant Ray McCarthy took his statement. Miller was at the corner of Western and Selby about 9:30 P.M. Saturday night when he overheard the women talking. "I bet my life that Tim O'Halloran is the man that committed that crime," one said to the other. "It must have been someone acquainted with the hotel to get in there in the night and do what he did do and he was a world war veteran and he was a patient in the Aberdeen when the government had it for a hospital."

When her friend suggested she should tell the police, the first woman replied, "I wouldn't for the whole world because my name would be in all the headlines of the papers."[9]

Miller did not know the two women who were talking and there was no easy way to identify them, leaving another potential clue open ended. Miller's statement underscored Mayor Gehan's concern that citizens were withholding information from the police. It also suggested another area where suspects might exist—among the hundreds, maybe thousands, of men who had been patients when the Aberdeen was a veterans hospital.

On Sunday afternoon, as the murder investigation continued in St. Paul, in Grantsburg, Wisconsin, friends and relatives gathered to say goodbye to Ruth Munson. An estimated 500 mourners, including seventy-five people from the Twin Cities, filled the sanctuary of the English Lutheran Church. They listened solemnly to hymns sung by a quartet, a duet, and a soloist. The Reverend H. P. Walker conducted the service.

"We have gathered here today with something more than grief in our hearts," Reverend Walker began. Mourners listened as Reverend Walker summarized Ruth Munson's life. She was born in Sterling Township, Polk County, Wisconsin, on March 13, 1906. She was baptized in the Lutheran faith and later confirmed in 1920 at the Lutheran church in Frederic. Ruth attended public schools at Hopkins, Minnesota, and Wolf Creek and Frederic, Wisconsin, before transferring to Grantsburg, where she graduated the teachers training course in 1925. She taught school in Trade Lake, Wisconsin, for two years, then taught in Beldenville, Wisconsin, for another two years. Having little interest in teaching, she moved to St. Paul to find employment. She worked at Miller Hospital for seven years, and then she worked at the Union Depot for the past year and three months. Ruth was laid to rest in the Riverside Cemetery on the edge of town.[10]

According to the *St. Paul Daily News*, two St. Paul detectives were in attendance "with the idea that the slayer might turn up to see the effects of his evil deed." At a quiet moment during the long and difficult afternoon, the detectives showed the broken bracelet to Ruth's sister, Helen. Helen examined it and definitely identified it as Ruth's.[11]

Back in St. Paul, Detective Lieutenant Joseph Heaton and Detective Ralph Merrill checked out a report that a man living at 286 Dayton, near Ruth's apartment, "left hurriedly on the morning of Dec. 9," the day of the fire. The detectives located the man, Christian Christianson, who, it turned out, had only "hurried" to 427 Portland, where he worked as a janitor. But Christianson told the detectives an intriguing tale. On December 9, at 12:30 A.M., nearly seven hours before the fire, he was walking home from 427 Portland. On Virginia Street, near the rear of the Aberdeen, a car was parked facing south toward Selby. A man was pacing back and forth on the sidewalk. "God damn it, how long do I have to wait?" the man complained as Christianson approached. Christianson laughed sympathetically. "It's kind of cold to have to wait for your girl friend." "What's it to you?" the man snapped. "Nothing," Christianson replied and kept walking. He described the car as a new dark coach or sedan with a built-in trunk, possibly a Chevrolet. The man was twenty to thirty years old, five feet eleven inches tall, with a red, full face. He wore a bulky overcoat.

There were no residences nearby where the man's girlfriend might be. Was it possible this man was standing guard outside the hotel while others were inside attending to murderous business? If Ruth had left the Ace at 11:30 P.M., it was theoretically possible for her killers to have lured her or carried her into the hotel by 12:30 A.M. Or was the man just waiting—impatiently—for someone, not necessarily a woman? Heaton and Merrill noted that they had been unable to identify either the man or the automobile.[12]

Meanwhile, Detectives Alfred Jakobson and Herman Schlichting interviewed several staff members at Miller Hospital. A rumor had circulated through the hospital that Ruth had left her job because she was pregnant, but one employee had determined that Ruth Munson had returned to work from a vacation, worked about four days, and then quit. She had started at the Union Depot shortly thereafter, making it unlikely she was pregnant. A housekeeper provided a list of eight other employees who had worked with Ruth. Several of them were eventually interviewed, though none provided any new information.[13]

Throughout the day, Detective Jakobson filed a series of solo reports that touched on several major themes of the investigation. Because he neglected to record the time of day on his reports, it is impossible to determine their exact order.

At 276 Dayton, Ruth's building, Jakobson talked to Mrs. Otto Hoenhouse in Apartment 13. On the morning of the murder, she was awakened at about 2:00 A.M. by loud talking on the street in front of the apartment. She looked out and saw a man about five feet four inches in height, of medium build, and wearing a light tan coat and hat. He was very drunk. He entered the building and came out shortly thereafter. He was met by two men who had approached the apartment on foot from the west. One said, "For Christ's sake let's get going." They assisted the first man to a sedan parked about a hundred feet to the west. A woman got out of the rear seat and spoke to someone in the car and then got into the front seat with the first fellow. His two companions got in the rear, and the car drove east on Dayton. Hoenhouse could not provide descriptions of the woman or the two men. The hour of this incident fit within the seven-hour time gap detectives were trying to fill.[14]

Hoenhouse also told Jakobson about "two girls" who had knocked on her door on the afternoon of the fire. They claimed to be friends of Ruth Munson. They seemed "excited" and tried to verify that the body found at the hotel was Ruth's. The young women said they had tried to talk to Ruth's landlady, but she wouldn't say anything. The descriptions Hoenhouse gave of the two women did not match descriptions of Ruth's companions at the Ace. The young women left, saying they would return later. A moment later, Mr. Hoenhouse came into the building and found the two women studying the mailboxes in the hallway.

Jakobson checked with Ruth's landlady and another of her tenants. Neither of them recalled a visit by these two women. The women never returned. The detective concluded that the women may have been reporters.[15]

Jakobson interviewed Mrs. Grace Swanson at 272 Dayton, Apartment 1. She recounted an incident reported to her by James Dunworth, a bartender at the Covered Wagon, located at 320 Wabasha, where they both worked. One evening a few weeks ago, Ruth Munson was riding the Selby streetcar up from downtown. "A negro," Detective Jakobson wrote in his report, "also riding on the same car got off at her corner and as soon as they were off car, [the] negro walked up to her and started talking to her on [the] corner." Mrs. Swanson had no further details.[16]

The police had not released any information about the Black men taking cabs to Ruth's Ramsey Hill neighborhood. Indeed, as the investigation continued, the department largely kept information about Ruth's relationships with Black men out of the public eye. Nevertheless, Mrs. Swanson took it upon herself to share with police what amounted to nothing more than secondhand information about a white woman and a Black man riding the same streetcar and talking on a public street corner.

Other white St. Paulites were also willing to point accusing fingers at other people of color. Over the course of the day, police received three separate complaints about men of Chinese ancestry. Mrs. Evelyn O'Connor and her daughter Mrs. E. Brobeck reported that on Western Avenue between Iglehart and Marshall Avenues they were followed by a man whose ethnic identity is not recorded in the report. Mrs. O'Connor screamed for police. Responding patrolmen took them in the squad car and toured the district but did not spot the man. Then Mrs. Brobeck stated that a month earlier at the "Chinese Laundry" the "Chinaman unbuttoned his trousers and exposed himself to her." She ran out of the place but didn't report the incident. "She now thinks this man may have some bearing on the Munson case," the officers noted. Mrs. George S. Nadeau reported that when she lived at 286 Dayton Avenue some time before, "a Chinaman did at different times stop or follower [sic] her daughter on Selby Avenue." Mr. E. V. Nelson reported to Officers Louis Burg and Arthur Pagel that while shoveling the sidewalk in front of the Aberdeen, he saw a 1931 Ford coupe with a man at the wheel parked in front of the hotel for some time. He described the driver as "an Oriental." After a short time, two white girls got in the car with the man and drove away.[17]

The hour was late. Another name from the first day of the investigation suddenly reappeared. At 11:00 P.M. Detectives John Baum and Erwin Jahnke met with Mrs. Betty Warnicke, 302 Arundel, who shared some information about Willard Wolf, the owner of the garage next door to the Aberdeen. Wolf's story about the man who had tried to buy gasoline had received coverage in newspapers, making him a momentary celebrity and touching off a search for this mystery man. Warnicke told Baum and Jahnke she took care of Mrs. Wolf's baby on occasion. She told them that Wolf was a woman chaser, that he had been married several times and divorced. He did not stay home nights with his family, but slept on a cot in his garage.[18]

Like a bad penny, Willard Wolf would keep coming back as the investigation continued, each time a little more tarnished.

While Detectives Baum and Jahnke were meeting with Mrs. Warnicke, Det. Lt. Cullen took a statement at police headquarters from Bernard E. Boerger. Boerger was foreman at Kirsch and Gillis, a nightspot located on University Avenue in the city's Midway district. He had called police earlier in the evening and had come down to the police headquarters to provide more details about his story.

"About 8:30 this evening," Boerger began, "Sam Webster, the man in charge, told me that Alice Mayes had told him that she knew who done the job and she was waiting to have the reward increased before she would give any definite information. So, Sam told me that and I called up the police department."

"Who is Alice Mayes?" Det. Lt. Cullen asked.

"She's a colored woman. She has charge of the toilet and she has a source of information back there." Summarizing the conversation he'd had with Sam Webster, Boerger added, "She says somebody talked too much back in the toilet."

Cullen showed Boerger the photo of Ruth Munson that had appeared in the December 10 issue of the *Pioneer Press*. "Have you ever seen that girl in the place out there?"

"Yes, she's been there. I've seen her face." He could not recall the last time he'd seen her or who she was with.[19]

Boerger's statement raised many questions for detectives to ponder. Was there anything to Alice Mayes's assertion? Kirsch and Gillis's clientele was primarily white. In St. Paul, Black folks and white folks did not socialize, so presumably the speaker was a white woman who had stepped into the ladies' room, perhaps with a friend. Black women in service positions were all but invisible to their white clientele, who often talked to each other as though the attendants were not there. Did this woman who "talked too much" know something, or like so many others, was she merely speculating? (On December 18, Det. Lt. Joseph Heaton and Patrolman James Cook would talk to Alice Mayes. "The only information she could give is that some patron of this beer parlor stated she knew Ruth Munson," the detectives wrote in their report. If the detectives took her words, or lack of them, at face value, or wondered if she was holding something back, they made no mention of it in their report.)[20]

The day ended as it had begun, just after midnight. This time it was Detectives Kennedy, Carrier, and Harkness who haunted the Friendship Club in search of patrons who knew Ruth Munson. Ed Schockey of Minneapolis had danced with her a couple of times. She always came with two girls, he said, and she picked out the best dancers and talked to them so she would have them to dance with. She always went home alone. Schockey had never seen Ruth with a redheaded girl "except her sister, and she used to be there every week end." Ruth had introduced her sister to Schockey. (Since neither of Ruth's sisters had red hair, either she introduced someone else with red hair as her sister, or Schockey's memory was faulty.)[21]

Leo Smith, a St. Paul resident, also had danced with Ruth and her two girlfriends on occasion. The two women who accompanied Ruth, he said, would know any other friends she had over at this place.

Frank Kenny, the club manager, told the detectives Ruth had been coming to the dancing club for quite some time and almost always came with the same two women. She had come on occasion with Whitey Unglamb, and once with Dick Das. Her sister was with her a few times, but she was never with a redhead. When she first started coming to the club, she was "a very nice girl," Kenny told the detectives. She frequented the place regularly until about nine weeks ago. Then her attendance fell off. Recently, Ruth and Ella Wormley had been coming at a later hour, as though they had been someplace else and finished the evening here. They showed signs of drinking. On one occasion, Kenny had admonished Ruth for "being in an intoxicated condition," and he had given her black coffee "to try and straighten her out."[22]

Kenny's wife saw her in this condition as well and had observed that "there was a big change in Ruth in the past nine weeks."[23]

Monday, December 13, 1937

Monday, December 13, the fifth day of the investigation. A sensational headline story greeted readers of the *St. Paul Pioneer Press*. Ruth Munson had predicted her own death! Violet Thoreson, a coworker at the St. Paul Union Depot and self-proclaimed "close friend," said that Ruth had told her "I'll never live to see Christmas!" She offered no further details about Ruth's statement, other than to note that "Ruth often said she wasn't the least bit afraid to come to work at 6:10 each morning." Thoreson also told the newspaper that Ruth Munson had fended off a purse snatcher a few weeks before her death, a claim later substantiated by others—but the event appears to have happened several years earlier. It is unclear whether detectives were aware of Violet Thoreson and her claim prior to the newspaper's story. Ruth's green address book and the long list of birthdays written in her diary did not include Violet Thoreson, although other coworkers were listed. It would be several days before detectives interviewed Thoreson. Nevertheless, the woman's story gave the newspaper a headline for the day.

The *Pioneer Press* zeroed in on a gruesome theory that the killer had partially dismembered Ruth's body at the time of her death. The suggestion that her legs had been severed was first advanced by the firemen who discovered her body. Two firemen insisted there were no traces of the lower legs amidst the debris, although remains were found of her arms, which had been burned off. "There positively were no ashes or remnants of the legs," Captain William Davenport told the *Pioneer Press*. "They couldn't have washed away because no water was played upon the spot where the body was found. Remains of the arms still were near the body. If traces of these members were found, why not those of the legs?" Davenport's account was confirmed by fireman Joseph Harris, who had discovered the body.

Ramsey County Coroner Dr. C. A. Ingerson did not rule out the idea that the legs were severed rather than burned off. "We tried to determine what type of instrument might have been used, had the legs been cut off at the knees, as indicated," he told the *Pioneer Press*. "However, the charred condition of the body made this impossible."[1]

Having disagreed about whether Ruth Munson had been sexually assaulted, the county coroner and the police criminologist were once again at odds over the condition of the body. Dr. John B. Dalton, noting that portions of the right leg and the shoe heels were found in the fire debris, discredited the idea that the victim's legs were cut off. The press quickly abandoned the dismemberment theory.[2]

Despite Assistant Chief of Police Charles J. Tierney's public appeal, the women who accompanied Ruth Munson to the Ace remained silent. The *St. Paul Dispatch* observed, "Police cannot explain the girls' silence except on the supposition that they are afraid to talk or may be embarrassed by having been at the tavern."[3]

The Ramsey County Board of Commissioners had been unable to offer a $500 reward for clues leading to the arrest and conviction of Ruth's killer, as Mayor Mark Gehan had requested. State law limited such awards to $200, an amount the board quickly approved. The crusading *St. Paul Daily News* announced its own $500 reward on Monday, upping the total reward to $700 "in the hopes of speeding the solution of the torch-murder at the old Aberdeen hotel last Thursday." To encourage immediate public response, the newspaper announced it would decrease the amount of the reward by $100 each Monday, beginning at noon on Monday, December 20.[4]

Assistant Chief Tierney took up a handwritten letter from Detective Oran Stutzman, dated December 12. The note concerned a person already familiar to the investigation—garage owner Willard Wolf. Detective Stutzman wrote that "Dan," the bartender at the Short Line Inn on West Seventh Street, had recognized Wolf's recent picture in the newspaper as a former bar patron. According to Dan, Wolf had dated numerous nurses who stopped in after work from nearby Ancker Hospital. The bartender had given Stutzman the names of several nurses, and Stutzman included them in his letter.[5]

This information, echoing the testimony of Betty Warnicke, further threw Wolf's character into question. Detectives Boyd Carrier and Frank Kennedy were dispatched to Ancker Hospital, where they interviewed several of the nurses. "Big Bill" was a heavy drinker, the women said. When inebriated he became very loud and told "dirty stories to see if the girls would react to them." He was a "good spender and chased after the nurses that came into the tavern." All of the nurses interviewed confirmed Wolf's reputation.

The detectives added a personal note about their own encounter with Wolf on the morning of the fire. "Thursday morning when we went into his (Wolfe's) garage at 370 Dayton to call Dr. Dalton, Wolfe did not seem very much concerned over what had happened at the hotel. He would be a good man to be brought in for questioning. He is separated from his wife who lives at 298 Arundel and [he] sleeps on a cot in the garage."[6]

In the meantime, Detectives Herman Schlichting and Alfred Jakobson began the laborious task of canvassing the neighborhood. Canvassing involved knocking on every door, whether it was a single-family house or an apartment building divided into forty individual rooms, and asking the resident if he or she knew anything that might help the investigation. If no one answered, the detectives jotted down a note and made a return visit. At the end of the day, each detective completed a report detailing the addresses covered and the names of the individuals who answered their knock. If a resident had helpful information, the detective completed a separate miscellaneous report.

The two detectives began their canvass on Dayton Avenue, near the building where Ruth had lived. Detective Schlichting worked the odd-numbered addresses on the north side of the street, while Jakobson worked the even-numbered addresses on the south side. As the days passed, the canvass would eventually cover seventy-five blocks in the neighborhood and involve additional detectives.

As the morning progressed, two new pieces of information came across the desk of Detective Lieutenant Ray McCarthy regarding Ruth Munson's possible connections to Black men. At a barbershop at Grand Avenue and Lexington Parkway, a "colored porter" was doing a lot of talking about the Munson case. Det. Lt. McCarthy sent Detectives John Schroeder and Raymond Schmidt to investigate. The detectives interviewed the porter in question, eighteen-year-old Harold White of 277 Rondo Avenue. They quickly established that his only knowledge of the case came from his father, Arthur White. The elder White was a fireman at Engine 9, which had responded to the Aberdeen fire alarm. The detectives concluded that Arthur White had merely shared his personal experience in fighting the fire with his son.[7]

From the barbershop, Detectives Schroeder and Schmidt drove to the Minnesota State Capitol building to investigate McCarthy's second piece of new information. Luverne Van Voorhis told them that a friend of his, Arnold Igo, was a bartender at the Ambassador Inn, 169 North Dale Street. Igo had told Van Voorhis that he knew a cabdriver who had driven a Black man from the Union Depot to 276 Dayton Avenue on Wednesday night, meaning the night Ruth was murdered. Detectives Schroeder and Schmidt talked to Igo himself. He denied Van Voorhis's assertion that he knew the cabdriver. Igo maintained that he had merely overheard two cabdrivers talking in Clem's Sandwich Shop on Selby, near Dale Street. At that intersection, the detectives talked to the driver of Blue and White cab #44. The driver offered no information other than the observation that "Ruth Munson was well known at the Keystone Hotel."[8]

The detectives had no need to provide details about the Keystone in their reports. The hotel stood on the corner of Western and Carroll Avenues, in the heart of Rondo. The Keystone advertised in the *St. Paul Recorder*, a newspaper serving the city's Black community, offering "neatly furnished rooms" at "$2.50 a week and up"—an inexpensive housing option for underpaid Black workers. It was known to police as a hub for illicit activities. For Ruth Munson to be well known there only added to the growing suspicions about her proclivities.[9]

In addition, two cabdrivers had reported driving Black men from the Union Depot and the Lowry Hotel to Ruth's address. There were few facts here, but inferences could be drawn by those inclined to do so. In St. Paul, there were plenty of people who would look at the Rondo community and draw such inferences.

Det. Lt. McCarthy was having a busy day dispatching various detective teams to gather information. Around 10:00 A.M., he sent Detectives Robert Murnane and Axel Soderberg to the Ace to get information concerning a man known as Boots. Detective Ralph Merrill had reported that Boots was supposed to have taken Ruth Munson out at various times. He also owned a Ford with yellow wire wheels; and he had not driven it since the night of the murder.

At the Ace, the detectives established that Boots was Herman Hasse, who lived nearby at 769 Pelham Boulevard. They picked him up and drove back to police headquarters.[10]

Hasse was immediately questioned by Detective Lieutenant Frank R. Cullen, who treated him like a suspect. Hasse said he was currently unemployed, having been laid off from his job as a riveter three weeks earlier.

"Do you go to the Friendship Club in Minneapolis?" Cullen asked.

"I used to go there about a year ago."

"Did you take a girl home that lived at 276 Dayton, or that got off in that vicinity?"

"No sir, mostly all Minneapolis girls."

"What kind of car do you drive?"

"I haven't got a car now, I used to have a Ford, A model."

"Has it got yellow wheels?"

"Yes sir." Hasse explained that he had been driving a girl home from a dance "a week ago last Saturday" when the car's transmission went out. He had sold the car the following Monday afternoon for $20. Cullen showed him the now familiar picture of Ruth in the December 10 issue of the *Pioneer Press*.

"Did you ever see that girl?"

"I don't remember seeing her. I was in the Ace Wednesday night too, but I don't remember seeing her."

"What time were you in the Ace?"

Hasse explained that he often spent evenings there, usually alone. On Wednesday, he had been there from 8:00 until closing time, about 12:50.

"You don't recall seeing this girl at any time?" Cullen demanded.

"No sir."

"Do you recall seeing her at the Friendship Club in Minneapolis?"

"No sir."

"We have information that you have taken Miss Munson home on several occasions with that old car."

"I never even remember seeing her."

Further questioning didn't shake Hasse's assertion that he didn't know Ruth Munson from either the Friendship Club or the Ace. Cullen asked a round of background questions, then returned to the subject.

"Do you recall ever dancing with Miss Munson?"

"Never."

"You're sure of that?"

"Yes sir."

"Do you know anything about Miss Munson at all?"

"I do not."

"Did you tell anybody that you did?"

"No sir."[11]

Cullen appeared satisfied that Hasse knew nothing that would help the investigation.

A picture of Ruth Munson's social life was emerging. According to entries in her diary, she went out almost every night. Her own accounts of her social life were supported by miscellaneous reports filed by detectives and statements given by her friends and coworkers.

She took some of her meals at work, but others she purchased in restaurants near her apartment building. This raised a question. On a waitress's wages, how could Ruth Munson afford the life she lived?

It was common practice for people to apply for credit at individual businesses. Assistant Chief Tierney assigned the job of investigating Ruth Munson's finances to Detectives Michael Sauro and Alvin Johnson. The detectives began their investigation at the Golden Rule, St. Paul's premiere department store. Ruth had applied there for credit before she moved to the city. Over the course of their investigation, the detectives determined that she had opened an account at Newman's and applied for credit at Globe Finance Company and the Local Loan Company. The detectives did not record the balances on her accounts at any of these businesses.

The detectives then visited Lincoln Finance and Field-Schlick & Company, another popular St. Paul department store. She had not applied for credit at either location, but Jean Fliessner at Field-Schlick shared an interesting story with the detectives. About 11:30 P.M. on Saturday, December 12, she was in the ladies' room at Victor's, Sixth and St. Peter. She overheard two women talking. One said, "Do you supposed that could have been _____ that murdered her." The other replied "For God's sake, don't mention it." Fliessner, the detective wrote in their report, did not hear the name mentioned distinctly but knew it ended with 'ny.' " It was not much of a clue to go on.[12]

In the early afternoon, McCarthy's busy day suddenly got busier, with the arrival of Elvin Gordon Garrison. Following a brief discussion, McCarthy summoned a stenographer to record Garrison's statement. Garrison, thirty-five and married, lived at 837 Desoto Street on the city's East Side and worked as a switchman for the Milwaukee Railroad. McCarthy showed Garrison pictures of Ruth before the formal interview began.

"As you told me on the night of December 8th that you were out to the Ace Box Lunch with your wife and two girl friends and you were dancing."

"Yes, twice, once with each girl."

"And you told me that about 11:05 you went out to warm up your car; is that right?"

"Yes."

"And what did you see?"

"There was three girls in a sedan '35 or '36 model, looked like a Chev or Plymouth a black car, and [they] sat in the front seat of the car directly behind mine. They drove up and bumped into my car and then backed away and drove down University Avenue towards St. Paul. I saw them when they got into their car; two of them were about 5 ft. 6 and the other one was shorter; of course it was dark and I could not be able to distinguish the features of anyone. I didn't scrutinize them at all when I was dancing."

"Before you went out to warm your car had you seen these girls dancing at the Ace Box Lunch?"

"I had noticed two of them dancing in this place."

"Did either of these girls look like Ruth Munson?"

"One of them was about her size and build as far as features were concerned[,] I had paid no attention."

"Didn't you say that one of these pictures resembled one of these girls that you had seen in the Ace Box Lunch?" McCarthy asked.

"One of these girls could fit that picture very well."

McCarthy zeroed in on the two women who had accompanied Ruth. Garrison could not remember seeing a redhead. He remembered only that one of them was shorter than the other, a now familiar detail. Garrison had talked to his wife and their two friends about the evening, but none of them could be positive that they had seen Ruth and her two friends.

"Well in your own opinion, you could not say for sure whether this is Ruth Munson that was out there [in the car] or not, is that it?" McCarthy asked.

"No I could not."[13]

Despite Garrison's uncertainty, his statement was filled with intriguing possibilities. The Ace bartenders had estimated the trio's departure time as between 11:30 and 12:00. But H. A. Nielsen, manager of the Arions, claimed to have seen two of the women standing in the front with their coats on "in the neighborhood of 10:15 or 10:20." Garrison estimated the time he went to warm his car at about 11:05—halfway between the latest time suggested by Nielsen and the earliest time of their departure. The vague description of the car as a black Chevrolet or Plymouth was similar to descriptions of cars seen on Dayton Avenue some three hours later. The women's car had driven off toward both the Aberdeen and Ruth Munson's apartment building.

If these three women were, in fact, Ruth and her companions, for the first time, police had a piece of information that fell within the seven-hour gap between the time the women left the Ace and when Ruth's body was found in the Aberdeen. It also suggested that the three women drove their own car, which might help in identifying the two unknown women.

Fortified with information accumulated through dozens of interviews and statements, detectives reinterviewed people they had spoken with in the first hours of the investigation, hoping to trigger new revelations. Among these was Ruth's landlady, Clara Broughton. Detective Thomas Grace conducted the interview at police headquarters at 2:50 P.M.

Broughton had lived in the third-floor, seven-room apartment for nine years. To help meet expenses, she rented out three rooms, including one to Ruth Munson. In response to Detective Grace's questions, Broughton described Ruth's activities on Wednesday, December 8. She had slept until noon. At 12:30 she left the house. While she was gone, one telephone call came in, between 2:00 and 3:00. Ruth returned around 4:00, her arms loaded with bundles. Broughton told her the "girl with the weak voice" had called. At 5:45 P.M. the telephone rang, and Ruth answered it. The caller was Ruth's boyfriend, Dick Das. Broughton knew it was Dick Das because he had told her on Friday night after the murder that he was the one who called. Ruth left between 6:00 and 7:00 P.M. When she left, she was in her usual quiet mood. She didn't say where she was going. Right after she left, a man called. He left no message.

"Do you ever recollect hearing this man's voice over the telephone before?" Grace asked.

"I don't remember of ever hearing it."

Broughton described Ruth as secretive, one who never gave details or repeated names. When she was home, she kept her door closed, but she left it open when she was gone. She received many telephone calls a day. When taking telephone calls, she kept her voice low.

"You would never know what she was talking about," the landlady said. "And at times she would talk in Swede if it was important."

"And of course that left you out of what she was talking about," Detective Grace observed.

"Absolutely," the landlady agreed.

Regarding visits to the apartment by Ruth's gentlemen friends, they would stay an hour or two hours at the most. They usually came between 8:00 and 8:30, leaving about 10:00 or 10:30. She never heard any arguments or quarreling between Ruth and a boyfriend; in fact, always the opposite—laughing and talking. Most recently, Ruth had been visited by Dick Das. Whitey made visits for a couple of months in

July and August. Before that, there was someone whose name Broughton didn't know.

"Have you ever heard Ruth mention to you or to any one else about having any financial difficulties or trouble of any kind?" Grace asked.

"Never; but I know she never earned very much because she told me once if I raised the rent she couldn't pay it. She was making $9.00 a week," but she always paid her rent a day early.

The detective turned his attention to new information the police had learned about Ruth Munson.

"Have you at any time when you were either coming into the building where you live at 276 Dayton or when you might have been coming out, see [sic] any colored men in front of that building."

"I haven't. I myself never have, and I never heard that there were any. It seems to me if there were ever any seen I would hear something about it."

"Has at any time you answered the telephone and an inquiry was made for Ruth by a man[,] has the voice of that man in your judgement ever sounded like a colored man?"

"No, I don't think so, I never thought of such a thing. I'll tell you right now her friends were all Scandinavian or Swedes. Every man and every girl that ever came up here I think were Swedes."

"Have you at any time observed a lady visitor with Ruth that might have had red hair?"

"Oh yes."

"Was it the same person or different persons?"

"There was just one girl that ever came there that had red hair; the kind of red that you would notice. That was a year ago last summer, in July or August. I think at that [time] the redheaded girl was living next door."

"Ruth never introduced you to this redheaded woman?"

"No, in fact I didn't like her very much. I would take her to be kind of a bold woman. I let her in two or three times and I just sized her up at a glance." The last time she had seen her was in August of 1936.

"Were you familiar with the sound of this woman's voice?"

"No. I knew voices but I didn't know which is which. She may have called Ruth quite often but Ruth never gave me any names, she never gave me the names of any of those girls. When she got a call she always asked me what kind of voice. I would describe the voice and 'Oh, yes, I know who that is,' she would say."

"Now when Ruth left on the night of December 8, 1937 between

6 [and] 7 P.M. did she say she was going out to eat or that she was going to be home early or pass any remark when she left your apartment?"

"She never said one word, never looked in. My door stands open all day long. Ruth called [a] Midway number to talk to some girls. I never heard any names. She talked so low. Sometimes if she thought I might catch a word then just 'Yes . . . no . . . maybe . . . sure . . . seven o'clock . . . Okey Doke,' and maybe a word in between in Swede. When she talked over the phone I didn't pay much attention."[14]

Broughton's interview had not helped much, but she did mention something that had potential: Ruth called a "Midway number to talk to some girls." It wasn't clear whether she meant that Ruth made those calls in general or on Wednesday evening before she went out. Either way, checking the telephone numbers of women Ruth knew may have led police to one of the two women with her that night. There is no record showing that detectives pursued this opportunity.

As the evening crept in, Detectives Jakobson and Schlichting returned to police headquarters and filled out reports on their day's canvassing work. Detective Schlichting had made contact with fifty-six people and did not pick up any leads that required a follow-up report. Detective Jakobson had better luck among the fifty-five people he had interviewed. Two of his interview subjects touched on themes important to detectives. Neoma Reiswieg, in Room 6 at 286–288 Dayton, told the detective that on the morning of the fire she was unable to sleep. Between the hours of 2:00 A.M. and 4:00 A.M., she was wide awake reading and did not hear anyone scream. She was positive that had anyone screamed during that time she would have heard it. Her claim, Detective Jakobson noted in his report, discounted the story of Oscar Loberg. Mary O'Brien, living in Apartment 6 at 300 Dayton Avenue, said she went to work at 5:00 A.M. Several times recently she had seen a shiny black car parked on Virginia between Selby and Dayton, facing south—close to the gate at the rear of the Aberdeen. She was unable to give any further description of the car and did not see anyone inside. "There are no buildings about this vicinity where people would have any reason to park a car in this particular spot," the detective noted.[15]

Ruth Munson's interactions with Black men were quickly becoming a central theme in the investigation. At 8:00 P.M. Detective Lieutenant Nate Smith dispatched Detectives Frank Martin and Herbert Olson to Rossini's, a bar across Sibley Street from the depot, to investigate a report that "three white girls" who worked at the Union Depot had been coming in and ordering six beers. Once the drinks were ordered, "three negros would come in and drink with them."

Proprietor Dan Rossini denied this scenario had ever occurred to his knowledge. However, bartender Benny Rossini stated that he knew Ruth Munson and that she often came in, usually in company with a girl named Gladys or one named Kathryn. Frequently all three were together. Benny told the detectives that Gladys had left the Union Depot and was employed, he thought, at either the Mayfair or Macey Apartments as a telephone operator. Detectives Martin and Olson checked those locations and located a tenant at the Macey Apartments named Gladys Wicklund, but she was not home. The next day, Detectives Schroeder and Ernest Woodhouse added a postscript to the detectives' report. Gladys Wicklund had been located, and she would come into headquarters at noon. Further, a Katherine Mueller at 201 Goodrich Avenue, Apartment 4, said she only knew Ruth Munson by sight, had never been out with her any place off duty, nor had she ever seen her talking to any man.[16]

The hour was late. At 9:58 P.M., Detective Erwin Coates filed a report about Celia Starr, a singer in nightclubs in Minneapolis and St. Paul. She had been missing since 7:15 P.M. Saturday. According to Coates's report, Starr was a redhead and weighed about 140 pounds. "This description fits generally with the red headed girl mentioned in the Munson murder," Detective Coates wrote.[17]

Coates's report raised immediate questions. Was this the redheaded woman seen with Ruth Munson at the Ace? Was her disappearance connected to Ruth's death? Would this missing woman suffer the same fate? Once again, women's vulnerability in St. Paul came into question.

Apparently, that mystery did not last long and had a satisfactory outcome. No further police reports were made about Celia Starr, nor did local newspapers carry any stories about her.

Tuesday, December 14, 1937

Cab rides, socializing over beers, workplace friendships. Withholding these leads from the public, detectives began to look into Ruth Munson's relationships with members of St. Paul's Black community.

Acting on the rumor that Ruth was friendly with the porters at the Union Depot, the police acquired a list containing the names, addresses, and telephone numbers of thirty-six employees. Robert Brown literally topped the list as head porter. Ruth's diary entry for June 10, 1937, noted, "(Bob Brown [indecipherable]) Alma, Ella and Whitey called." In the entry, Brown's name was followed by illegible letters or a word, all written in smaller script and enclosed in parentheses—as if added in afterthought. A photographic enlargement made by police was no clearer. The June 10 diary entry also included the note that "Bertha [Ella], Joan, Sue and I went to Hunters. Bob there." Ruth's green address book included the entry "Bob Br," and the telephone number DA 0946. The telephone number proved to be the number for a saloon belonging to Jim Williams, located in the heart of the Rondo district at Kent Street and St. Anthony Avenue. The establishment was a popular nightspot.[1]

At 1:00 A.M. on Tuesday, December 14, Detective Lieutenant Nate Smith and Patrolman Lewis Schultz "arrested Bob Brown (colored) 42 yrs. of age at Kent and St. Anthony." Brown was taken to police headquarters and "put on the hold book for Assistant Chief Tierney." This meant that Brown would remain in custody at least until he was questioned.[2]

Exactly what triggered Brown's arrest at such a late hour is unclear. While other rumors about Ruth Munson and Black porters and waiters mostly involved unnamed men, her own diary and address book contained Brown's name and a telephone number for reaching him. For police struggling to find leads in the case, now one hour into its sixth day, having a Black man's name was evidently good enough reason to make an arrest. Brown would not be questioned until midafternoon.

At 2:00 A.M., after the Ace closed for the night, Smith and Schultz met with bartender Gus Gavanda. Gavanda told them that at around

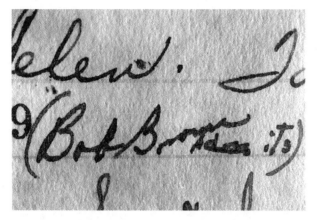

A close-up of the page from Ruth Munson's diary showing her indecipherable note about Bob Brown. *SPPD*

7:00 P.M. on the evening of Wednesday, December 8, the night before the murder, three women stopped at 834 Raymond Avenue, two blocks north of the Ace, to enquire about renting a room. Gavanda said he had gotten this information from an Ace patron named Toney, who roomed there. The two policemen turned the information over to headquarters for further investigation at a more decent hour.[3]

Around 9:00 A.M., Detectives Robert Murnane and Robert Vick interviewed Gus Gavanda. Earlier, Mrs. Hagen, 1486 Taylor, had called the station and reported a friend of hers, whose name she would not disclose, had told her that Gavanda had said Ruth's two friends who accompanied her to the Ace were "Nurses at Miller Hospital," where Ruth once worked. According to Hagen, Gavanda claimed "the hospital authorities had sent the girls out of town to keep unwelcome publicity away from the hospital." Gavanda denied making any such comment. He then told the detectives the same story he had told Smith and Schultz.[4]

Murnane and Vick drove to 834 Raymond and spoke with the landlady. She thought one of the three women looked like Ruth Munson. She described one of the other two women as "very small, weighing less than 100 lbs., and having dark hair." The other woman was a "tall blond." The landlady noted that the woman who looked like Ruth Munson said she had a room and it was the other two who sought the room. The three women did not call each other by name during the encounter. The landlady said she had only a single room and advised the women to try 853 Raymond Avenue. The women said they had been there and were informed the room was only rented to men. The detectives checked at that address and learned the three women had not been there.[5]

It was an intriguing lead. According to her landlady, Ruth had left her room at 276 Dayton between 6:00 and 7:00 P.M., making it theo-retically possible for her to have been at 834 Raymond Avenue "around 7:00 P.M.," and then at the Ace at 8:30 P.M. But the descriptions of the two women given by the landlady at 834 Raymond Avenue had little in common with those offered by Ace patrons. Both the landlady and Ace patrons described one of the two women as taller than the other. Several Ace patrons mentioned blondish hair in describing one of the women. Ace patrons—observing in a room with at least some light—were consistent in describing one woman as a redhead. It is possible that if the three women did not go inside the house, in the darkness of a winter night, the landlady may have mistaken a redhead for someone with dark hair. As was often the case, there was not enough informa-tion to take the lead any further.

For some newspapers, the lack of progress evoked the unsolved murder of Laura Kruse, which bore eerie parallels to the Ruth Munson case. Laura Kruse was also from a small town. Pine City, Minnesota, was located just seventeen miles west and slightly north of Grantsburg, Wisconsin. Kruse moved to Minneapolis to attend beauty college in 1936. On March 19, 1937, the eighteen-year-old woman attended a Min-neapolis party and then took the streetcar home. About 12:30 A.M., a scream was heard near 14th Avenue South and 51st Street. Her body was found at about 7:50 the following morning. Despite an intensive investigation by Minneapolis police, the case remained unsolved.[6]

These two unsolved murder cases encouraged a waitress to come forward and tell the press a harrowing story about being kidnapped and assaulted. The morning papers combined her story with accounts of both unsolved murders. The previous August, the *St. Paul Pioneer Press* reported, a thirty-eight-year-old waitress got off work at 2:00 A.M. While she was waiting for a streetcar, a male customer offered her and a coworker a ride home. They accepted. The man dropped off the coworker first. Then, instead of taking the waitress home, he drove her out to rural Dakota County. "He told me there wouldn't be any tomor-row for me," the waitress recalled. "He talked about the Kruse murder in Minneapolis and said that I was going to be the victim of another unsolved murder. When I tried to talk to him, he told me to shut up and he hit me in the face. I was so scared I didn't know what to do and I started to cry. He kept telling me to shut up and hit me in the face again and again."

When the assailant stopped the car next to a cornfield, the waitress jumped out of the car and hid in the field. The man searched for her for about fifteen minutes before giving up. The waitress waited another hour before she started an eight-mile walk through the night to get home, hiding in fear each time a car approached. Though she was seen by a doctor and had told her story to Dakota County authorities, she had requested no reports be made, "fearing the results of publicity." At her request, the press also withheld her name. Armed with information she had given, authorities were now looking for her assailant.[7]

Tuesday morning's editions also reported new police theories about the Munson case. Even as detectives continued to pursue new leads, they increasingly revisited territory they had already covered. On Monday, detectives had literally returned to the scene of the crime by reexamining the Aberdeen Hotel inside and out. Outside the hotel, detectives decided that entry was probably made through a rear basement door, facing Selby Avenue. Once inside, detectives were hampered in their search by an inch of ice covering both the stairs leading to the door and the second floor where the body was discovered. The ice "eliminated any usual condition that might serve as a clue." To aid their search, floodlights were brought in to illuminate the areas to be searched. The additional light failed to penetrate the ice and spotlight something—anything—that could be turned over to the department's crime lab for analysis.[8]

Though it yielded no new evidence, the reexamination of the Aberdeen gave the police the opportunity to offer the morning papers new theories about the case that would reassure the public they were making progress on a resolution. The *Minneapolis Tribune* dramatically reported that "Re-enactment of the crime showed there was a clear path between the basement door and the hallway two floors above where the body was found." The *Pioneer Press* was equally dramatic, noting, "The fact that the girl was found on the second floor was regarded by police as an indication of the excitement of the murderer. Police said only a strong man or a mentally unbalanced one could have carried an inert weight of 140 pounds 200 feet and up two flights of stairs." The press's sensational reporting often moved beyond outlining police theories and into interpretations and speculation.[9]

Establishing the identity of the two women who were with Ruth Munson at the Ace on Wednesday night remained the key to unlocking the mystery. From these two women, the *St. Paul Daily News* reported, the police hoped to discover "where the trio went when they left the café, if they were with someone, by what manner of car or streetcar they traveled, and where and at what time they separated." At 11:00 A.M., the search for the two women received a potential boost from a driver for a White Bear Lake taxicab company. The driver told Assistant Chief Charles J. Tierney he had picked up two women on Saturday night, December 11, along Highway 61, just a few miles from the city of White Bear Lake. At their request, he took them to the town's railroad station. The women said they were taking a midnight train north. While they waited for the train, they asked the driver to pick up some lunch for them at a restaurant a block away. Later, the cabdriver talked to a driver for the Twin City Motor Bus Company and mentioned his two passengers. The bus driver said he had picked up the two women in St. Paul and they had departed the bus at the same spot where the cabdriver had found them.[10]

There was no guarantee that these two women were Ruth's companions, but after hitting many dead ends, at least police had a new trail to follow. The detectives would need to determine if the women had indeed boarded the northbound train and then determine where they left it. Like everything else, tracking down these women would take time.

During the morning, Detectives Boyd Carrier and Frank Kennedy went to the field office of the Federal Bureau of Investigation to get information the bureau had collected regarding Apartment 13 at 276 Dayton Avenue, located two floors below Ruth Munson's apartment. In February and April 1937, its occupants had been targeted by the bureau as part of its "white slavery" investigations.

First passed by Congress in June 1910, the White-Slave Traffic Act, also known as the Mann Act, made it a felony to engage in the interstate or foreign transfer of "any woman or girl for the purpose of prostitution or debauchery, or for any other immoral purpose." Despite the law, prostitution continued to flourish over the next two decades. With the repeal of Prohibition in 1933, prostitution became a profit center for organized crime. In the summer of 1936, FBI Director J. Edgar Hoover had launched a nationwide campaign to fight organized sex trafficking. The bureau had conducted investigations in the Twin Cities throughout much of 1937, which resulted in a series of convictions. Newspaper accounts indicate that federal agents arrested several Black men from Minneapolis, St. Paul, and Duluth and processed them through the court system. While enforcement of the Mann Act was the work of federal authorities, St. Paul police on occasion made arrests for violations of the federal law; they had made at least three such arrests in 1937—two Black men and one man presumed to be white. One Black man was transferred to federal authorities, the other turned over to Minneapolis police. The third man was not prosecuted.[11]

The bureau's investigation at Apartment 13, 276 Dayton Avenue, produced interactions with seven residents. Agnes Fahrner and Evelyn Anick, whose maiden name was Mallette, were "picked up." Fahrner became a government witness and was relocated to the Arcade Hotel in Sioux City, Iowa, while Anick was taken into custody. In Evelyn's room, bureau agents had found "pictures of men and women in a compromising position." The bureau also contacted other roomers, including Victor Peterson, Bernard Dahlberg, Kenneth Dahlberg, and Mrs. Victor Abarham.[12]

It probably was coincidental that Ruth Munson and the FBI's suspects lived in the same building at the same time. None of these individuals were connected to the Munson case. In gathering this information from the FBI, Carrier and Kennedy were simply covering all the bases. Nevertheless, in a different way, the fear surrounding the "white slavery" issue would influence the investigation in the future.

Around noon, Carrier and Kennedy made a stop at the Tunnel Hamburger Shop at 315 Selby Avenue, where they spoke with proprietor Guadalupe (Wally) Yniguez about Ruth Munson. He did not know her by name, but he told the detectives she ate breakfast there three or four times a week. Alyene Stivers, a waitress, told the detectives Ruth came in around 7:00 P.M. on Tuesday, December 7. She often had supper there, the waitress said. The detectives arranged for the proprietor and waitress to go to police headquarters that afternoon to give statements.[13]

Mindful that the afternoon dailies were always looking for a fresh story, the police department released details about the bracelet the Martins had found in the street and turned over on Saturday.

Both of St. Paul's afternoon newspapers made the most of the story. Along with a headline story, the *St. Paul Daily News* ran three pictures, one of the bracelet itself, one of Assistant Chief Tierney examining it, and one of the front of the building where it was found. The article described the bracelet as "a yellow gold band, hinged, set with a black onyx ornament, and engraved in simulation of an antique piece." Hinting at violence, the article noted that "the guard chain was broken and the hinge sprung." The police had valued the bracelet "at about $5."

The *Daily News* also detailed several theories about the case that police had developed after confirming that the bracelet was Ruth's. She may have been walking home on Dayton when she was seized. She resisted, losing the bracelet in the struggle, and was taken by force to the Aberdeen, where she was killed and burned. Police also theorized that if the spring was already broken, the bracelet may have slipped off her wrist as she walked. Or it may have been thrown from a passing car or dropped by the killer after the crime was committed.[14]

For the *St. Paul Dispatch*, Mrs. Martin added some embroidery to the account of hearing two screams that she had previously given to police. "The first one was an agonized, suffering yell, very loud," she said, "while the second was very much weaker. I turned out the light and walked out onto the porch, but I saw nothing. The only noises I heard were from the beer parlors on Selby Avenue and the street traffic on Dayton."[15]

Robert Brown had been arrested at 1:00 A.M. At 2:40 P.M., he was questioned by Detective Thomas Grace. Brown, forty-five years old, was married and lived in a house that he owned at 933 Rondo Avenue. He drove a 1935 Ford V-8 sedan, black with green wheels. He had been employed at the Union Depot since 1920 and was currently head porter.

"Now Bob," Grace said, using an unusually familiar form of address as he turned to the business at hand, "did you know a white girl by the name of Ruth Munson who worked for the Union News Company and was employed in the restaurant at the Union Depot?"

"Yes, sir, I never knew her last name—all I knew was that her name was Ruth." Brown had known her since February 1937, since he started working the hours 7:00 A.M. to 3:00 P.M.

"Have you had at any time any conversation with this girl named Ruth about going out with her?"

"Once."

"When did this conversation take place?" Detective Grace undoubtedly knew about Ruth's diary entry for June 10 and that Brown's name was in her address book, along with a telephone number.

"First of June this year," Brown replied.

"And did you at any time during this conversation with Ruth give her a telephone number so that she could call you up?"

"I did."

The telephone number Brown had given her was not his home number, but the number for the saloon where he had been arrested.

"Now what was the conversation that took place between you and Ruth at the time you gave her this telephone number?" Grace asked.

"She was talking about going out some time and I asked her and she said she would let me know later and wanted to know if there was any place that she could call me—that's how I come to give her this number."

"Did she ever call you at this number?"

"No sir."

"Did she give you her telephone number?"

"No sir."

"Have you ever called her at her home at 276 Dayton Ave.?"

"No sir." (Brown couldn't have known about Ruth's cryptic June 10 diary entry suggesting he had called.)

"Have you ever met her at any time and gone with her to any place?"

"No sir."

"Did you suggest to her about going out or did she suggest it to you?"

"She suggested it to me."

"And to the best of your recollection, just what did she say?"

"She said how is chances of going out sometime—then I asked her when and she didn't know for sure and wanted to know if there wasn't any place she could call me so I gave her the telephone number, Dale 0946."

"Have you at any time seen her at any beer parlors that you happened to be in?"

"No sir."

"Now you're [sic] object if you did go out with her and kept the date you planned on having intercourse with her, didn't you?"

"I am not sure but I suppose so."

"Now did you at any time either in September or October have a date with Ruth which was called off?" Grace was referring to a September 27, 1937, entry in Ruth's diary: "Supposed to meet B.B. in eve. But didn't feel well."

"No sir."

"Did you know whereabouts she lived?"

"She told me that she lived on Dayton Ave."

"Had you asked her where she lived?"

"I asked her where she lived and she said she lived on Dayton Ave."

"What was you [sic] reason for this inquiry as to where she lived?"

"Well, I saw her catch a Selby-Lake Car always and I asked her whether she lived in St. Paul or Minneapolis."

Grace asked a number of unimportant questions and then returned to the purpose of the interview.

"You are sure there is nothing else about Ruth that you haven't told me?"

"No sir," meaning there was nothing else.

"You have never had intercourse with her?"

"No sir."[16]

Brown later read the transcript of his interview and signed it.

At 3:00 P.M., Detective Lieutenant Frank R. Cullen began to interview the Tunnel Hamburger Shop employees whom Detectives Carrier and Kennedy had briefly questioned during their noon visit. Proprietor Guadalupe (Wally) Yniguez, age thirty-six, said that Ruth Munson ate breakfast there several times a week. She had eaten there on Monday or Tuesday morning, ordering two eggs, toast, and coffee. She always ate alone. Yniguez had never seen her sit with anyone. He had never seen her in the company of a redheaded woman.[17]

At 4:40, Cullen interviewed waitress Aylene Stivers. She said that Ruth came in "practically every night" between 7:00 and 8:30 P.M. She had last come in on the Tuesday night before the murder. She always looked "neat and clean." Dorothy Yniguez, Wally Yniguez's estranged nineteen-year-old wife, was interviewed at 4:50 P.M., and Dorothy Mondar, a former waitress at the shop, was interviewed at 5:00 P.M. Neither added any new information—although, in a second interview on December 17, Dorothy Yniguez would say that her husband had a fascination with fire.[18]

The Tunnel Hamburger Shop employee interviews followed a frustrating pattern, by now all too familiar. Ruth Munson, detectives knew, regularly visited many places. She patronized restaurants where she took most of her meals. She went to bars and dance clubs almost every night. Many people at these establishments knew her by sight or by first name. They could offer small details about the regularity of her habits. They described her friends and acquaintances vaguely. They could only make guesses about her personality, her likes and dislikes. To a person, no one seemed to know her well enough to offer detectives solid information with which they could move forward. Or, if they had information, it may have been that they were unwilling to share it.

Citizen complaints about suspicious men continued to pour into police headquarters. Among them was a complaint by a Mrs. Dobner who said that when she was at Midway Recreation recently (the night Rudy Vallee performed there), she was followed by a man in a new Chevrolet sedan. Twice on Snelling Avenue he stopped his car beside her and tried to get her into the car. A block from her home at 1515 Blair Street, he got out of the car and chased her all the way home. This man, she said, waits in front of Midway Recreation for women who are not escorted.[19]

Some time earlier, Emery Preston had reported to Detectives Michael Sauro and Alvin Johnson that Jack Ellsworth, a caretaker at 300 Dayton, had tried to rape Preston's wife after he had left for work. At the time Mrs. Preston refused to talk to the detectives about the assault. However, after reading about the Munson case, she thought Ellsworth might have some connection to it. Sauro and Johnson interviewed her at Montgomery Ward, where she worked, and she confirmed the assault as it was originally described by her husband. Mrs. Preston told the detectives that the only reason Ellsworth failed in his assault was the fact that she was "dressed in riding breeches and she threatened to scream." The detectives put Ellsworth on the holdbook for investigation of attempted rape. A handwritten amendment to their report noted that he was released on "advice of County Atty's office no evidence."[20]

Along with the murder case, the influx of citizen complaints about sexual attacks no doubt influenced Police Chief Clinton Hackert's decision to contact Warden Leo Utecht at the Minnesota State Prison in Stillwater. "Will you kindly send us a list of men released from your institution within the past five years who had been convicted of sex crimes," the chief requested. "We would appreciate having a photograph of each with the description, date of commitment and release and where committed from," he wrote, adding that he "Would deem it a personal favor if you will send us this list as soon as possible."[21]

Throughout the day, Detectives Alfred Jakobson and Herman Schlichting had continued their canvass of the neighborhood, working addresses on Dayton Avenue. At day's end, Jakobson filed several follow-up reports of interviews. Martha Fischer, living in Room 38 of 290–292 Dayton Avenue, informed the detective that her boyfriend, Hilding Nelson, had danced with Ruth Munson on one occasion. Based on her discussion with her boyfriend, Fischer was of the impression that the "character of Ruth Munson was not too good."

In Room 42 at the same address, Ivory Satre reported that on November 7, he and his wife left their apartment about midnight. On the landing, they encountered "a very drunk woman lying on the floor." The woman wore a green dress and, he believed, a fur jacket—garments similar to what Ruth Munson wore the night of the murder. Once outside, the woman walked east on Dayton Avenue, which was in the direction of 276 Dayton. Satre thought the woman resembled Ruth Munson, and Jakobson advised him to visit police headquarters and look at some recent photographs of her.

Catherine Ryan, Room 43, had information about a man familiar to the investigation, one Willard Wolf. While she was living at 395 Dayton two years earlier, Wolf was also living there and claimed to be unmarried. He was in the practice of having women up to his room several times a week. "This practice was O.K.'d by landlady," Jakobson noted.

According to Eleanor Martin in Room 47, very early on December 9, the morning of the fire, she was awakened by a woman crying out. To Martin, "it sounded as if she was silenced by someone putting something over [her] mouth." She was certain of the time, 2:30 A.M., because she turned on a light and looked at the clock. After the woman's cry, she heard a car door slam and then a car drive away. Martin's memory of the time of the cry matched roughly with the times other neighbors had reported hearing screams. Like those of other witnesses, her description contained no information that helped police take the lead further.[22]

That evening, December 14, Policewoman Catherine Olinger, Detective Boyd Carrier, Ace bartender Fred Meyer, and two of Ruth's friends, Linda Best and Ella Wormley, journeyed across the Mississippi River to the Friendship Club in Minneapolis. Both women had already given statements. The party's goal for the night was "to try and contact some girls who knew Ruth Munson and who also were known to the above girls."

Though they stayed late, both Best and Wormley thought the evening's crowd was small. They did not see anyone they knew except "Cliff" and "Ade." They danced with them. Cliff said that a month before at a club dance, he had seen Ruth "with a 'red headed girl'" but at that time he did not dance with her." Meyer did not recognize any woman as an Ace patron.

During the evening, Ade asked Best if she knew who killed Ruth Munson. Best replied that she did not, "and if she did, she would inform the police." Did he, Best asked? Ade replied that "he was not telling all he knew." Best later informed Policewoman Olinger and Detective Carrier that Ade had been drinking and "maybe was just talking."[23]

Policewoman Olinger and Detective Carrier did not file their report until the next morning. Before that day was out, police would give Ade the chance to tell them whatever else he knew about the case.

Wednesday, December 15, 1937

The investigation now moved into its seventh day. A handful of arrests had been made, potential suspects had been questioned and released, and no murder charges had been filed. The *St. Paul Pioneer Press*'s front-page coverage of the case was a rehash of details previously reported, including the neighborhood canvass that was underway, the discovery of the bracelet, and the assumption that Ruth Munson was attacked where the bracelet was found. The paper captured the frustration of the detectives working the case, reporting that "Scores of clues have been given police, but most have led to nothing. Citizens anxious to assist in the search for the killer send in reports of every variety concerning girls. A check usually proves those clues to be cases of mistaken identity." The *Minneapolis Tribune* buried its coverage on page eleven. Paraphrasing Assistant Chief Charles J. Tierney, the paper noted "recent developments in the inquiry have not reached a point where any announcement would be advisable." The discovery of the bracelet and the reporting of screams in the night at the same location, the *Tribune* continued, "have not led to anything beyond assumption that the girl was attacked at that spot."[1]

By the time the afternoon dailies hit the city's streets, several things had come to light that shook up the investigation. Previously, the dailies had reported that the reexamination of the second floor of the Aberdeen had yielded no new evidence, but today's afternoon editions reported (to the displeasure of police) that the search *had* yielded a new clue, which the investigation was keeping secret. Exactly how the *Daily News* discovered the new clue is unclear, though it is possible Assistant Chief Tierney was indirectly the source. He had telegraphed FBI headquarters in Washington, DC, reported the *Daily News*, requesting the loan of "a combination microscope-camera, capable of enlarging the photographed subject manyfold." The device was expected to arrive in St. Paul by Thursday, December 16. One way or another, the reporter had got wind of the request.

"A new clue which may point out the killer of Ruth Munson has been found by detectives on the second floor of the vacant Aberdeen hotel where her body was burned," the *Daily News* announced. Although Tierney declined to identify the clue, the newspaper described it as "a small object, found frozen in the ice formed on the second floor by water used to fight the fire." The object would remain in the locked hotel, embedded in the ice, until it was photographed with the requested equipment.

Quoting an unnamed police official, the *Daily News* reported that "This is one clue which the murderer or the flames did not destroy. We have examined it carefully under flood lights, and it looks very promising. When we get it to headquarters, we believe we can trace it to its owner. It's something the killer left behind." The unnamed official said the object would be photographed immediately after the camera arrived, then cut out of the ice and taken to the crime lab for further examination.[2]

The new clue consisted of three small metal shear pins, each about one and a half inches long. Shear pins are used in complex machinery. Their function is to break or "shear," to prevent serious damage to a machine when it is under stress.

From the beginning, the case had been investigated as a sex crime, meaning sex was the motive behind the killer's actions. Now, the *Minneapolis Journal* proclaimed, the search for Ruth Munson's killer had "narrowed to the circle of her acquaintances today." And police had a new hypothesis. "Hope for the solution lay within this circle, police believed, as they advanced a theory that the young woman's death was plotted and planned in minute detail. Revenge, they believed, was the motive behind the murder, rather than attack."

The *Journal* credited the new theory to the "startling disclosure" that a light had been seen on the Aberdeen's second floor on the eve of the murder. The disclosure may have been "startling" to the press, but police had known about the light in the Aberdeen since Mrs. Martin described it four days earlier. The *Journal* declared, "The presence of someone in the building at that early hour led police to believe the murderer had prepared the scene of his crime far in advance of the murder. Double doors of the building and an outside gate had been jimmied."[3]

The *Journal* cited other "bits of evidence" it claimed supported the theory that the murder was planned and "that the murderer was known to his victim," including the "agonized scream" heard during the night, "the discovery of Munson's bracelet" in the snow, and the discovery of a "black mask." The mask had been found the day after the murder by a man walking on Western Avenue near the Aberdeen. The finder said he had walked on that sidewalk just ten minutes earlier and the mask was not there. Like other objects, the mask had been turned over to Dr. John B. Dalton in the crime lab for examination. How much credibility the police actually assigned to the mask as a significant clue is uncertain, but it made for a nice detail in the *Journal*'s story.[4]

The *Journal* also noted that the "revenge theory" was the reason detectives were searching for a "state employee" who reportedly knew about a man Ruth Munson had claimed to fear. On December 14, the paper had reported that the state employee had been sitting on a porch with Ruth when another man stopped at the curb. "I'm afraid of that man," she supposedly said. Police efforts to locate and interview the state employee had been unsuccessful.[5]

Although the *Journal* had a scoop about the state employee, new revelations about the bracelet had apparently not yet made it across the river. Both the *Daily News* and the *St. Paul Dispatch* reported that a woman had stepped forward to claim ownership of the bracelet, casting doubt onto what had been considered a promising clue. The woman who claimed the bracelet said she had lost it a few days earlier. At press time, police had not released the woman's name. If her claim of ownership was verified, it meant police could no longer assume that Ruth had been attacked at that location.[6]

The woman's claim raised new questions: Police had no reason to doubt that Ruth owned a similar bracelet, so where was it? Her purse had been with her, consumed by the fire. Did the killer take her bracelet, believing it was something more than costume jewelry?

Both of St. Paul's afternoon papers reported details about an earlier attack on Ruth Munson in 1934. One morning as she was walking near the St. Paul Cathedral on her way to work at Miller Hospital, a man accosted her. Ruth suffered a cut lip and broke her watch in the scuffle, but she escaped. The man was never caught.[7]

News of this earlier attack once again raised questions about the safety of women on St. Paul's streets and by extension how seriously police took the issue. The *Daily News* pointed out that police had recorded the incident as a robbery attempt, even though the assailant "tried to drag her toward an automobile."[8]

After two days' work, detectives were finally able to interview the "state employee" referenced by the *Minneapolis Journal*. Detectives Raymond Schmidt and John Schroeder identified Irving Hanson by talking to the reporter, then tracked him down and interviewed him. Hanson had met Ruth Munson about three years earlier at the Friendship Club, and he had driven her home several times. The previous March or April, he had taken her home around 1:00 A.M. He didn't remember the exact address on Dayton Avenue. While they were parked, talking, a black sedan pulled alongside their car. "Immediately Ruth became frightened," the detectives wrote in their report. Hanson asked her if she was married, and she did not answer. The sedan's driver got out of the car, walked in front of Hanson's car, and disappeared between two apartment buildings, reappearing about five minutes later. He got in his car and drove away. "All the time this man was out of car," the detectives reported, "Ruth watched him and would not talk to Hanson, and after [the] man drove away she seemed to watch every car that came down the street." Hanson told the detectives that he had never been "familiar" with Ruth or made any "advances" toward her.[9]

Ironically, in their report, the detectives did not record Hanson as quoting Ruth saying she was "afraid of that man," leaving the authenticity of the comment somewhat in question. Hanson described the sedan's driver as thirty years old, with dark blond hair, wearing a chauffeur's cap with a leather visor and a dark mackinaw jacket with leather sleeves.

During his canvassing work, Detective Alfred Jakobson had "found two 'red-heads.'" Betty and Beverly Boyer lived in Apartment 4 at 280–282 Dayton. Both women fit the general description of the redheaded woman at the Ace. Jakobson took the two women to see Clara Broughton, Ruth's landlady. The landlady said that neither of the women had visited her tenant, "although the hair and build of Betty resembled the red-haired visitor to some extent. But she was positive they were not the girls." Detectives Jakobson and Frank Kennedy then took the two women to the Ace. A bartender there noted a resemblance, "but was positive they were not the girls who accompanied Munson."[10]

At police headquarters, a clerk-typist took an anonymous report about Mrs. Fred E. Melichar, living at 1915 St. Clair Avenue. Mrs. Melichar had told the anonymous informant in a previous conversation that "she had been at the Munson apartment several times and that she had a very good idea who the two women were who were with her [Ruth] the night of the murder, but that she did not care to get mixed in with it."[11]

Detectives Jakobson and Herman Schlichting were sent to interview Mrs. Melichar. The only name she gave them was Ann Noren, a friend of Ruth's whom other detectives had already interviewed.[12]

In a note to Assistant Chief Tierney dated December 15, Patrolman Edmond Kane went back two years to 1935 to name a man as a potential suspect solely because of the color of his skin. "When Cook and myself were working in the Rondo district," Patrolman Kane wrote, "we had a pick-up request from out of town on a Ramsom Blakey, 522 W. Central Ave, a colored man (young), wanted for rape." The request had originated in the Dakotas or Montana, the patrolman recalled, and in the end, he and Cook were unsuccessful in locating the suspect. Nevertheless, "If Blakey is in town," the patrolman concluded, "he might be a suspect in the Munson case."[13]

St. Paul resident Eldon Luger also reached back several years to inform police about "a girl that used to live with a colored man." He told Detective Lieutenant Bertram Talbot that in 1933 or 1934, the woman worked at the Eat Shop at 383 Robert Street in downtown. A woman named Mary Wicker also worked there, and Luger sometimes drove the two women home. He used to let the first woman out on the corner of Virginia and Iglehart Streets. She walked north in the direction of Carroll. Whether Luger had the Munson case in mind specifically when he came to the station or he was simply making a general accusation is unclear. But the police viewed his story as a possible lead based on the fact that a Black man was involved. Luger was shown Ruth's picture, and according to the police report, "He said it looked like her." Det. Lt. Talbot later talked to Mary Wicker and determined that the woman Luger was thinking of was Dorothy Jackson, who lived on Carrol Street, two doors east of Virginia.[14]

That Luger thought a white woman living with a Black man was worthy of police attention was not unusual in the city, the state of Minnesota, or even the nation. "Living with a colored man" indicated a sexual relationship. In 1937, among the forty-eight states in the union, thirty states had laws on the books prohibiting either cohabitation or marriage of mixed-race couples. Eleven states had repealed such laws by 1887. Minnesota was one of seven states that had never enacted a miscegenation law, but not for lack of trying. A bill was introduced into the Minnesota House of Representatives in 1913, but no action was taken on it. In 1918, District 31 legislative candidate Dr. Henry Wuerzinger indicated that if elected he would introduce a bill preventing interracial marriage. He lost the race.[15]

Nevertheless, it was not unusual for mixed-race couples to be singled out for both prosecution and persecution. In 1915, for example, Minneapolis police raided a dance of the Maple Leaf Club, "an organization of Negro men married to white women, who being denied the privileges of public amusement, held their dances at private residences and at Kistler's Hall." The host was fined $50 and guests were fined $10 for "being found in a disorderly house."[16]

A decade later, a white man living in St. Paul's Merriam Park neighborhood unsuccessfully sought to have his new marriage annulled "because he discovered that his wife was not white and that she had deceived him." Until the groom made his discovery, the couple "had lived together very happily."[17]

A 1936 editorial in the *Minneapolis Spokesman*, the city's Black weekly, pointed out "a growing tendency" among police officers "to molest without cause men and women of both races who happen to be in the company of others of different nationalities." According to the editorial, a "young white attorney in company with two Negro University students, a young woman and a young man," were harassed by police simply because they happened to "be Americans of a different racial stock." "This must stop," the editorial declared. "As long as a man or a woman is orderly and is a law-abiding citizen no police officer has a right to subject him to humiliation and abuse simply because one or the other of them does not happen to be of the same race."[18]

At 3:00 P.M., Detective Lieutenant Frank R. Cullen introduced himself to Elmer Unglamb, who had driven to St. Paul from his home in Arlington, Minnesota. Unglamb went by the nickname "Whitey," and under that moniker he had already popped up several times in the investigation. On December 10, he had called police to tell them about a letter he received from Ruth written on December 7. Unglamb explained that he had recently lived in Minneapolis, where he worked for Clover Leaf Dairy. In early November, he had undergone gallbladder surgery and was living in Arlington during his recovery. The state of his health and the fact that he lived out of town eliminated him as a murder suspect, but the police realized that he might know something about Ruth Munson that would help the investigation.

Unglamb gave Det. Lt. Cullen the December 7 letter from Ruth. In a neat, precise hand, Ruth responded to a letter he had sent her, saying she was glad to hear from him and she had been wondering how he was getting along. She apologized for not visiting the hospital again to see him. In answer to his thoughts about returning to Minneapolis, she advised, "I am sure it would be better for you to stay at home than to come to the city to stay," adding, "A person gets lonesome and discouraged in the city too."

She wrote that she had not been to the Friendship Club in over two weeks. "That place just doesn't appeal to me anymore. They couldn't get a crowd on Tuesday nights so they don't dance on Tues. And I understand the Thurs. night crowds are not so good either." She closed with "Be sure to call me if you come down, I shall be waiting to hear from you. Glad to hear that you have gained. Hope you continue to improve. As ever, Ruth."[19]

Unglamb said he had known of Ruth Munson in Wisconsin, but his "first personal contact was at the Friendship Club sometime in April 1937." They usually met at the Friendship Club on Sunday nights.

"How did she get back and forth?" Cullen asked.

"On the street car. She was never afraid to go from the car line to her home."

He said he had visited Ruth "most every Tuesday night since I have known her. I called her over the phone two or three times a week." Before his surgery, when he visited her in St. Paul, they took walks down to Western Avenue or sat on the cathedral steps.

Cullen did not ask Unglamb if they had had intercourse, as he did the other men he questioned. Instead, his questions focused on trying to establish Ruth's preferences for getting around the neighborhood.

"When you and Ruth used to walk what route would you usually use for going say west from where she lives?" Cullen asked.

"Ninety percent of the time we would go down Dayton toward Western Avenue . . . should we have wanted to go over to that little drug store over on Selby and Western and have a Coke there. Other times we would use that little quarter block, that short cut to go alongside the Aberdeen Hotel from Selby up to Dayton, [but] she never wanted to walk that way."

"Did she ever express a reason for not wanting to go by the Aberdeen or the corner where it is located?"

"No she said she didn't like to walk up along that street."

"Did she ever express any reason for not wanting to take the side of the street on Western Avenue that was close to the Aberdeen?"

"No."[20]

After Unglamb departed, Cullen had a few minutes to contemplate the significance of what he had learned: for some reason Ruth Munson was afraid to walk by the Aberdeen. And in her own hand, she had written, "A person gets lonesome and discouraged in the city too," as if she were speaking from personal experience.

At 4:15 P.M., Cullen questioned Adolph (Ade) Hultgren. He was thirty-one years old and worked as a guard at First National Bank; he had been brought to police headquarters at 11:50 A.M. so he could elaborate on his cryptic statement at the Friendship Club that he was not telling all he knew.[21]

Hultgren met Ruth Munson the previous year at the Friendship Club and had gone out with her a few times, including on New Year's Eve. He last talked to her over the phone "a long time ago."

"Did you know any of her girl friends?" Cullen asked.

Hultgren had seen a couple of her women friends, one who worked at the Union Depot and another who "went to school or something." He recalled seeing a redheaded woman, but he had forgotten the names of all of them. Ruth had mentioned a boyfriend, "a big tall blond fellow. She was very interested in him."

"Did you ever have intercourse with Ruth?"

"No."

"Would you know these two girls, this red headed girl, if you seen her again?"

"I might know her. As a rule I can remember faces very well."

"Did she ever express fear of anybody to you?"

"No. . . . She told me once . . . that she was never going to get married. She did make the statement, 'I'll never get married.'"

"Is there anything else that I haven't asked you that you can add to this statement at this time?"

"She acted different than other girls. I don't know in what way; I couldn't say exactly. She seemed to be a little bit odd."

"In what way?"

"She talked about dances all the time. I like to talk about interesting subjects and that didn't seem to appeal to her. Talking about dances and fellows. She seemed to be interested in fellows. She didn't mean anything to me. I just happened to go out with her a couple times, that's all that's to it."

"Is [there] anything else?"

"That's all I can add."[22]

For someone who had hinted that he wasn't telling all that he knew, what Hultgren did know did not amount to very much.

Detectives Boyd Carrier and Frank Kennedy took Ruth Munson's friends Ann Noren and Ella Wormley to the Ace at 9:00 P.M. Detective Carrier and Ella Wormley had been to the Friendship Club the previous night, which had stretched into the early hours. The detectives hoped the two women might "see anyone there who resembled Ruth Munson." They did not explain exactly why they hoped to see someone who resembled her, but it hinted at a new theory: the possibility that Ruth

Munson had been mistaken for someone else and seized and killed in error. "We sat around for several hours," the detectives later wrote, "but no one came in who looked like Ruth."

The detectives spoke with the waitress "who was supposed to wait on Ruth," but she said she did not see her there on Wednesday night. She claimed that she did see her on Monday night, just before 9:00 P.M. Both Ann Noren and Ella Wormley disputed the waitress's claim. They insisted they had had telephone conversations with Ruth that evening around 8:30 P.M., a claim verified in Ruth's diary entry for Monday, December 6.

The foursome also kept watch for women who matched the descriptions of Ruth's two companions. Once again, they met with disappointment.[23]

Detectives Carrier and Kennedy were not the only policemen to visit the Ace that night. At 11:00 P.M. Detective Robert Vick and Patrolman Frank Welander stopped by to chat with the bartenders. They learned that Bob McDougal, a bar employee, had passed the corner of Virginia and Dayton about 1:30 A.M. on December 8. He saw a car parked there at that late hour. He had not yet been interviewed at police headquarters.[24]

The duo dutifully noted MacDougal's comment in their report. Always, it seemed, there was one more lead to follow.

Thursday, December 16, 1937

The Ruth Munson murder case cast a shadow over the investigation of every incident involving an attack on a St. Paul woman. At 1:29 A.M. on Thursday, December 16, Lieutenant Joseph Schmitz and Detectives Karl Salaba, Robert Vick, and Maynard Welander responded to a radio call for a domestic incident involving a Black couple on St. Anthony Avenue, between Dale and Kent Streets in the Rondo neighborhood. The complainant, Mrs. Ferrell, told the detectives her husband, Willie Ferrell, had been drinking and started to beat her up. Mr. Ferrell, the detectives learned, previously had been arrested in San Francisco for "slapping down a colored woman." He arrived in St. Paul in September 1937 and had married the complainant on October 25. Mrs. Ferrell told the detectives that a week ago, her husband "had been drinking and tried to force her to go down on him." Mr. Ferrell was told to pack some clothes. He was taken to a friend's house nearby after being booked for "investigation on suspicion of disorderly conduct." The friend had "a car similar to the one seen in the vicinity of the Munson murder," Detective Welander wrote in the report, inferring a connection to the Munson case.[1]

The shadow of the Munson case also loomed over a pair of incidents involving women that occurred late Wednesday night. Thursday's morning newspapers carried the news. In the first, three women had been skating at the St. Paul Auditorium. At 10:30 P.M., just as they started their car, they were accosted by a Black man who displayed a revolver and threatened to shoot. The women sped away without injury. Minutes later and a few blocks away, two nurses were stopped by the same man as they were on their way to work at St. Luke's Hospital. A suspect (identified days later as Charles Moore) was arrested shortly after the second incident, but he was released when none of the five women could identify him. The assailant was described by the *St. Paul Pioneer Press* as "a slim Negro six feet tall, quite thin and wearing a short black jacket and a dark cap." He displayed "a nickel-plated revolver." According to the paper, "Police believe the man might have some connection with the slaying of Ruth Munson."[2]

The police seemed to be linking these incidents to the Munson case for no reason other than the suspects were Black. The disposition of the incident involving Willie Ferrell was handled separately from the Munson case, but as the days passed, the two robbery cases would become intertwined with the murder investigation and the suspect in the attempted robberies would also become a suspect in the murder case.

The *St. Paul Daily News* was moved to address the vulnerability of St. Paul women on its editorial page:

> Molestation of five girls by a man, apparently bent on robbery, has further aroused women and men in St. Paul. It does not appear that the man who attempted these robberies had any connection with the Munson murder but almost everything which takes place now bears some relations in the public mind to that horrible crime.
>
> More to the point is the growing apprehension of women. They are afraid to venture forth on the streets after dark.
>
> Clearly their only reassurance can come from some positive police action in the Munson and other cases.[3]

The arrest of the assailant in the robbery attempts fueled rumors that an arrest had been made in the Munson case. St. Paul's afternoon dailies trumpeted both the rumor and a subsequent denial by police in the same article. MUNSON CASE ARREST? NO, POLICE SAY read the headline in the *St. Paul Dispatch*. "Wild rumors that the murderer of Ruth Munson was under arrest filled St. Paul today," the paper reported, "but [they] were denied by police. The rumors were based apparently on the arrest of a man, later released, in connection with threats against five girls Wednesday night." According to the *Daily News*, St. Paulites "were electrified" by reports "the Ruth Munson killer has been caught," but in the next breath the paper admitted that "Police denied the rumor."[4]

While scores of citizens had stepped forward to offer tips, the two individuals detectives most wanted to hear from remained silent. And unidentified. It seemed logical to assume the women remained silent because they feared they might suffer the same fate as their friend. In public, at least, Assistant Chief Charles J. Tierney and Mayor Mark Gehan did not address such fears. Rather, they attributed the women's silence to a fear of violating cultural mores about women's social behavior. "Both officials promised to do all in their power to protect the young women from publicity," the *Minneapolis Journal* observed, "if fear of publicity in connection with their presence in a tavern has motivated their silence and kept important clues from police."[5]

Both afternoon St. Paul newspapers zeroed in on the most promising lead to identify the two women—the possibility that they had been seen in White Bear Lake on Saturday evening, December 11. The facts were meager. Two women had left St. Paul by bus. In White Bear Lake, they got off the bus and took a taxi to the city's train station, where they enquired about purchasing tickets for a northbound train. There the trail ended. While there was no guarantee that these two women were in fact Ruth's companions, the timing of their departure from St. Paul certainly aroused suspicion. "Significance is attached to the report because the flight apparently occurred a short time after newspapers first announced discovery of the visit to the Ace café the evening of the killing," the *Daily News* reported, adding, "One of the women is described as having red hair."[6]

As the day progressed, Detective Robert Murnane pursued this lead in White Bear Lake. He learned that the women, who seemed to have plenty of money, said they were going to Superior, Wisconsin, but purchased tickets for Duluth. He also secured descriptions. One was forty years old, five feet five inches tall, weighing about 180 pounds, with a dark complexion, dark hair, dark hat, and a black fur coat. The other was twenty-five to thirty years old, five feet four inches tall, 150 pounds, with a dark complexion and dark hair, wearing a green turban hat and a black fur coat. Neither woman had red hair. Despite this inconsistency, the police didn't abandon the search for these two women.[7]

The *Minneapolis Journal* gave its readers an update on the "mystery clue," noting that the police indicated it was "the most important clue developed to date in their search" for the killer. The police had kept details secret to avoid helping the killer "cover his tracks provided that—as they believe—the 'mystery clue' was actually left behind by the murderer in his flight." According to the *Pioneer Press*, ownership of the gold bracelet "would be determined today." In addition, detectives were working with two dentists to establish a legal identification of Ruth Munson through "dental work in the dead girl's mouth." These minor developments aside, the *Pioneer Press* observed that "the seventh day of the Munson murder mystery had passed on Wednesday, with the police no nearer a solution," due to "a complete lack of real clues."[8]

With few other leads to work on, detectives collected information about the 1934 attack, on the chance it could be linked to Ruth's murder. Detective Lieutenant Frank R. Cullen interviewed Mr. and Mrs. Peter Gustafson at 11:00 A.M. The Gustafsons had met Ruth Munson in 1929 through her former boyfriend Olaf Anderson, but they had not seen much of her since the couple broke up.

"Did she tell you what she thought was the reason for this attack?" Cullen asked.

"There was a boy that worked at Miller Hospital he was very fond of her and wanted to take her out and she said maybe he hired a man to scare her," Mrs. Gustafson recalled.

"So that she would let him walk home with her, is that the sence [sic] of it?"

"I don't know, but it seemed that way," Mrs. Gustafson said. "He wanted to take her home and take her out, but she always refused." She did not know his name, but remembered Ruth saying "he was an Italian fellow and he sang and played." What he played she didn't know.

"Did Ruth ever express fear of this fellow?"

"Yes she did, she was afraid of this man because [after that] there was a Squad car parked up there about four or five nights in the morning when she went to work but they never did find out who he was. It was on Summit Ave. near the Miller Hospital."

Mrs. Gustafson's recollections about the 1934 attack did not give detectives much new information. Asked if she could think of anything else, Mrs. Gustafson turned the conversation in a different direction. "The only thing I can think of is the two girls; one girl looks like her." One of the two women was named Beatrice, the other Clara, Mrs. Gustafson elaborated. Beatrice was the one "who looks so much like Ruth."[9]

Mrs. Gustafson's wording suggests that the "two girls" subject had surfaced in a discussion before the stenographer began to transcribe the interview. More than just a vague reference to the two women who were with Ruth the night of her murder, Mrs. Gustafson's response hinted at another angle detectives seemed to be pursuing. The foursome who had visited the Ace had been on the lookout for women who resembled Ruth. The search for women who looked like Ruth Munson suggests detectives were considering the possibility that Ruth had been mistaken for someone else.

The resemblance angle also appeared in a report filed by Detectives Boyd Carrier and Frank Kennedy, who were working many aspects of the case. "This morning we contacted Maybell Darling at 30 Iglehart and from what information we received she does not know Ruth Munson," the detectives wrote. "She gave us a picture of Hazel [Bohen] and

Ruth [Willmar] who live at 302 Sherman and who resemble Ruth Munson quite a bit. Maybell does not know Ruth Munson and never saw her around the Keystone Hotel."[10]

As if it were common knowledge among sworn officers, the detectives did not bother to explain in their report who Maybell Darling was and how she was connected to the Keystone Hotel. Neither did they offer any further details about the two women in the picture she gave them. What the detectives did with the photograph is unknown.

Although Detective Thomas Grace had extensively questioned head porter Robert Brown and released him two days earlier, the investigation was not finished with him. To learn more about Brown, Detective Lieutenant Roy Coffey and Patrolman Louis Schultz interviewed both the superintendent and the depot master at St. Paul Union Depot. The two police officers were shown Brown's personal file and found it contained "no record of any mis-conduct on his part." Brown's supervisors spoke "very highly of him as an employee." At one time a woman named Ethel Vanderpool, employed by Travelers Aid, was discharged for "associating with negro porters." Brown's employers did not know if he was acquainted with her. Further checking about Ethel Vanderpool revealed she had left Travelers Aid three years before.[11]

The two officers also checked out an automotive license plate number that had appeared in a notebook "taken from one Robert Brown, colored." The officers did not record how and why they had taken Brown's notebook. License plate B-367-871 was for a 1936 Chevrolet coupe owned by bookkeeper Florence Porier, 1727 Berkeley Avenue. According to the officers' report, "she knows no one by that name and has no idea where he obtained it. She has never been employed where any colored help have worked." The officers added a note of personal opinion and racial judgment to their summary: "She does not appear to be the type that would be acquainted with Brown." A handwritten note later scrawled at the bottom of the typed report noted that "number obtained through accident of car," indicating the car had been in a minor collision.[12]

Separately, Det. Lt. Cullen had followed up on Ruth's June 10 "Bob Brown" diary entry, which referenced a trip to Hunters and noted: "Bob there." Cullen had requested that Joseph Scheer, manager of the Hunters Club at 757–759 Mississippi Street, come to the station. Neither Scheer nor two waitresses employed there who accompanied him could recall seeing Ruth Munson at the tavern. None of the three employees had worked at Hunters longer than six months, meaning they probably were not present on June 10. But, Cullen learned, it might not have made any difference. According to what Scheer told him, it was Hunters' policy "to refuse to serve colored people." In Scheer's memory, on only three occasions had a "colored man . . . come to the bar asking for beer." In addition, "there have been no mixed couples in the place since he has been in charge."[13]

At 1:15 P.M., Detective Thomas Grace questioned Robert Gatzke in the presence of Patrolman James Cook and Detective Frank Kennedy. Though it was not standard procedure, it was not uncommon for a witness to be interviewed in the presence of detectives. Hastily scribbled notes accompanying Gatzke's typed transcript suggest the detectives had questioned him earlier and thought his comments were worthy of a formal statement. Gatzke was reporting on a conversation he had with his friend Davis Thoreson, who was married to Violet Thoreson. Violet, Ruth's coworker, had told the *Pioneer Press* on December 13 that Ruth Munson told her, "I'll never live to see Christmas." Grace wasted no time getting to what the witness had to say.[14]

"Will you relate in your own words any information that you might have pertaining to the Ruth Munson Case?"

Gatzke responded:

I went over to Davis Thoreson's place last night, and while talking to Thoreson, Thoreson told me that while he was in St. Joseph's Hospital last summer that he became acquainted with a night watchman from the Union Depot and that the watchman knew Violet Thoreson, Ruth Munson and a girl by the name of Frances. This watchman said that when the Hiawatha Train would come in there would be a negro on that train and when he was through working he would get off the train and pick up this Ruth Munson and Frances and get on a taxi and leave and also that Violet told Mr. Thoreson that this negro also bought a lot of clothes for the Munson girl. Thoreson also told me that the Munson girl wore an engagement ring and was supposed to be married before Christmas or on Christmas and that about four days before the murder Violet said to Ruth, aren't you glad or happy and Ruth said, No—I don't think I'll live that long. Mr. Thoreson worked at Seeger Refrigerator Co and Mrs. Thoreson took him to work about 10:00 or 10:30 o'clock in the evening of the day before Ruth Munson was found and Mrs. Thoreson got him about 7:00 or 7:30 in the morning of the day that Ruth Munson's body was found and Thoreson said he does not know whether she was out that night or where she was—whether she was home or not he couldn't say. Violet went to work that day and when she came home after work Violet said, I got a feeling that Ruth got killed last night and Mr. Thoreson said that she made that remark before the murder was made public. Last spring Thoreson told me he couldn't trust Violet because she stepped out with other men—she said she stayed home all night but he had checked the speedometer and there were about 25 or 30 miles in the morning that wasn't supposed to be and also that Violet didn't know about this.[15]

Gatzke's statement gave the detectives a lot to consider. Though the information was secondhand, and in some parts thirdhand, it suggested Violet Thoreson knew more than she had told the newspaper reporter. The statement also suggested that she might not be a trustworthy witness. Like several other witnesses, Gatzke hinted at a relationship between Ruth Munson and an unnamed Black man connected with the railroad. Despite the spectacular nature of Gatzke's statement, it would be days before detectives questioned Violet Thoreson.

At 2:30 P.M., Willard Wolf reappeared in the investigation—not in person, but as the primary subject covered during an interview with one of his associates. For the previous two months, Earl Carl Gussman, twenty-four years old, had worked Wednesday and Saturday nights at Wolf's Dayton Avenue Garage, parking the cars of neighborhood residents who rented overnight space or winter storage space there. When he worked, he stayed all night, sleeping in the back seat of one of the cars. He was working on the night of Wednesday, December 8. Cullen was obviously checking Wolf out, independently trying to nail down his movements around the time of the murder. What nights did Wolf generally stay all night at the garage, Cullen asked. Generally, the nights that Gussman wasn't there parking cars. But he stayed there that Wednesday night? Yes. When he stayed, where did he sleep? On a cot on the first floor. Was Wolf there in the garage on Wednesday night, December 8, and Thursday morning, December 9? Yes. Was anyone else there? Jim McGinley, an old gentleman who rooms at the garage for free. Did Wolf leave during the night? At 12:30 A.M. he went out to get a bowl of chili, returning at 1:00. He went to get breakfast at 6:30. Did he go to the Aberdeen when he learned about the fire? Yes, but he came back in five minutes. Did you see or hear anything out of the ordinary on the night of December 8? No, nothing out of the ordinary, was the answer, no strange cars or unusual noises.[16]

In terms of Wolf's activities on the night of December 8, Cullen determined he had been at the garage all night, staying there on a night he normally went home. He had left at 12:30, returning at 1:00 A.M.—which just happened to be around the time some witnesses had heard screams. He'd left again at 6:30 in the morning—just before the fire was discovered. These details would come in handy if and when Wolf himself was questioned.

True to the *Pioneer Press*'s prediction, the ownership of the bracelet was settled during the afternoon. At 3:00 P.M., Bureau of Identification superintendent John J. Tierney, brother of the assistant police chief, took a statement from Helen Laska, 464 Dayton Avenue.

"You reported on the 15th of December that you lost a gold bracelet in the vicinity of your apartment?" the superintendent asked.

"Yes," Laska answered.

"When did you lose this bracelet?"

"Dec. 8th, about 11:30 P.M." Laska explained that she had gone bowling at 8:30 P.M. The bracelet wouldn't stay on, so she took it off. She left at 11:20 P.M. and realized she had forgotten the bracelet. "I had to come back for it, and that is when I put it (bracelet) in the toe of the bowling shoe. When I arrived at the apartment, I parked on North side of Dayton Ave. opposite my apartment, took my shoes and bowling ball and walked to my apartment."

"When did you first miss this bracelet?"

"Thursday morning, Dec. 9th."

"You were shown a bracelet in the office of C. J. Tierney, Asst. Chief of Police. Do you believe that that is your bracelet?"

"Yes I do."

Asked how long she had owned the bracelet, Laska said it had been in her possession for about a week, but belonged to her sister, Mrs. Dorothy Bell of St. Cloud.[17]

Superintendent Tierney could hardly help but recognize the irony. Laska had lost the bracelet late in the evening on December 8, within three hours of the time police had originally estimated Ruth Munson had been attacked. With the bracelet ownership apparently settled, it was clear Ruth had not been attacked, screamed, and lost her bracelet in front of at 450–452 Dayton Avenue on the night she died. The seven hours between the time when Ruth left the Ace and her body was found the next morning was once again a gaping hole that needed to be filled. In this regard, the investigation was back to square one.

Through the late afternoon and evening hours, investigators worked on three separate leads that all pointed at Black men. In the first, an undated note bearing a disturbing message and addressed to the chief of police had appeared. Detectives Alfred Jakobson and Herman Schlichting, stalwarts in the Munson investigation, inherited the task of looking into it. The penmanship and grammar were as ugly and uneducated as the message.

> To the Chief of Police
>
> A Mind Reader told me that the Dirty Black Janitor of the First National Bank Bldg is the Cold Bloody slayer of the Poor Munson Girl and he is worth to be Lynched by Sunrise the Dirty Black Cur.
>
> a Broken Hearted Girl Friend[18]

Around 4:30 P.M., the detectives secured the name and address of the janitor from the building superintendent at First National Bank. He was Ivor Shelby, who lived at 321 West Central Avenue. The two detectives drove to that address and spoke with his wife. She informed them that Mr. Shelby "had left her about three weeks ago and she did not know where he was staying."[19]

The detectives were stymied for the time being. Coincidentally, however, Shelby was the subject of a separate complaint filed later in the day. At 8:00 P.M., Detective Lieutenant Ray McCarthy was visited by Charles Sitzoff, who claimed that Ivor Shelby fit "the description of the colored man who pointed a gun at three girls near the auditorium on Dec. 15th." Sitzoff also told Det. Lt. McCarthy that the janitor owed him five dollars, a fact that led McCarthy to suspect the complaint "may be a case of a grudge."[20]

At 9:30 P.M., George Nado arrived at police headquarters to give a statement about the tip he had phoned in on December 13, discussing events at Rossini's, the tavern on Kellogg Boulevard and Sibley Street. Det. Lt. Cullen, who had been on duty since morning, opened the interview with the usual questions about the subject's background. Nado was thirty-three, married, and a resident of West St. Paul. He had worked for three years in the railroad mail division for the US Post Office.

"Do you know Ruth Munson?" Cullen asked.

"No."

"You called the station last Monday, 7. P.M., stating that you had some information you thought might have some bearing on the Munson case. Will you go ahead and tell what that information is?"

"We came to Rossini's and the waitress Evelyn told us she had something good to show us—she said there are three girls who work at the depot who came in, ordered six beers and took them to a booth—a few minutes later three negroes walked in, went to the booth sat down with the girls and drank beer. This waitress remarked these girls had a lot of nerve only going across the street to pull that. We went past the booth to take a look but we didn't look enough so I can't recognize any of them. As we were going out Harry Rossini, one of the proprietors, mentioned that these girls had come in there and ordered the beer and paid for it, so it couldn't have been a common occurrence or he wouldn't have noticed it."

According to what Rossini had told Nado, the Black men worked at the depot as porters, also known as red caps.

"You couldn't identify Miss Munson as being one of the girls?"

"No."

"How long ago was that?"

"Three weeks to a month before Miss Munson was murdered."

"Would you be able to identify the two other girls if you saw them[?]."

"No."[21]

At the same hour, a Roxy Café bartender told Detective Oscar Enebak that Wally, a driver for the Blue and White Cab Company, had been in the café and remarked that he had driven Ruth Munson in the company of "colored men" on several occasions. At the Blue and White office, the operator identified "Wally" as Walter Couture, age twenty-seven. Detective Enebak had then directed the operator to call Couture in, and he took him to police headquarters to make a statement.[22]

At 11:00 P.M., Cullen, still on the job, took Couture's statement. Couture had driven a taxicab for five years. He claimed he did not know Ruth Munson and he never went into the Union Depot restaurant where she worked.

"You told some people that you hauled Miss Munson on a number of occasions when she was accompanied by colored people—is that correct?" Cullen asked.

"I don't remember saying anything like that."

"Were you drinking?"

"Yes."

"Where at?"

In a rambling answer that named other establishments, Couture never mentioned Roxy Café. Despite being pressed, he remained adamant that he had never driven Miss Munson, and even took his denial a step further.

"I never hauled a colored man and white woman together since I have been driving," he declared.[23]

A Black man who had no apparent connection to the Ruth Munson murder case or a robbery attempt on three women, yet was singled out as a target by two different people, one even calling for him to be lynched. At a typical city tavern, white women and Black men socializing at 4:00 in the afternoon, a sight so unusual that a waitress regarded it as "something good" to show others—even as she criticized the women as having "a lot of nerve." A taxi driver bragging to others about hauling mixed couples in his cab, only to deny it when questioned by the police.

These three incidents on the shank of the day typified the state of race relations in St. Paul as police continued the Ruth Munson murder investigation.

"A Long Hard Drag"

Friday to Sunday, December 17–19, 1937

On Friday, December 17, the *St. Paul Pioneer Press* relegated coverage of the case to its second section, predicting its future in the headline: LONG HUNT FOR CLUES IN MUNSON CASE SEEN. According to the article, "Weary detectives grimly settled down Thursday night to what they termed 'a long hard drag' in the attempt to solve the killing of Ruth Munson." While the search for her two women friends continued, "police were beginning to despair that they would be found soon."[1]

With no new developments to report, the other dailies revisited the search for the two women, repeating yesterday's details. "The bus arrived at White Bear village at midnight," the *Minneapolis Tribune* reported. "The women were reported to have inquired about trains, but it was said that they did not take one in the station in the village." The *Minneapolis Journal* would report later in the day that the "trail of two girl companions who had been with Miss Munson in a St. Paul tavern . . . was apparently lost at White Bear Lake." The *Journal*'s wording strongly and inaccurately hinted that the two women who took the bus to White Bear Lake *were*, in fact, Ruth Munson's friends. Further, the account incorrectly reported that the women "answered descriptions of her companions."[2]

While the press focused on the White Bear Lake angle, within the police department detectives were pursuing other potential leads. Detectives Frank Kennedy and Boyd Carrier contacted Mr. F. B. Bauer at the National Battery Company. Bauer informed them that he and his wife had dismissed a maid named Luella Hersch "on account of hanging around the Ace Box. She has been known to have been out there at least four times a week." Hersch had implored Mrs. Bauer "to let her keep on working by promising to stay away from there." In the end, however, Mrs. Bauer decided to let her go. She described her former employee as "a good liar and a pretty smooth talker." The detectives also talked to Mrs. L. S. Cline, 946 Osceola, who told them that Luella Hersch's sister, Marion, had left her employment around the same time the former was dismissed from the Bauer household. "These two girls answer the general description of the girls seen with Ruth Munson at the Ace Café," the detectives concluded in their report.[3]

In the meantime, Detective Lieutenant Roy Coffey and Patrolman Louis Schultz were checking out an anonymous letter sent to the chief of police. "If you will pick up this woman Bea Roberts 587 W. Central you will have the redhead that was with Ruth Munson," the anonymous writer declared, noting that "the other is a jew girl—this Roberts woman has a house, white women for colored men, so take this in consideration. They went to Jim Williams often, this Bea, is absolutely no good. So please see about this, the bartenders can identify Bea. Ask at Jim's also. Do not pass this up." "Jim Williams" was both the informal name of a bar in the Rondo neighborhood and its owner-proprietor. The two police officers first brought the subject of the anonymous letter, Bea Roberts, to the police station, then took her to 56 West Summit Avenue, where Ace bartender Gus Gavanda lived. The bartender told the officers that the redheaded woman he saw with Ruth at the Ace on December 8 had the same shade of hair, but was heavier and shorter than Bea Roberts. The officers' report did not indicate whether they followed up by taking Bea Roberts to Jim Williams's bar, but she was later released to her attorney.[4]

If Willard Wolf was the bad penny of the investigation, Ruth Munson's friend Whitey was a strip of flypaper that seemed permanently stuck to it. On December 16, Detectives Frank Martin and Herbert Olson had received information from a Minneapolis police officer that had directed them to the home of Mrs. Valentine Wiegand in that city. Wiegand had told them that her boyfriend, Weston Hill, was in a St. Paul bar a week earlier and overheard two women talking about the Munson murder case. One named "Gene" stated she had been interviewed at police headquarters and had "neglected to inform the Police that Ruth Munson had told her that she feared for her life, because of a boy friend by the name of Whitey." "Gene," the detectives wrote, supposedly had remarked that Whitey had just been released from the hospital and he had told Ruth "that if she ever turned him down she wouldn't live to tell about it." Wiegand told the detectives that her boyfriend would be able to provide more information.

Detectives Martin and Olson took Wiegand to police headquarters, where she gave a statement to Detective Lieutenant Frank R. Cullen. She recounted the same basic story, adding that Whitey wanted to marry Ruth Munson, but Ruth didn't want to marry him and was afraid of him. Wiegand added that her boyfriend, Weston Hill, had asked if this information had been turned into the police, and "Gene" had said she had not been asked.[5]

Det. Lt. Cullen's interview of Whitey Unglamb on December 15 had confirmed he was living in Arlington, Minnesota, and recuperating from surgery at the time of the murder. Nevertheless, there was always the possibility that Cullen had missed something upon which Hill could shed some light. Cullen sat down to question Weston Hill at 10:55 A.M. on December 17.

Weston Hill was twenty-four years old. Though Valentine Wiegand had referred to him as her boyfriend, like Wiegand herself, he was married. The week before, he had been at Matt Weber's, a tavern on East Seventh Street, and started talking to three women. One of the women, who he thought was named Jean or Joan, was a waitress at the Union Depot. Her last name, Hill said, was similar to "Levorn."

Cullen no doubt understood that Hill was talking about Joan Pivoran, Ruth's work colleague and friend, whom he had interviewed on December 9, the day of the murder.

"I asked if she had given this information when she was up here," Hill said, referring to Ruth's fear of Whitey, "and she said she wasn't asked. I told her I wanted to see it cleared up and why didn't she tell them that. She said she wasn't asked and besides he (Whitey) just got out of the hospital and he was too weak to do anything like that."

"Did she say that Ruth had told her that this Whitey asked Ruth to marry him?" Cullen asked.

"She said Ruth told him that they didn't have nothing in common."

"Did she say whether or not Whitey made any threats against Ruth at any time?"

"No, she didn't."

"You don't recall her saying this Whitey had said he would kill her if she went out with anyone else."

"No."

"Did Jean [sic] intimate to you that Ruth appeared to fear for her life because she didn't continue to go with Whitey?"

"No she didn't."

Weston Hill had just nullified all the secondhand claims Valentine Wiegand made. Cullen began to wrap up the interview.

"Is there any other information that you have on this case?"

"Not concerning that." Hill then proceeded to share information passed on to him from his friend Phillip Meath, 290 Dayton Avenue, about Willard Wolf. (In the transcript, the stenographer spelled the name as "William Woulfe.") According to what Meath told Hill, Wolf "had been married five times and each of his wives had left him."

"Did he intimate that he (Meath) knew anything definite in reference to Woulfe?" Cullen asked.

"No. He said he knew Woulfe and he said he was known for his different acts around there some way or another. He had a good suspicion. He said a fellow came in with a can and he said Bill Woulfe told [the man] he didn't handle gas and he showed him where a filling station was to get some gas and when this fellow left[,] he went the other way and Phil said it looks like Woulfe is trying to cover some tracks, because a man wouldn't go in the opposite direction he was told."[6]

It is not clear whether Cullen put any stock in this secondhand assertion that Wolf in essence had made up a phantom suspect to deflect suspicion from himself.

As the day proceeded, the police department received a message from the Munson family in Grantsburg that Ruth's bracelet had been found among her effects at the family home. The police could shelve the once promising lead and focus on other clues.[7]

Primary among them was the "mystery clue" still embedded in the ice on the second floor of the Aberdeen Hotel. Who knew what else might be buried in the sludge under the inch-and-a-half layer of ice? The challenge, of course, was how to melt the ice without disturbing whatever else lay in the muck beneath it. On Friday afternoon, police attempted to use a "steam apparatus" to melt the ice "without disturbing clues which might remain." This method quickly proved to be unworkable and was abandoned.[8]

On Friday evening, to reduce the area that had to be heated to melt the ice, carpenters began to board off the second-floor area burned in the fire. The new plan was to employ charcoal-burning heaters known as salamanders to warm the air enough to melt the ice.[9]

While efforts at the Aberdeen continued late into the evening, elsewhere in the neighborhood other sworn officers were going about their work. At 10:05 P.M., Patrolman Robert Williams filed a report stating he had arrested a Black man, William Lawrence of 447 Carroll Avenue, at the Keystone Hotel on a complaint that he had made a remark that he knew who killed Ruth Munson. "This man frequents different beer parlors and possibly might have heard someone discussing this murder," Patrolman Williams wrote, adding, "He was put on hold book for general investigation."[10]

In terms of solving the murder case, the arrest and subsequent release of William Lawrence would prove to be insignificant. However, the arrest was significant in another way.

Among the more than 300 sworn officers on the St. Paul police force, Patrolman Robert Williams was one of a handful of Black officers. A resident of Rondo, he was appointed to the position of patrolman on December 4, 1920, at the age of forty-one. For many years, he worked out of the Rondo substation. Patrolman Williams's arrest of William Lawrence marked the first time in the Ruth Munson murder investigation, now in its ninth day, that a Black officer had filed a report on the case—even as the investigators pursued leads that took them into the Black community.

In making the arrest, Patrolman Williams appeared to have acted within the scope of his regular duties, as opposed to being assigned any task related to the investigation by the white administrators who were directing it.

By midday on Saturday, December 18, work on boarding up the Aberdeen's second floor was wrapping up. Four salamanders were installed and fired up. The wait for the ice to melt began. The *Minneapolis Star's* update on the Aberdeen project carried a hint of optimism, noting that detectives were "hopeful that ice covering the floor and stairs of the hotel will contain some clue." The *St. Paul Dispatch* looked ahead to the next steps. "After the ice is thawed and the floor dried, all ashes will be sifted by Dr. John Dalton, police criminologist, for telltale traces of the murderer."[11]

While the ice slowly melted, out on the streets, detectives continued the neighborhood canvass. The effort now included twelve detectives, knocking on doors from 8:00 A.M. to 10:00 P.M. The seventy-five-block area being covered extended west from the St. Paul Cathedral for more than a mile to Lexington Parkway. With Marshall Avenue as the center axis running east and west, the canvass area extended three blocks north to Rondo Avenue and three blocks south to Laurel Avenue. Within these boundaries were various sites associated with the murder, including Ruth Munson's apartment building, the Aberdeen Hotel, the blocks where screams were heard in the dark hours of the night, and the Keystone Hotel.[12]

One of the doors that Detective Herman Schlichting knocked on was Apartment C at 203 Virginia Street, where Mr. and Mrs. E. J. Farrell lived. Their apartment was located directly across the street from the front of the Aberdeen Hotel. Detective Schlichting asked the

Farrells if he could view the Aberdeen through various windows within their apartment. From one apartment window, he observed, "There is a reflection of light which is caused by street lighting that shines on the [Aberdeen] window and may have given some women the impression some one had a light burning in same."[13]

Detective Schlichting's observation raised a question: Were neighbors who reported seeing lights burning in the hotel on nights before and after the murder in fact only seeing reflections? On Wednesday, December 8, the eve of the murder, had Mrs. Martin actually seen lights burning on the hotel's second floor as she made her way to the grocery store on Selby? Burning lights offered the possibility that at that hour the killers were inside the hotel preparing for the attack. A mere reflection offered no such possibility.

Detective Schlichting asked Mr. and Mrs. Farrell about the evening of December 8. "Everything was quiet and peaceful as far as they knew," he later wrote. Other building residents he interviewed also said nothing unusual occurred that night.[14]

Tips about the two women with Ruth Munson continued to come from the public. On December 18, Detective Lieutenant Joseph Heaton and Patrolman James Cook investigated a tip that two women had suddenly moved out of 265 Dayton on December 14 or 15. They learned that the women had given a month's advance notice, which indicated they were not Ruth's two friends.[15]

With little else to report on in the way of developments but the ongoing neighborhood canvass and the ice melting effort in the Aberdeen, the December 18 *Dispatch* focused on two recent "dates" Ruth Munson had had with "gentlemen friends." Attributing the information to sheriff's deputies in rural Ramsey County rather than the St. Paul police, the newspaper noted that she "was seen with an escort at one tavern four nights before the murder . . . and is known to have been at a different tavern with another man two weeks before her body was found." One of the men's identity had been established, and he was "being sought for questioning."[16]

While this information may have been a development for sheriff's deputies not familiar with the case, the St. Paul police already had in their possession full details of not two, but three recent dates Ruth had with "gentlemen friends"—provided someone had taken the time to review existing files carefully. Her diary entry for November 29 noted she had gone to the Paramount Inn with "Cliff." Cliff Sorenson was listed in her address book as living at the YMCA.

On December 1, her diary noted that "Bill called. To Hugo for dinner—then to Midway." "Bill" was Ruth's former fiancé, William Nelson. During Nelson's interview, he had acknowledged that they had driven to Hugo and had dinner at Louie's on December 1.

On December 4, Ruth wrote in her diary that she and her current boyfriend, Dick Das, had gone to the Wagon Wheel.

Furthermore, the trips to Hugo and the Wagon Wheel were mentioned in Ruth's December 7 letter to Whitey Unglamb, which he had given to police when he was interviewed on December 15. All it took to discover these details was for someone to have read all the materials.

Whether the police had identified these details is unknown, but the situation points out a potential serious challenge in the investigation. Who among all of the sworn officers knew everything? Each detective or detective team accumulated knowledge of the case from their own assignments. But detectives did not always know what others had learned.

The four men who usually received copies of all reports connected to the investigation were Police Chief Clinton Hackert, Assistant Chief Charles J. Tierney, Public Safety Commissioner Gustave H. Barfuss, and Ramsey County Coroner C. A. Ingerson. This made them the most likely candidates to have access to everything related to the investigation. At the same time, these men had other significant and time-consuming duties to perform. Did they have time to study everything, or did they assign that task to one of their assistants?

The potential for important details to go unnoticed raised a deeper question: Was the resolution to the Ruth Munson murder case buried somewhere in the department's own paperwork, rather than still lurking out on the street?

Melting the ice on the Aberdeen's second floor proved to be a very slow process. Detective Fred Nielsen arrived at 3:00 P.M. to start his shift and restocked the salamanders with charcoal. The fires burned into the evening. "Checked fires at 6 and 9 P.M.," Nielsen noted in a report. "When Detective G. Murphy arrived at 11 P.M. we fixed the fires again, and I turned the keys over to him."[17]

While Nielsen was on duty at the Aberdeen, Detective Lieutenant Bertram Talbot and Patrolman Robert Williams drove to 607 St. Anthony Avenue. Running parallel to Rondo Avenue, St. Anthony Avenue was part of the Rondo neighborhood, housing Black families and Black-owned businesses. Upon arriving at the address, the officers "Brought in [to police headquarters] . . . Pat White who runs the place," along with Norene Beasley, age twenty-seven, and Annette Martin, also twenty-seven years old, "who lived there with her." In their report, the officers did not specify whether the "place" Pat White ran was a simple boardinghouse, a house of prostitution, or some other type of establishment. The officers did note that "All these are white women and associate with negros." The three women were questioned by Assistant Chief Tierney, who was interested in what information they could provide about Ruth Munson. They had nothing to offer and were "not held" according to the officers' report.[18]

At 12:20 A.M. on Sunday, December 19, Detectives Donald Kampmann and Cecil Stow were sent by the dispatcher to check on a report of lights burning on the second floor of the Aberdeen Hotel. To their surprise, Detective George Murphy unlocked the Aberdeen's front door and admitted the two detectives. Murphy had relieved Detective Nielsen at 11:00 P.M. The mystery of the burning lights was immediately solved, but dutifully Kampmann and Stow "went through the place," finding the second floor "lighted up by portable lighting plant and four salamanders burning." The detectives informed the dispatcher that "Everything was O.K." and went on with their shift.[19]

The plan to install salamanders on the hotel's second floor to melt the layer of ice had been publicized in Saturday's morning and afternoon newspapers. It is also probable that details about the project circulated among the sworn officers. That neither the dispatcher nor Detectives Kampmann and Stow seemed aware of the ice-melting project indicated that within the St. Paul Police Department the right hand did not always know what the left hand was doing.

At the same time Kampmann and Stow were checking out the Aberdeen, Detectives Darwin Morse and LeRoy Tynan were pursuing a lead supplied by Detective Harry O'Keefe that had the potential to break open the case. At 12:45 A.M. the two detectives went to Bibeau's Tavern at 624 Wabasha Street to talk to Mrs. Mary Van Ness. She told the detectives that her nine-year-old daughter had a ten-year-old friend named Barbara Bushinski. Barbara had told Mrs. Van Ness's daughter that her mother, Betty Bushinski, "was out with Ruth Munson the night she was murdered." The Van Ness girl did not believe what Barbara had said at first, but Betty Bushinski told her that it was true.

The detectives took Mrs. Van Ness to her own apartment at 186 West Summit Avenue and spoke with her daughter. Then, mother and daughter rode with the detectives to point out the location where the

Bushinskis lived, 156 Pleasant Avenue. The detectives drove Mrs. Van Ness and her daughter home, then returned to the Bushinski residence. By this time, it was 3:30 A.M., and Mrs. Bushinski said she had not been home very long. The detectives told her that "the man in charge at headquarters wanted to talk to her," but they made no mention of the Munson case. Mrs. Bushinski, Detective Tynan later wrote, seemed neither surprised nor inquisitive "about what she was wanted for." On the way, they asked if she had any idea why she was going to headquarters. "Oh, I suppose they want to know if I knew Ruth Munson," she surmised.

At headquarters, Mrs. Bushinski was questioned by Detective O'Keefe. She said she was twenty-nine years old and separated from her husband. When asked for recent places she had lived, she gave seven different addresses. She denied knowing Ruth Munson. "She did impress us as being truthful," Detective Tynan observed, expressing a rare opinion on a report form. Nevertheless, the detectives put her on the holdbook for Assistant Chief Tierney.[20]

In terms of new developments, December 19 proved to be a slow day. The Sunday *St. Paul Pioneer Press* announced that the salamanders had "sufficiently melted the ice to permit careful investigation of the spot where the body was found. Detectives today will begin the task of sifting debris." Exactly when the "sift" began and how it was conducted under the supervision of criminologist Dr. John Dalton is unknown. Dr. Dalton did not file any reports documenting his process or his findings. In subsequent days, some details about the "sift" would be shared with the press.[21]

Throughout Sunday, the neighborhood canvass continued with no new revelations. Similarly, detectives continued their fruitless search for leads that would identify Ruth's two women friends.

Since arriving at the Aberdeen at 7:45 A.M. on the morning the body was found, Detectives Carrier and Kennedy had filed twenty-eight reports about the case. Their twenty-ninth documented yet another witness's account of a scream heard during the wee hours of the night. "On information we received," the detectives interviewed Mrs. Jessie Hanson. Hanson, a nurse, had a patient on the third floor of the Angus Hotel at Selby and Western Avenues. The patient's room was on the hotel's northeast corner; the Aberdeen Hotel was on the northeast corner of the block to the northeast, and so about a block away. Hanson told the detectives she was a light sleeper. On December 9, at 1:30 A.M., "she heard a woman scream twice as though scared, like some

The Angus Hotel at Selby and Western, 1925. *MNHS*

one being grabbed or struck." Hanson was sure of the time because she checked the clock. She also heard "an auto start up and a door slam at about the same time."

Mrs. Hanson added one new detail to the now familiar story. At 4:00 A.M., she got up and noticed "smoke coming out of the chimney" of the Aberdeen. "This is the larger chimney of the three that she can see from her window," the detectives wrote in their twenty-ninth report. "She described smoke as going straight up—not very black and about ten inches wide."[22]

With the bracelet clue discredited, the scream and accompanying reports of a strange car were the only known clues that had potential to close the seven-hour gap. Like the other witnesses' accounts, Jessie Hanson's version unfortunately contained no information that helped detectives take additional steps to track the scream to its source.

The "long hard drag" to find Ruth Munson's killer continued.

12 Dead Ends

Christmas week: St. Paulites prepared to celebrate the holiday. Over the weekend, efforts to melt the ice on the Aberdeen's second floor had proved successful. On Monday morning, December 20, the *St. Paul Pioneer Press* reported that workers had scooped up twelve bushels of debris from the floor. The muck was transported to the crime lab at police headquarters, where Dr. John B. Dalton began "a microscopic examination" in search of "some tell-tale trace left behind by the killer." Dr. Dalton would also be on the lookout for "coins or other objects from the girl's purse."[1]

Beyond acknowledging the existence of the "mystery clue," the police department issued no reports describing new evidence retrieved from the debris. This absence of newspaper stories, along with a similar absence of reports issued by detectives following up on items discovered in the debris, suggests the extensive effort ultimately yielded no new physical evidence.

On the same day the crime lab's examination of the hotel debris got underway, the investigation abruptly turned in a new direction. A former Red Cross caseworker who had worked at the Aberdeen Hotel when it was a veterans hospital suggested to police that "a mental patient" at the hospital might have returned "to the neighborhood while deranged" and murdered Ruth Munson. The former caseworker indicated that all records of "these patients" were still on file at the US Veterans Administration offices, now housed at Fort Snelling.[2]

For an investigation struggling to come up with new leads, the caseworker's suggestion was appealing, even if the idea contradicted the department's recent theory that the murder was a carefully planned act of revenge.

Monday morning's *Pioneer Press* announced that Police Chief Clinton Hackert had detailed two detectives "to go over the records for leads in the case." According to the newspaper, the Veterans Administration claimed to "have authority to co-operate with the police in such matters," and the records would be opened without "the customary court order."[3]

By the time the afternoon *St. Paul Dispatch* hit the city's streets, the Veterans Administration had had a change of heart. "Officials of the United States Veterans administration denied today that records of mental patients at the old Aberdeen hospital will be opened to police for investigation in connection with the Munson murder," the *Dispatch* reported. The officials asserted that "mental patients . . . never were taken care of at the Aberdeen except briefly until they were transferred to the proper hospitals."[4]

The police department had already taken the first step in conducting a records search. The task of checking out the records was assigned to Detectives Boyd Carrier and Frank Kennedy. By 2:05 P.M. on Monday afternoon, the duo had returned from the Veterans Administration at Fort Snelling with a report. They had learned "that there were between ten and twelve thousand names in files and that they were not classified by their disability," which meant "We would have to check . . . the individual cases which would take from four to six months."[5]

The Veterans Administration's sudden lack of cooperation and the lengthy estimate for the work apparently caused Chief Hackert to reconsider the project. As abruptly as the department had announced its plan to review veterans' records, the effort was abandoned. The investigation continued to check out the status of men who had been arrested or convicted of sex crimes, but mental health patients once housed at the Aberdeen were never routinely checked out.

The investigation took a close look at Harold A. Creagan, who was being held at the state prison in St. Cloud. Creagan, twenty-nine years old, had been paroled in July. On December 3, he had killed a truck driver in Fargo, North Dakota, then fled to St. Paul, but soon returned to Fargo. He was arrested and sent to St. Cloud. On Sunday, December 19, Assistant Chief Charles J. Tierney interviewed Creagan at the prison, hoping to learn if he was still in St. Paul when Ruth Munson was murdered. The prisoner claimed he had left St. Paul on Monday, December 6, two full days before the murder. "Mr. Tierney today is checking Creagan's statements to determine if he was still in St. Paul Dec. 9," the *Daily News* reported, "but [he] would not explain why he suspects the convict."[6]

The task of checking out Creagan's alibi was assigned to Detectives John Baum and Cecil Stow. Using information Creagan had given Tierney, the detectives talked to Nyle Paulson, eighteen years old, who recounted an adventure with Creagan. Driving Creagan's car, the duo left St. Paul on December 6, headed for Fargo. They ran out of gas near Detroit Lakes, Minnesota. A trucker picked them up and gave them eight gallons of gas in return for helping him unload his truck in Detroit Lakes. Creagan drove on toward Fargo alone. Paulson returned to St. Paul the next day. Creagan's alibi had checked out, and he was eliminated as a suspect.[7]

Investigators continued to look at men in St. Paul's Rondo neighborhood. Ivor Shelby, the bank janitor who on December 16 had been fingered separately by two informants as the murderer of Ruth Munson and the would-be robber of five women, was given a second look. At 11:30 A.M., Detectives Herman Schlichting and Alfred Jakobson drove to 557 Rondo, where they had learned Shelby was staying, and "left word for him to report to Detective Headquarters." Assistant Chief Tierney and Inspector William McMullin questioned him, but because no report was made of this interview, it is unknown how extensively they asked about the Munson murder. Inspector McMullin released Shelby. In the meantime, the detectives had checked with the building superintendent of First National Bank. They determined that on December 15, Shelby was working at the bank from 6:00 P.M. to 4:00 the following morning. This eliminated him as a suspect in the attempted robberies.[8]

To detectives, no Black man was above suspicion, especially if he was connected to the Union Depot. "On information received," Detective Carrier investigated a report of "a colored man receiving first aid 12–9–37 at 5:55 P.M.," the day Ruth's body was found. The man in question, Charles S. Anderson, lived at 453 Rondo and worked as a porter at the Union Depot. He had sought treatment for a cut on the second finger of his right hand, after catching it as he was exiting the depot's swinging doors. Like Shelby, Charles Anderson proved to be a dead end in the investigation.[9]

The latest lead in the search for the two women with Ruth Munson at the Ace took Detectives Baum and Stow to South St. Paul, accompanied by that city's police chief, Edgar McAlpine. Through Dr. Bloomer, a veterinarian in charge of the sheep-dip at the stockyards, they connected with Kenneth Johnson, formerly of Grantsburg, Wisconsin. Johnson told the detectives that he knew Ruth, and that in the past, she was "very chummy" with Arlene Berglund of Grantsburg. According to Johnson, Arlene Berglund had carrot-red hair and was about five feet tall, with a "slender build when he knew her." He thought it "very possible" that Berglund "may have been the red head described as with Ruth at the Ace Box and later took the train for Duluth from White Bear Lake."[10]

Johnson, like the papers, assumed the two women who went to White Bear Lake on December 11 were the same two women who accompanied Ruth to the Ace three days earlier. Like other leads about Ruth Munson's two women friends, this one was another dead end.

True to its word, Monday's *Daily News* reduced its reward for information leading to the capture of Ruth Munson's killer by $100. The reward now stood at $600—$200 from Ramsey County and the remainder from the paper.[11]

On Tuesday, December 21, the newspapers had nothing to report but day-old information about Tierney's interest in Harold Creagan, even though the man's alibi had already been verified, a fact the newspapers never reported.

At police headquarters, there was new interest in the Aberdeen Hotel and its neighboring business, the Dayton Avenue Garage. Because firefighters had destroyed the crime scene, exactly how the killer gained access to the Aberdeen remained a mystery. The vacant hotel was on the beat of Squad 7 Patrolmen Emil Arndt and John Doth, who worked the 11:00 P.M. to 7:00 A.M. shift. The two patrolmen were asked about the state of the building when they made their rounds prior to the murder. "We have always found the front doors locked (padlocked)," they wrote in a report to Assistant Chief Tierney. "The only entrance to [the] building that we found open is rear door on west and adjoining the garage." On the Virginia Street side, they sometimes found the back gate wired shut—and then standing open several hours later. The patrolmen noted that they had received "several complaints of larceny from this building" of metals, wires, and fixtures. In an effort to catch the burglars, they sometimes parked their white squad car on the street and kept watch.

"On December 9, we parked on Virginia Ave. about 20 feet south of Dayton, facing south from about 4:10 to 4:45 A.M.," the patrolmen recalled. They were positive no one entered or exited the hotel grounds from Virginia Street during that time. While their notes did not shed much light on which door the killer entered, they did clear up a report of a mysterious white car parked along Virginia Street in the early morning hours of December 9.[12]

What door the killer entered may have been on the minds of investigators when they decided to question two men associated with the Dayton Avenue Garage, Jim McGinley and the owner himself, Willard Wolf. It is also likely that Weston Hill's story about Wolf's possible invention of a man who sought gasoline on December 8 inspired investigators to dig further into Wolf's activities on that night. On Tuesday morning, December 21, Detectives Carrier and Kennedy made two trips to the garage to pick up the men.[13]

Detective Lieutenant Frank R. Cullen had already questioned garage employee Earl Carl Gussman on December 16, concentrating on Wolf's presence at the garage on the night Ruth Munson was murdered. It seemed logical that he would question these two men, but the task fell to Detective Lieutenant Nate Smith. He questioned McGinley first, asking him about his background and past association with the Aberdeen Hotel. McGinley, who was seventy-two years old, had lived in a room above the garage's office for a little over a year, doing odd jobs in exchange for lodging. He had been a caretaker of the Aberdeen for several years, dating back into the 1920s. Asked about connections between the hotel and the garage, McGinley said there was no way to get from the annex, which housed the hotel's laundry, into the garage. To get from the hotel to the garage, one had to go outside.

Smith began asking McGinley questions about Willard Wolf. Was he married? Yes. Had he been married before? Yes.

"Do you know why Mr. Wolf stayed in the garage nights instead of staying at home with his wife and family?" Smith asked.

"Yes. He's doing that to save money." Wolf himself supervised parking cars in the garage at night, hiring an assistant a couple nights a week "to let him get a rest at home."

"Do you know if Wolf ever had any women come to the garage to see him nights?"

"No."

"Has he ever had any women come to see him that you know of?"

"No, his wife and her friend come down once in a while in the evening and talk for a half hour or so. While his other wife was with him she used to come down for a half-hour visit or so. Outside of that there were none that I know of."

"Have you ever noticed anything unusual around the Aberdeen Hotel nights since you have been around there?"

"No I have noticed youngsters running around. I imagined they were trying to get in or something like that."

"You have never seen anyone in the hotel?"

"No."

"Is there any knowledge that you have at this time which may help the Police in the solution of the murder of Ruth Munson?"

"No there is none."

"If you have any would you give it to the Police?"

"Yes sir."[14]

Armed with information gleaned from this interview, Smith questioned Willard Wolf at 2:05 P.M.

Wolf was thirty-nine years old. He had been running the Dayton Avenue Garage since September 1935. Times being what they were, he had been staying at the garage nights since April 1, 1937, to save money.

"Do you stay at your garage every night?"

"No. I go home one or two nights a week; it depends how busy I am." On nights he went home, McGinley was there, and, lately, so was Gussman.

"Are you married?"

"Yes sir."

"Have you any family?"

"Yes; one child." Wolf acknowledged he had been married three times. His first wife had died. He was divorced from his second wife. He had been married to his current wife for two years.

"Did you stay at your garage all night the night of Dec. 8, 1937?"

"Yes sir."

"What time did you go to bed on December 8, 1937?"

"I laid down at ten minutes to one, got up at one o'clock to let a car in, went to bed; that was the last car in."

"Do you recall what time you got up on the morning of Dec. 9, 1937?"

"About twenty minutes after six." He had walked over to Curt's Hamburger Shop about 6:30 and got something to eat, returning by 6:45. Both McGinley and Gussman were there when he returned.

Next, Smith turned to the subject of the phantom gasoline purchase.

"On the night of Dec. 8 or the morning of Dec. 9th, 1937, did someone come to your garage and want to buy gasoline?"

"On the night of December 8th."

"What time of night was that?"

"About 7 P.M."

"Did you know who this man was?"

"No I didn't then, but I have heard since that it was Tom O'Day."

Det. Lt. Smith did not ask which direction the would-be purchaser went after he left the garage. Instead, he asked if Gussman was in the garage all night on December 8 and if he could have left without Wolf knowing it. Yes, he was and no, he couldn't, were Wolf's answers.

"Have you any knowledge at all at the present time that might help the police in a solution of the Ruth Munson murder?"

"No, anything I have I gave it to them"—a reference to his previous interviews.[15]

Questioned separately, Earl Gussman, Jim McGinley, and Willard Wolf had all told the same story.

Around the same time on Tuesday afternoon that Det. Lt. Smith was questioning Wolf, Detective Grace was questioning a man about his relationship with Ruth Munson. Horace Dupont was mentioned in a June 28, 1937, entry in Ruth Munson's diary.[16]

Dupont was thirty-four years old and lived with his mother. He was unemployed, having last worked at the cigar stand at Reddy's Café for four months. He had met Ruth Munson there five months ago "in a casual way." She was there with another woman, whose name he didn't know. He had seen her at Reddy's about five times. She had told him that she worked at the Union Depot, and he had telephoned her there.

"Do you recall when?"

"Well I imagine the month of July or August."

"Could it have been on or about June 28, 1937?"

"Yes, it could." His reasons for telephoning her were "to have a visit with her—social." He acknowledged that he had also met her at Dahill's—evidently a bar or café—after calling her at the Union Depot and making "an appointment" to meet her there. After spending a half hour at Dahill's, they had gone to Steve's, a nearby café and bar. Ruth drank beer and he drank bourbon. They were there from 4:00 to 8:00 P.M. He did not take her home and couldn't remember whether he left Steve's first or she did. He confessed to being "under the influence of liquor but not exactly intoxicated."

"Did you make any advances toward her?" Detective Grace asked, finally addressing the likely reason for the interview.

"No."

"Did you at any time ever have intercourse with Ruth Munson?"

"No."

"Have you taken, as I asked you before, any unduly [sic] liberties with her such as feeling her up or anything like that?"

"No."

"Was there ever any conversation between you and Ruth Munson about having intercourse at any time?"

"No."

"Was your object at the time when you called her up at the Depot and made the date with her to have intercourse with her if you could?"

"No."

"What was your object for wanting to meet her at Dahill's?"

"Social."

"How many social dates do you have in a year?"

"That is pretty hard to say."

"Quite a few, isn't that right?" Detective Grace seemed to have secured additional information about Dupont from other sources.

"Yes."

"Now you mean to say that your acquaintance with Ruth Munson started through her visits at Reddy's is that correct?"

"Yes."

"Is that the only date you ever had with Ruth?"

"Yes."

Dupont had no other information about Ruth Munson, and he had never seen her in the company of any other man.

"Have you ever been in trouble?"

"No, not serious."[17]

Detective Grace did not pursue the nature of the "not serious" trouble Dupont might have experienced. He was aware that previously Dupont had had many "social dates." It wasn't much of a stretch for Grace to wonder whether the man was making "an appointment" as opposed to a date with women for the purpose of engaging in sexual intercourse, whether it was part of a romantic relationship or a simple business transaction. Either way, of course, sex outside of the institution of marriage was viewed culturally as a sin. As a business transaction, it was illegal. Like other men the detectives had interviewed, Dupont had reason to lie about his relationship with Ruth Munson and how intimate it may have been. Once again, there was no one to contradict him.

As for Ruth herself, a woman interested in "dances and fellows," her very brief relationship with Dupont raised questions. After one date, had she simply concluded that she was not interested in seeing him again? Or was their one meeting a business transaction? It made one wonder about the nature of her relationship with all the "fellows" that she knew.[18]

On Tuesday evening, Patrolmen John Conroy and Joseph McDonnell in Squad 7 received a radio call directing them to 449 Fuller Street. Once there, they met Mrs. M. Dilger. At 6:11 P.M. Mrs. Dilger had gone to the store at Arundel and Aurora Streets to make a telephone call. On her return home, as she walked south on Arundel, "a negro stepped out from behind a shed in the center of the block and asked her where she was going," according to the patrolmen's report. Mrs. Dilger said she started to scream and ran. "The negro crossed the street and ran east through the alley," the patrolmen wrote. Mrs. Dilger described the man as "6 ft., slender build, short coat, probably kahki [sic] color, wearing a cap." Patrolmen Conroy and McDonnell drove around the neighborhood but were unable to locate the man. Though the incident had no obvious connection to the Munson case, the patrolmen's report was added to Offense File 33436, the nature of the report noted as "Negro molesting woman."[19]

In writing up their reports, police routinely identified Black folks as "colored" or "negro." The absence of such a label was indication that an individual, in this case Mrs. Dilger, was white. The incident illustrates the mutual fear that existed between Black folks and white folks in St. Paul—if for different reasons. The white woman encountered a Black man at night on the street, screamed, and ran in fear of attack. The Black man, in turn, crossed the street and ran into the alley, determined to escape, well aware of what could happen to him if he was suspected of assaulting a white woman.

The newspapers carried no stories about the Munson case on December 22. At police headquarters, Detective Herman Schlichting spent the morning filling out reports on his canvassing efforts. Most recently he had been working a block north of Dayton, in the 200 and 300 blocks of Marshall Avenue. In all, he had talked to thirty-two people. At two apartments, the tenants were out, which meant a return visit. The detective found three interviews worthy of follow-up reports.[20]

Miss Dorothy MacDonald in Apartment 21 at 233–235 Marshall reported that she had seen another woman who worked at the Golden Rule department store "eating her noon day luncheon with Ruth Munson."[21]

At 506 Sherburne Avenue, Miss Irene Giesen told the detective that a Mr. Famion, living at 384 Bay Street, had told her he had seen Ruth Munson "with a colored man." Giesen asked that her name not be mentioned.[22]

Miss Jule Miller, Apartment 16 at 229–231 Marshall Avenue, told Schlichting a provocative story. She said that in New York, "it is customary to have a colored person do the first thing in [the] new year for a white person." At 1:00 A.M. on January 1, 1937, she had asked Daniel Faulkner "to deliver her some packages to her right after mid-night." Faulkner did so, but he was "under the wrong impression—he thought he was supposed to go down on her so he wanted to do so." Miller declined. She then questioned Faulkner, who told her that "a colored man by the name of Lindsey had got him started," and that Lindsey "lost his women callers" to Faulkner because he gave "so much better service to the ladies."

According to Miller, Faulkner was employed as a porter at the Apothecary Shop in downtown St. Paul. She had "seen many white women talking to Faulkner," presumably "making a date for his services." She described Faulkner as "a sex degenerate" and asked not "to have her name mentioned," though she was willing to be contacted for further information.[23]

Other than the investigation's interest in Black men, Faulkner had no obvious connection to the Munson case. Nevertheless, the report was added to the Munson case file.

In the meantime, Detectives Axel Soderberg and Earl Harken were sent to downtown St. Paul's Minnesota Building in regard to another Black man who had a more direct link to the investigation. At 2:44 P.M., they spoke with Mr. Walsh, who told them a client of his, a waiter at the Lowry Hotel, had informed him that another waiter, "a colored man by the name of Ewing," was "claiming to know who Ruth Munson was out with." Further, Ewing said he "knew of no reason why he should tell the Police Dept. all he knew." Walsh said the white girls who worked in the dining room were afraid of Ewing because of his remarks. Recognizing that the name matched one of the men who had supposedly taken a cab to Ruth's apartment building, the detectives immediately went to the Lowry, picked up Merton Ewing, and took him to Assistant Chief Tierney's office.[24]

At 4:00 P.M., Detective Grace began to question the waiter. A native of Omaha, Ewing had lived in Minneapolis since 1915. He was forty-three years old and currently separated from his wife. He had been a waiter at the Lowry for four years.

"Do you know a white girl named Ruth Munson?" Detective Grace asked.

"No."

"Did you ever take a taxi cab here in St. Paul at all and go to any flat or house where a white woman lived?"

"No sir."

"Have you ever been in any taxi cab here in St. Paul?"

Ewing stated that he had not taken a St. Paul cab in the last five years, other than taking one to work when he was employed by Northern Pacific Railway.

"Now you stated that you got a lady friend, Madeline Williams, at 742½ Rondo St. St. Paul?"

"I used to go with her but I don't go with her any more."

"When were you up there last?"

"Latter part of August 1937."

"Now you were brought in here a week ago last Sunday night for questioning by Asst. Chief Tierney, were you not?" Grace was referring to December 12, when Detectives Raymond Schmidt and Ernest Woodhouse drove cabdriver J. E. Brooks to the Lowry Hotel, where he picked out Ewing and Lawrence Louis as the Black men he had driven from the Lowry to 276 Dayton on December 2.

"Yes sir."

"You were released by him, is that right?"

"Yes sir."

"After you left here and since then did you pass a remark or words to this effect: 'Why should I tell those God dam coppers or dicks what they wanted to know about the Munson case?'"

"No sir."

"What remarks did you make that would be similar to the one that I asked you about just now?"

"I only made a remark that I knew nothing about the Munson case."

"Isn't it a fact that you told me while in my office this afternoon that you did make this remark: 'If they crowded me I would tell them who takes cabs.'"

"Yes."

"By them who did you mean?"

"The persons who I gave you the names of."

"And these names were what?"

"_____ Gray, Walter Brown, Ike Hackman, Lee Washington, and Wilbur Randall." Either Ewing didn't remember Gray's first name, or the stenographer missed it.

"These are all colored waiters at the Lowry?"

"All colored waiters, yes sir."

"Those colored waiters take a taxi cab and go where?"

"Out Rondo, just where they live I don't know."

"Have you ever heard of any colored waiters in the Lowry or any place else talk about taking taxi cabs and visiting white women on the Hill?"

"No."

"Sure about that now?" Grace pressed.

"Only thing I heard them say was they were out for a ball, a [phrase] for having a good time."

"Would this be with white women?"

"They didn't say; they said they had a ball."

"Well I asked you about these colored fellows visiting white women in St. Paul?"

"I never run around with any of those fellows."

"I didn't ask you that; I asked you did you ever hear any of those colored waiters talking about visiting white women here in St. Paul?"

"No."[25]

Ewing read and signed his statement and then was released without charge, just as he had been on December 2.

In midafternoon, Detectives Carrier and Kennedy picked up bartender Fred Meyer at the Ace and drove to White Bear Lake, where they met a deputy sheriff. The deputy escorted them to 41 Shadylane, where, the detectives later wrote, "a Wilma Taylor or Therrin lived." The woman supposedly resembled one of the women who had accompanied Ruth, but bartender Meyer said "she was not one of the girls." Wilma Taylor and a woman named Mary Barrisford of Antigo, Wisconsin, were known to have been at the Keystone Hotel, "on different occasions," but "they never knew Ruth Munson," the detectives wrote.[26]

If either of these two women were the ones who had "fled" St. Paul by bus on December 11 and got off in White Bear Lake, the detectives did not note it in their report. They did note that Patrolman Robert Williams had questioned Wilma Taylor at the Keystone Hotel a week earlier. No report documenting Williams's interview of Wilma Taylor was added to the Munson file.

With nothing new to report on the Munson investigation, on December 23, the newspapers carried no stories about the case for the second straight day. The neighborhood canvass had continued through the week. Now, two days before Christmas, detectives were catching up on their reports. Working the even-numbered addresses on the 200 and 300 blocks of Marshall Avenue, Detective Jakobson recorded forty-six people on his canvass report. Knocking on doors on the 400 block of Laurel Avenue, Detective Ralph Merrill reported interviewing sixty-five people. Between them, they had talked to 111 people, and each conversation was a dead end. Neither detective encountered information worthy of a follow-up report.[27]

A follow-up canvass report filed the previous day, however, caught someone's attention at headquarters. At 11:30 A.M., a bare twenty-four hours after Detective Schlichting filed his report about Jule Miller's account of her year-old encounter with Daniel Faulkner, Detectives Carrier and Kennedy picked him up at the Green Gate Café where he worked. He was brought to headquarters and put on the holdbook "for investigation of molesting women." No record exists documenting any statement given by him. Faulkner was released by Detective Grace the following day, Christmas Eve, for "lack of prosecution."[28]

On Christmas Eve, the *Daily News* paused to look back on the year. Beneath the headline MURDER, POLITICS, AND LABOR ARE BIG NEWS IN 1937 the paper declared the death of Ruth Munson to be "one of the most mysterious murders in St. Paul history." With few hard facts to report, the newspaper instead focused on what was not known—and took note of the unsolved murder of Laura Kruse in Minneapolis on March 20.[29]

At police headquarters, Detectives Schlichting and Jakobson each filed a report documenting individuals they had talked to on Marshall Avenue as the canvassing project ground along. The results were as discouraging as the day before. Between them, the two detectives had talked to 126 people without learning anything new on the case.[30]

On the day after Christmas, while riding the streetcar to work, Patrolman James Axness picked up a lead about the two women who accompanied Ruth Munson to the Ace. "I was talking to a man who knows one Arthur Conlin, living near Kent and Holly," the patrolman later reported. The man told Patrolman Axness that Arthur Conlin worked in a South St. Paul packinghouse and knew "the two girls that were out with Ruth Munson that night she was murdered in the Aberdeen." Conlin claimed, "These two girls, are living with negroes that are working at Union Deport." Patrolman Axness noted that his seatmate on the streetcar "would not give me any further information when he saw that I was interested."[31]

Det. Lt. Heaton and Patrolman Cook were later sent to check out Patrolman Axness's report. "We questioned this man [Conlin] and he denied all knowledge of this report," the officers wrote in their own report. "He did say he knew Ruth Munson by sight as she rode the same street[car] he did for a period of two years."[32]

One more dead end—or closed door—in the investigation.

13 Focus Areas

December 27, 1937–January 7, 1938

By the last week of the year, the investigation had settled into several focus areas: the search for Ruth Munson's illusive companions; the neighborhood canvass, inching farther and farther westward, away from the scene of the crime; departmental checks on men who had been arrested or convicted of sex crimes during the year; the mystery clue, freed at last from the ice and literally under the investigation's spotlight; and Ruth's secretive relationships with Black men.

Even as they looked ahead, detectives continuously looked back at leads that in one way or another seemed unfinished. Detective Lieutenant Bertram Talbot took up some of these, allegations relating to Violet Thorson. On December 13, she told the *St. Paul Pioneer Press* that when she and Ruth were Christmas shopping, Ruth said, "I'll never live to see Christmas!" Three days after that, Detective Thomas Grace had taken the explosive statement from Robert Gatzke. Gatzke recounted that Violet Thoreson's husband, Davis, had told him several things he had heard from Violet: that Ruth and a woman named Frances left the Union Depot by taxi with a Black porter; that the porter was said to have "bought a lot of clothes for the Munson girl"; that Ruth wore an engagement ring and was to be married by or on Christmas Day. Finally, on the day the body was found, but before the news was made public, Violet supposedly said to her husband that she had a feeling that Ruth had been "killed last night."[1]

On December 27, Det. Lt. Talbot finally brought Violet Thorson into the station to be questioned. He did not take a formal statement, but he did write up a report. Violet had known of Ruth Munson for about six years, having seen her at dances at the Strand Ballroom in the company of a man, presumably Olaf Anderson. Ruth had uttered her death premonition "about three weeks ago" at the Emporium department store. Ruth's comment had "astounded" Violet, in part because Ruth "never seemed to be worrying about anything." The *Pioneer Press* had portrayed Violet Thoreson as a "close friend" of Ruth's, but Det. Lt. Talbot noted that she "didn't know Ruth's name was Ruth until she went to work with Ruth at Depot. Ruth was uncommunicative with Mrs. Thoreson."[2]

In the end, the unfinished business with Violet Thoreson would remain unfinished. The subjects Det. Lt. Talbot covered while questioning her essentially matched what she had told the *Pioneer Press*, with a major exception. Ruth Munson's premonition about her death was mentioned but left unexplored. He also did not ask about Ruth's rumored relationship with the porter and potential marriage, as well as Thoreson's own premonition that her friend had been killed. It is quite possible Det. Lt. Talbot was unaware of Gatzke's statement and did not know these issues were at hand. Less likely, but still possible, Det. Lt. Talbot may have purposefully withheld from his report the answers he received to questions based on Gatzke's statement in order to protect some part of the investigation.

At the same time Thoreson was being interviewed, Detective Lieutenant Joseph Heaton and Patrolman James Cook were checking out a report from Blue and White Cab Company driver Leo Allison that turned into a lead about Ruth's two friends. Allison reported a conversation he had had with "Mrs. Moore," an Omaha Railroad employee. The officers then interviewed Mrs. Moore, who told them about sisters Helen Overby, a reddish blond, and Ronnie Overby, who was dark haired. Based on newspaper articles she had read, Mrs. Moore was "impressed" that these sisters might be "the girls that were with Ruth Munson out at the Ace Café the night of the murder." Mrs. Moore wished no publicity regarding this information. Apparently she got her wish, as no one appeared to have followed up with an interview of the sisters.[3]

The following day, Tuesday, December 28, Detectives Alvin Johnson and Michael Sauro checked up on two men who had been arrested for sex crimes. One, who had received a suspended fifteen-day sentence on June 15 for indecent exposure, was employed at Hansen Fuel Company. He was instructed to report to Detective Lieutenant Nate Smith on December 29. The other man, who had pleaded guilty to assault on June 16 and received a year in the workhouse, was out of town looking for work. Over the next ten days, different detectives would be assigned several names to check out. None of the men would be linked to the murder investigation.[4]

Detectives Alfred Jakobson and Herman Schlichting filed reports documenting their efforts on the neighborhood canvass, covering the

300 and 400 block of Dayton Avenue, the 200 block of Marshall Avenue, and addresses on Western Avenue. Only one of the residents contacted had information that merited a follow-up report. June Zelik, 208 Western Avenue, told Schlichting that about a week before the murder, a neighborhood boy, George Meade of 161 Nina Avenue, was playing with other boys in the Aberdeen. The boys saw the so-called coffee can that was pictured in the newspapers in the days immediately following the murder. The coffee can was lying in the hallway, the boy said. The statement underscored the investigation's earlier realization that the coffee can was not the vessel in which the killer had transported the flammable liquid used to start the fire. The canvass effort would continue over the next ten days. Occasionally a follow-up report would be written, but for the most part the effort proved fruitless.[5]

Detectives Boyd Carrier and Frank Kennedy spent Tuesday afternoon following up on several earlier leads and reports. Although Heaton and Cook had already connected with Arthur Conlin regarding the story that Ruth Munson's companions were "living with negroes," Carrier and Kennedy paid him a visit at 4:30 P.M. Rather than talking about Ruth's companions, Conlin told them a new story. In the "spring or fall of 1936," he was walking along Laurel Avenue near Mackubin Street at about 2:10 A.M. He saw a woman being followed by a man. He judged them to be a married couple who had had a fight. The woman turned into a house and the man kept walking. As Conlin passed the house, the woman emerged and asked him to walk her home to 489 Holly Avenue. The man, she explained, had been exposing himself. Carrier and Kennedy went to 489 Holly, but with more than a year having passed, they could find no trace of the woman. They also checked for her at the buildings next door.[6]

At 5:30 P.M., the detectives took up the previous day's follow-up report filed by Detective Schlichting regarding a Mr. Famion. The detectives located and questioned George Famion, who denied that he knew Ruth Munson and that he had seen her with a "colored man." The only thing he had ever said about the case was that he had delivered parcel post in that neighborhood on various occasions.[7]

As the day ended, the detectives could look back on their busy afternoon with the satisfaction that they had completed some unfinished business. But at the same time, they had found nothing to move the case forward.

On December 29, Detective Robert Costello reported that in 1930 or 1931, Ruth Munson had received medical treatment from Dr. Nellie Barsness, whose office was in the Lowry Building. How Costello obtained such private information is unknown, but it is possible he learned of the doctor visit through a collection agency while looking into Ruth's finances. From January 25 to August 26 of 1933, Costello learned, Ruth paid the balance due of $13 in small amounts through a collection agency. While the reason for her treatment was not disclosed, the detective's findings suggested Ruth was pressed for money at that time—or that her financial priorities lay elsewhere. Detective Lieutenant Roy Coffey and Patrolman Louis Schultz would later interview Dr. Barsness, who confirmed that she had treated Ruth Munson six years earlier but refused to discuss the reason for her visit, other than to state "that it would have no bearing on the case." "From her conversation," the detectives concluded, "we surmised it was some female complaint."[8]

On Wednesday, December 30, Sheriff George Iverson of Grantsburg, Wisconsin—Ruth's hometown—paid the St. Paul Police Department a visit. He was accompanied by Grantsburg resident Peter Polli. Polli was a barber looking for a shop to purchase. The day before, Polli had visited a place he thought was for sale in Harris, Minnesota, about forty miles north of St. Paul. "This man"—a barber, who had already purchased the shop—"had his hat on and acted very strange," Polli said. Rather than cut his own hair, the barber asked Polli to give him a trim. Doing so, Polli noticed that the barber's hair was burned in the front. When he asked what happened, the barber said only that he had been burned in a gasoline fire. Polli estimated that his hair had been growing back for about three weeks, roughly the same length of time since the Munson murder. During the haircut, the barber asked Polli "if he had heard any news about the Munson case." Polli had found the barber's behavior and his burn to be suspicious.[9]

Had this burn been suffered during the murder? Detective Lieutenant Nate Smith, who had met with Sheriff Iverson and Polli, must have regarded the latter's story as a "hot tip." Joined by Detective Lieutenant Frank R. Cullen and Detective Thomas Grace, Smith drove to Harris that same day to question the barber. The three men had taken dozens of statements from people connected to the Munson case. The fact that they left headquarters to investigate this new lead suggests the importance they assigned to it.

Like so many other leads, this one was a dead end. C. C. Everson, the only barber in town, had purchased the shop on December 21. Before that, he ran a barbershop in New London, Minnesota. While still in New London, he had tried to fix his gasoline hot water heater, and his

hair accidentally caught on fire. "He was unable to give us any information on the Munson case," the officers' report noted. "All he knew about
it was what he had heard from people coming into his shop."[10]

Among the proposed theories of the case was the suggestion that the
murder was an act of revenge. To date, the investigation had neither
documented a potential suspect looking for revenge, nor constructed
a scenario in which someone might wish to seek revenge upon a seemingly quiet waitress who was mostly interested in "dances and fellows."

At 9:30 P.M., Detectives Donald Kampmann and Cecil Stow interviewed Dorothy Wagner, an employee of Ancker Hospital. She stated
that while at work, she had overheard "Miss Cox, an occupational
theraphysicist [sic] say to Miss Lucas, colored, [of the] City Physician's
office, that 'it is reported that Ruth Munson was going out with the
captain of the porters at the depot and that *they* (meaning the porters)
think the wife of the captain hired two men to kill Ruth Munson.'"
According to Dorothy Wagner, Lucas's reply was noncommittal, along
the lines of "is that so?" or "isn't it terrible?"[11]

The rumor marked the first recorded reference to anyone seeking
revenge against Ruth Munson. Dorothy Wagner's language was somewhat imprecise in referring to the "captain of the porters." The head
porter at the Union Depot was Robert Brown, with whom detectives
were quite familiar. In his signed statement, he had admitted, "I'm not
sure but I suppose so," to Detective Grace's question whether his objec-
tive "was to have intercourse" with Ruth Munson—but he insisted that
he had not.[12]

Rumor that it was, the story was ripe with opportunities for further
investigation. As usual, five copies of the Kampmann and Stow report
were made, one each going to the Records Division, Commissioner
Gustave H. Barfuss, and Police Chief Clinton Hackert. Two copies went
to Assistant Chief Charles J. Tierney, director of the investigation.
Whether the investigation actively pursued this rumor is unknown.
The investigation's leaders seldom wrote up reports on their activities. No reports were filed by detectives working the streets regarding
follow-up interviews with Cox, Lucas, the porters at the Union Depot,
or the wife of the "captain of the porters." The investigation would continue to collect information about Robert Brown in areas that were not
connected to this rumor.

On the last day of 1937, Detectives Carrier and Kennedy filed their
forty-sixth report on the Munson case. A week earlier, the detectives

had picked up Daniel Faulkner, who had seemed to have no connection to Ruth Munson. How they linked him to her is unknown. They interviewed Maud Krenick, who had worked at the Green Gate Café, Faulkner's place of employment, during July and August 1937. During her tenure, she had told Faulkner's fortune. He wanted to know if Ruth Munson would repay the $25 loan he had given her. Ruth had needed the money "to bail out a friend" after the police had conducted "raids on the Rondo district." Krenick told Dan he was foolish to lend money, but he said he had "loaned her money before and was always paid back." He also asked the fortune teller "if he was going to marry Ruth."

Maud Krenick told the detectives that "she couldn't understand why a good looking white girl would marry a negro." She had also told Ruth's fortune. Ruth did not ask about anything in particular, but Krenick thought "Ruth was afraid of something, although she did not ask her what it was."

According to Krenick, "Dan seemed to have a lot of white girls around him at the Green Gate" who did "the cleaning and scrubbing" after the café closed. She asked if the women were paid for their work and "was told that the girls like Dan." She mentioned two other employees of the Green Gate, Mrs. Glass, a cook, and Jessie, a waitress, "who could give some information" on his actions.[13]

Maud Krenick's comments raised more questions. Who was the friend Ruth Munson needed to "bail out" at the time of the "raids on the Rondo district"? What was the relationship between Ruth and this friend? What was her relationship with Daniel Faulkner? Was he the groom in the rumored Christmas marriage that Violet Thoreson mentioned? What "information on the actions" of Daniel Faulkner did Mrs. Glass and Jessie possess? And, finally, was Daniel Faulkner involved in any way in Ruth Munson's death?

These questions remained unanswered. Faulkner had been released on December 24, and no record exists in the Munson case files documenting further investigations of him. There are no existing transcripts of interviews of the two Green Gate employees Maud Krenick mentioned.

Following up on yet more leads, Det. Lt. Coffey and Patrolman Schultz investigated an anonymous letter that promised information concerning Ruth Munson's death after $500 was paid to "Smith" at the Frederick Hotel. The exact contents of the letter, when it was written, and how police received it is unclear. Coffey and Schultz spoke with Bob Smith, a dishwasher at the Frederick Hotel. He denied authorship of the note or any knowledge about Ruth Munson. He believed that a man he met on December 26 in a downtown bar had written the note because the man said to him, "How about an Aberdeen Hotel party." Coffey and Schultz determined that the man was Robert Blum, who lived "in the cheaper hotels" and was a "frequent visitor of beer taverns in the downtown district." Bob Smith, the officers noted, was "an honest citizen and we believe him to be telling the truth." Their efforts to locate Blum were unsuccessful.[14]

Three other homicides had occurred in St. Paul in 1937, one each in March, May, and August. All of them had been cleared with an arrest. The murder of Ruth Munson was the only one that remained unsolved at year's end.[15]

On Monday, January 3, 1938, the Munson murder case returned to the front page of the *Pioneer Press*. According to the two-paragraph article, "Microscopic examination of debris taken from the old Aberdeen hotel had given investigators their 'best clue yet uncovered.'" Chief Hackert declined to describe exactly what had been found, but claimed it was "the most incriminating" clue located since the murder was discovered.[16]

The clue was, in fact, the same clue that days before the press had labeled the "mystery clue": three metal shear pins, roughly one-eighth inch in diameter and just over one inch long. A shear pin is a piece of metal, easily replaceable, designed to be inserted in a machine and to break under stress, thus preventing or reducing damage to the machine or its operator. The pins had been spotted in the ice, and the police believed the killer or killers had accidentally dropped them near the body.

On the same day that the *Pioneer Press* article appeared, Detective Lieutenant Thomas Jansen began the process of fully identifying the pins and, hopefully, connecting them to a suspect. At 1:30 P.M. Jansen showed one of the pins to F. R. Erickson, the outboard motor repairman at Park Machine Company on West Sixth Street. Erickson described the pin as made of "Tobin bronze" (a type of brass) and fashioned "from a length of 'welding rod' and cut with a side cutter." Using a micrometer, he measured the pin at 5/32 of an inch in diameter and one and 3/32 inches in length. Erickson said the pin's diameter was the same as the shear pin for a Neptune outboard boat motor, "a trifle longer than the factory pin" but still serviceable. He found the pin to be "the exact length of the pin used in the Johnson single twin or alternate firing

Three metal shear pins found in the debris at the Aberdeen Hotel. *Courtesy SPPD*

4 P.P. motors, but it is 1/64 of an inch less in diameter but is commonly used in these motors when a factory pin is not used."[17]

It would be several days before the police took their next step.

Meanwhile, other members of the force were pursuing leads associated with Ruth's two companions. Although most tips police received were about candidates for both women, other tips involved only one woman. Det. Lt. Heaton and Patrolman Cook were dispatched to investigate a tip forwarded by Superintendent Frank J. Hetznecker regarding Emily Dumminnee, who had picketed at a strike at Montgomery Ward and who was standing trial for assault and battery. Hetznecker's contact thought the woman "may be the girl that was with Ruth Munson the eve of the murder." The officers picked up Ace bartender Fred Meyer, now a veteran of several identification missions, and drove him to municipal court to see Dumminnee. Meyer said she was not one of the women at the Ace. The officers also spoke to Mrs. Gross, Hetznecker's sister-in-law. She told them "a negro called for Emily Dumminnee when she stayed at 425 Thomas St." Mrs. Gross lived next door at the time.[18]

Similarly, Detectives Carrier and Kennedy were informed that Lester Berglund, employed at Rogers & Company of South St. Paul, had a sister named Vernice, who worked on the first floor of St. Luke's Hospital. The only reason her name was put forward was because she was "a red-headed girl."[19]

Having finished his visit to Park Machine Company to learn about shear pins, Det. Lt. Jansen was ordered by Chief Hackert to make a forensic effort to determine the state of the Aberdeen before the fire. From 6:00 until 11:00 P.M. he interviewed firemen from Engine Company Number 1 and Hook and Ladder Company Numbers 1, 9, and 10. In all, he interviewed twenty-one firemen, asking each how he had entered the building and what equipment he had used fighting the fire and cleaning up after it was subdued. Firemen had entered by breaking through various doors and windows, making it difficult, if not impossible, to determine what entrance the killer might have used.

In addition to trying to figure out how the killer entered the Aberdeen, detectives were still trying to determine exactly how the body's skull had been crushed. Was it at the hands of the murderer, or from falling beams and timbers? Was it caused by the firemen with their implements? The firemen confirmed that they had used picks, pikes, axes, shovels, and other tools while battling the fire. No fireman admitted to accidentally striking or disturbing the body, though debris from their efforts had fallen on it by the time Detectives Carrier and Kennedy first arrived on the scene. One fireman from Hook and Ladder Number 9 admitted he "Later cleaned up with [a] shovel right up to body," but that was as close as Det. Lt. Jansen got to an answer.[20]

Four days into the new year, Detectives Patrick Lannon and John McGowan, along with Police Chauffeur Arthur Courtney, investigated not one, but two leads involving the search for Ruth Munson's two companions at the Ace. On January 3, Chisago County Sheriff Henry Stream had written to Chief Hackert, prefacing his tip all too accurately: "Undoubtedly in this case . . . you have so much worthless information to listen to, so here is just a little more." Sheriff Stream had heard secondhand information about a man named Anton Lind, who lived on a farm northeast of Harris, Minnesota. Lind's two daughters were "supposed to have been friends of Miss Munson and . . . they used to go out together, but . . . they never told any officers about this." The girls lived in St. Paul, but "their folks would have their address if you can't locate them any other way. Thats [sic] all I know, hope you can use it."[21]

The three officers drove to the home of Anton Lind near Harris. He confirmed that his daughters, Evelyn and Violet, were employed as maids in St. Paul. They both knew Ruth Munson, "but only to see her and [were] not personally acquainted with her and have never been out in company with her." Both daughters were home over the Christmas holiday, Lind explained, and talked about the Munson case, giving rise to the secondhand information Sheriff Stream had picked up. The officers left Harris empty-handed.[22]

The three officers also investigated an anonymous letter about red-headed sisters Marie and Irene Johnson. The officers interviewed Irene Johnson, who was employed in Clear Lake, Minnesota. Whether they conducted the interview in person or by telephone is not known. Irene Johnson had worked at Miller Hospital "about 6 years ago at the time Ruth Munson worked there" and had not seen her since then. She had visited her sister, Marie Johnson, on December 7, arriving at her residence at 244 Marshall Avenue at 7:00 P.M. and leaving at 9:30 A.M. on December 8, the eve of the murder. Irene's account was confirmed by her sister, Marie, and Marie's landlady, Mrs. Swenson. Detective McGowan's report noted that "Both Marie and Irene Johnson have red hair and both are extremely large girls—being 5′ 10″ or 11″ tall." The two women with Ruth at the Ace, McGowan noted, "were supposed to be about 5′ 4″ tall."[23]

By the end of the day, the three officers had eliminated both sets of women from further consideration in the case.

On the following day, January 5, Patrolmen Robert Williams and Robert Turpin followed up on a complaint by fellow officer George Poquette. Officer Poquette had seen Ira Dorsey, a Union Depot red cap, talking to Ruth Munson on several occasions and felt the man should be investigated. It is unclear if these two Black officers were assigned to question Dorsey, a Black man, based on the color of their own skin. In response to their questions, Dorsey admitted he had spoken with Ruth Munson because "he had charge of the football jackpot, and she had a chance on it." Beyond that, he insisted "he did not have anything to say to her."

The officers did ferret out a juicy piece of gossip that Dorsey might not have shared during an interview conducted by white officers. "This man is a bitter enemy of Robert Brown, who is Captain over him," the patrolmen wrote in their report. Enemy or not, Dorsey avoided speaking ill of his superior. "Dorsey states that he never saw Brown talking to Ruth Munson," the officers noted, "nor [has he] heard any of the 'Red

Caps' make any remark regarding any undue familiarity on the part of Brown with any of the white women help."[24]

At 3:00 P.M. that afternoon, Police Chief Hackert, police criminologist Dr. John B. Dalton, Dr. John F. Noble of Ancker Hospital, and H. H. Goetzinger, who worked for the Minnesota Bureau of Criminal Apprehension, met "in conference" to review available information the department had concerning Ruth Munson's cause of death. On the day after her death, the department and Ramsey County Coroner C. A. Ingerson had released contradictory opinions to the *Daily News*. Nearly a month after the murder, the police department remained uncertain about various circumstances surrounding her death. The police account disputed the coroner's assertion that Ruth Munson had been sexually assaulted. Exactly what injuries caused her death were also at issue. Det. Lt. Jansen's recent interviews of twenty-one firemen on January 3 were part of the effort to determine how she died.[25]

It is possible that some of these four men had attended the official autopsy. At the very least, they had had access to information compiled by Coroner Ingerson. At 9:00 A.M. on January 6, Dr. Dalton issued a "summary of opinions" expressed by Dr. Noble following the previous day's conference. Dr. Noble attributed the triangular skull fracture to "an outward blow from an ax after the fire." "The basal fracture," Dr. Noble believed, "may have been from the same source but probably was from another blow." Bloodstains on the floor and blood in the stomach "supported the theory of death by skull fractures." Cuts on the scalp may have been made before or after the fire. Due to the heat and cold, Dr. Noble did not believe the time of death could be established. "I do not think that you could even determine that she died that same day," Dr. Noble noted.

As a whole, the group believed "the removal of the girdles from the body eliminates the hit-run theory, although basal skull fractures may result from such an accident." In addition, "The blood stains on the floor about the body, on the girdle, and absence of other stains in the building, support the theory that she expired where found."

The issue of whether Ruth Munson had been sexually assaulted was also addressed. "Microscopic slides prepared from vaginal smears of Ruth Munson were examined," Dr. Dalton noted in his summary. "No sperm cells or recognizable fragments were found. No recognizable cells were found that did not belong in a normal menstrual smear. [Dr. Noble] expressed the belief that at least fragments should be found if sperm cells were present." Copies of Dr. Dalton's summary were forwarded to Chief Hackert, Commissioner Barfuss, and Assistant Chief Tierney. The county coroner, whose preliminary report had pointed to criminal assault, was not sent a copy.[26]

In short, the exact cause of death remained uncertain, but the skull fractures were caused in part by the firemen. Whether Ruth Munson was sexually assaulted could not be verified based on the evidence. The absence of sperm raised the possibility that the murder was not a sex crime after all, giving some credence to the revenge theory.

On January 7, Police Chief Hackert and Inspector of Detectives William McMullin paid the Dayton Avenue Garage and its proprietor Willard Wolf a visit. Afterward, Inspector McMullin filed a report describing their encounter. "We visited the workshop and incidentally carried on a conversation with the proprietor, Wm. Wolf," he wrote. When asked if he had a welding outfit, Wolf said he used to own one, but now he sent any welding he needed done to another shop. When asked if he had any welding material on hand, "he found 2 or 3 pieces about 8 inches in length. He explained that the pieces he showed us were brass, but that aluminum, iron and a composition was also used." Then they "asked Wolf if he thought this welding material could be used as shear pins for outboard motors and he replied 'Yes, I think I have 3 or 4 here that I cut for myself some time ago.'" Wolf searched his toolbox and a pocketbook within it, but was unable to find any pins. From one of the pieces of brass welding material, he cut off a piece approximately one and a half inches long and "said it was similar and would answer the purpose in emergencies of a shear pin."

While they were there, Chief Hackert and Inspector McMullin searched Wolf's shop for a piece of cutting equipment that made impressions similar to the impressions left on the shear pins found near Ruth Munson's body. They were unsuccessful. Later, micrometer measurements were taken of Wolf's samples and the shear pins found next to the body. Their diameters were different. "Our opinion," Inspector McMullin concluded, "was that both the pins found near Ruth Munson's body and the samples we obtained from Wolf were of brass but of a different grade or color."[27]

As cordial as the visit sounded from the inspector's report, it is obvious Hackert and McMullin were searching for any links between Wolf and the three shear pins found at the Aberdeen crime scene. It is not clear whether Wolf realized he had become a prime suspect in

The fire escape connecting the roof of the boiler room and upper floors of the Aberdeen. *Courtesy SPPD*

the Munson murder case. He had a reputation—accurate or not—as a ladies' man. The garage's proximity to the Aberdeen could not be ignored. As a mechanic, Wolf was the kind of man who might have three shear pins in his pocket at any given time. During the police chief's and inspector's visit, he had been unable to find shear pins he believed he had.

The same day the police chief and the inspector visited the Dayton Avenue Garage, Detectives McGowan and Lannon and Chauffeur Courtney checked all of the buildings in the vicinity of the Aberdeen for possible entrances into the hotel. There were none. For the Dayton Avenue Garage, the trio determined that "the only entrance would be up over the roof thru a second story window." Once again, former Aberdeen custodian and now Dayton Avenue Garage resident Jim McGinley was interviewed, and once again he could not identify any secret passageway from the hotel, through the annex, and into the garage.[28]

On January 7, Detective Ralph Merrill, Patrolman Louis Schultz, and Patrolman Thomas Shanley filed two reports concerning the Union Depot's head porter. In a report addressed to Assistant Chief Tierney, they noted, "We have information" that Robert Brown had been seen at the Union Depot at night, sometimes in the company of saloon operator James Williams, other times alone, "and has met Great Northern train No. 2 on its arrival from the coast. It is the belief of this party that they received a package from one of the porters on this train, and that the contents was dope." The unnamed party who gave them this information promised to call them "if they see Brown meeting this train again." No other copies of this report were made for distribution.[29]

In a second report sent only to Assistant Chief Tierney, the trio of police officers recounted a story "Boss," a local taxi driver, told them. At 1:00 A.M. on the morning of December 9, Boss had been called to the 38 Club, a downtown tavern. Upon arrival, he saw three men and three women talking. One of the women climbed into the cab and directed him to 282 Dayton Avenue. During the drive, she noted that she and the other two women had "started out on a little party by themselves, going to different beer spots and ending up at the 38 club." The three men had sat down at their table and ordered drinks. The women decided to let them stay at the table and buy their drinks. One of the men wanted the woman's telephone number, "and she told him it was Riverview 123-jump." When Boss reached the address, the woman paid him the forty-cent fare and got out of the cab. At the same time, a man came out of 276 Dayton Avenue and approached the cab.

When Boss offered his services, the man declined. According to the officers' report, the man "had his coat collar turned up and his hat pulled down over his eyes, so Boss could not see his face; but he noticed grey hair around his temples." Boss drove away and did not see where either the woman or the man went. The man, the officers wrote, was "40–45 years; 5'10" or 11", heavy set, stocky build; wearing dark fedora hat, a dark cloth Uster [sic] overcoat with large collar—could not tell if white or black."

"This description fits Robert Brown," the officers concluded. The woman was described as "25–30 years; 5'8" or 9"; light hair; light grey coat; and small light hat." The officers noted "We will follow this up" at the end of their report.[30]

Were these the same three women who had been at the Ace as late as midnight? Ruth's diary included a reference to the 38 Club on July 17, 1937, so the establishment was known to her. Theoretically, there was enough time for the three women to get from the Ace to the 38 Club in the downtown area by 1:00 A.M., although the amount of time to socialize with the three men would be minimal. The woman's destination, 282 Dayton, was a couple of doors west of Ruth's address, 276

Dayton. The description of the woman's clothing did not match the description of Ruth's green dress and black fur coat, but it did not necessarily need to be Ruth who took the taxi. Ruth could have been one of the two women who remained at the 38 Club.[31]

Was it wishful thinking on the part of the three officers that the rather vague description of the man who emerged from 276 Dayton Avenue matched Robert Brown?

January 8–January 19, 1938

While investigators remained interested in Robert Brown as a murder suspect, they turned their focus to others, too. A concerted effort began to link the shear pins—the investigation's one piece of physical evidence—to a suspect. In their efforts, detectives seemed less interested in tracking the pins to an individual than in connecting the pins to a known suspect: Willard Wolf.

Toward that end, several steps were taken on January 8, one day shy of a full month after the murder. Police Chief Clinton Hackert drafted a letter to Albert M. Pett in Miami, Florida, who ran a business on Selby Avenue. "While in the business of handling out-board motors on Selby Avenue, this city," the chief wrote, "in the past year, did you at any time make a sale to or purchase a used out-board motor, make unknown, from Willard or Bill Wolfe, proprietor of the Dayton Avenue Garage at 370 Dayton Avenue this city[?]." The chief concluded with "Any information given by you will be greatly appreciated."[1]

Inspector of Detectives William McMullin, who on January 7 had visited the Dayton Avenue Garage with Chief Hackert, sent Detective Lieutenants Thomas Jansen and Nate Smith, along with the team of Detectives Boyd Carrier and Frank Kennedy and Patrolman James Cook, to that location to retrieve "all the cutting tools available." According to their report, they "brought 32 different tools to Headquarters for further investigation."[2]

The intention was to put the crime lab to work making sample cuts with each of the tools, so analysts could study what kind of impression each left on the end of a piece of welding rod. If they found one that matched impressions on the shear pins found in the Aberdeen, it would definitely link Wolf to the shear pins. To perform the tests, the crime lab would need some welding rods samples to cut. Det. Lt. Jansen and Detectives Robert Vick and Oran Stutzman were sent to the Dale Street Garage to "get samples of welding rod." They acquired "one 3-ft length of bronze." Back at headquarters, they turned the rod over to the Records Division. The process would be time consuming, as each cut was made, studied under magnification, and compared to the evidence.[3]

Along with their suspicions about Wolf, detectives still had their doubts about his permanent guest, Jim McGinley. The team of Carrier, Kennedy, and Cook interviewed a Mr. Parshall, who now managed the vacant Aberdeen Hotel. The manager told the team that in 1931 he struggled to get McGinley to relinquish the hotel's keys. On April 14, 1931, the frustrated Parshall had finally contacted the St. Paul police, who brought McGinley to headquarters. McGinley surrendered the keys and was told to stay away from the hotel. Parshall then had all the locks on the hotel changed, giving the old locks and keys to McGinley. Parshall told Carrier, Cook, and Kennedy that he picked up thirty or forty packs of cards around the annex after McGinley moved out. He claimed that all the damage to the building—the removal of lead pipe, brass fittings, toilet bowls, and bathtubs—had occurred while McGinley was watchman. For the time being, Parshall turned the keys over to the three police officers.[4]

On Thursday, January 13, readers of the *St. Paul Dispatch* found a page one article about the capture of a "bandit suspect" named Charles B. (Big Slim) Moore. "At 1:30 P.M. today," Moore had been found hiding in the "sub-basement" of a vacant house at 312 Louis Street, near the St. Paul Cathedral—and about a block from Ruth Munson's apartment. At the time of his capture, Moore was no stranger to either the police or readers of St. Paul's daily papers.[5]

If the paper's stated time for his arrest was accurate, Moore was taken immediately to Assistant Chief Charles J. Tierney's office to be questioned. At 1:30 P.M., Tierney himself questioned the suspect in the presence of Chief Hackert and Det. Lt. Smith, who had also been present at the arrest.

"Are you willing to make a statement of the facts as asked you knowing that what you say may be used against you in court?" Tierney asked.

"Yes, I am," Moore replied.

Charles B. Moore was thirty-two years old, single, and Black. He had been unemployed since his release from a North Dakota prison in November after serving six years of a ten-year sentence for robbery. Most recently, he had been living at 225 Rondo Avenue, washing dishes and cleaning house there, while "trying to get some sort of a job."

"What crimes have you been responsible for since coming to St. Paul in November?" Tierney asked.

On the night of December 15, Moore had attempted to rob three young women at gunpoint outside the Auditorium in downtown St.

Paul. Minutes later, he had tried to rob two nurses on their way to work at St. Luke's Hospital.[6]

On Sunday morning, January 9, Moore had robbed a drugstore on University Avenue, severely beating the druggist, seventy-four-year-old Stephen B. Conger.

"I put this gun on him," Moore told Tierney, "and he said 'What's this?' and I said I wanted the money out of the cash register. . . . I must have been mentally unbalanced, I hit him. . . . I just kept on hitting him, I hit him 7 or 8 times." Moore eventually escaped with $15.

"Where did you get the gun?" Tierney asked.

"I bought that gun, I'm telling you the God's truth, from a little short n - - - - - , he said he works on the road."

"What is his name?"

"I don't know—they call him Blacky."

"Where do they call him that?"

"On Rondo St."

"Whereabouts on Rondo St.?"

"About Western Avenue up there by the beer parlor. He was standing on that corner."

"Blacky" sent Moore to 411 Rondo to see "Cyrod." There, he traded "Cyrod" a radio he had purchased for $6.50, plus $4.00 cash, for the gun, a .38. He later purchased twenty bullets for three cents apiece.

The police had originally attempted to take Moore into custody at 225 Rondo on January 11, but the attempt had failed.

"Tell me what happened at 225 Rondo, the day Mitchell and Smith went up there," Tierney asked. Detective James Mitchell was one of the department's few Black officers.

"He (Smith) asked me if I had a gun and I said no. He was curious and he walked over to the bed raised the pillow and saw the gun, so he picked it up and poked me right here (pointing to his left upper jaw). Then he got me scared and so I knew right then he wanted me—I had a hunch he wanted me for this robbery. I told him I wanted to get my overcoat. He didn't have any knowledge that I was going to run, and I figured I would just let him kill me and get it over with. I started to run toward the door and that moment's hesitation gave me my change [sic] to get away. I was running and figuring he was going to shoot me."

Assistant Chief Tierney turned the conversation from robbery toward the Munson investigation.

"Do you know where the Aberdeen Hotel is?"

"No sir, I don't. Unless it is in South Dakota somewhere."

"I said the Aberdeen Hotel in St. Paul."

"No I don't."

"Do you know where Virginia and Dayton Ave is?"

"No sir, Virginia, I know where it is."

"Do you know where the big vacant building is on Virginia, Selby and Dayton Avenues?"

"No sir."

The cat and mouse game between Tierney and Moore continued. After a series of questions, Moore admitted he knew where the corner of Virginia and Dayton was, but he still denied knowing the building.

"I don't know where it is. I read about that girl being killed."

"What girl?" Tierney asked.

"The girl that was murdered, they said something about a n - - - - - being involved."

"Where was she murdered?"

"In a building at Virginia and Dayton."

"Whereabouts on Virginia and Dayton?"

"I don't know only what the papers said."

"What did the papers say?"

"Papers say she was taken up in a building at Virginia and Dayton."

"What building?"

"I told you all I know is just what the papers say."

Tierney turned the questions toward Ruth Munson herself. He showed Moore a large picture of her.

"Did you ever see this girl before?"

"Saw her picture in the paper, it's the girl that was murdered."

"What paper?"

"Evening paper."

"Who is that girl?"

"That's the girl was murdered, Ruth Munson."

"How do you know that?"

"I saw the picture in the paper?" Moore suggested.

"Is that the picture you saw in the paper?"

"I don't think it was the exact picture, it looks something like her."

"You mean it looks like the picture of the girl? A few minutes ago you said it was the picture in the paper?"

"It is a likeness of her."

"Have you ever seen this picture before?" Tierney showed a smaller picture of Ruth Munson.

"This is the same thing as that one."

"Do you recall whether this is the picture you saw in the paper?"

"This one looks something like it."

"Is it the same woman?"

"It is a likeness."[7]

Tierney did not seem to be getting anywhere with his questions about the Ruth Munson murder case. He ended the interview for the time being.

As a suspect in the Ruth Munson murder case, Charles Moore fit none of the prevalent theories about the killer. He was not an acquaintance seeking revenge. His criminal motive had always been robbery, not sex crimes. It remained a possibility that Moore had tried to rob Ruth Munson and she had resisted, just as she did in 1934, this time with fatal results. Since he had beaten the druggist about the head, had he beaten her in a similar matter? The question made the exact cause of her skull fractures all the more important.

Moore did match up with one theory about the case. As a Black man, he fit easily into the police suspicion that Ruth Munson's death was somehow connected to someone in the city's Black community.

Under questioning, Moore had been evasive enough about the Aberdeen Hotel and Ruth Munson that Tierney considered him a prime suspect. So did the press. On Friday, January 14, the *St. Paul Pioneer Press* reported the murder investigation had been "reopened" by the previous day's questioning of Moore. His arrest and interrogation was certainly the newest development in the case, but for days investigators had doggedly been working behind the scenes, out of view of the press; the case had not been closed.[8]

The press got its next opportunity to cover the investigation that afternoon when Moore was one of seven criminal suspects put on exhibit in a "showup" held at the Public Safety Building. At 2:00 P.M., the suspects stood before "more than 200 victims of criminal activity," including "grocery and filling station proprietors, operators of taverns, taxicab drivers, street car conductors and motormen, householders, owners of stores and other business establishments, and victims of street holdups and purse snatching." The *Dispatch* wrongly noted that "Police assert that [Moore] has admitted molesting women"—in fact, he had tried to rob them. During the showup, the two nurses whom Moore attempted to rob on December 15 identified him as their assailant, although they had been unable to do so immediately after the encounter. At that time, the police released him, only to arrest him at a later date for the drugstore robbery.[9]

While the showup was underway, Detectives Raymond Schmidt and John Schroeder were trying to track down witnesses linked to an anonymous letter sent to the Minneapolis police chief on January 4. The letter included sparse but sensational information about Ruth Munson's personal life and the individuals responsible for her death.

> To the Chief of Police Mplis,
>
>   This may not be anything worthwhile but I thought it [ought] to be investigated. A patient at the Miller Hospital in St. Paul was told by one of the nurses there who was a friend of the murdered Munson girl that the Munson girl had a friend (mulatto) porter at the Great Northern R.R. she kept this a secret from her folks.—at a beer parlor where she had a date with her mulatto porter sitting at a table with him and at another table were 3 men one of which after an argument got up and gives the Munson girl a blow over the head. She became either stunned or killed. The men took her between them to Aberdeen Hotel—the man delivered the blow to the girl has left town and the other man who was the girl's boyfriend is afraid of being suspected of the killing and keeps low. As I said before this may or may not lead to anything but the woman who told me this is very trustworthy and not given to gossip or idle talk. The nurse who told this was at the time working in the Laboratory at the Miller Hospital of this I am not positive but this was a nurse at the [illegible] Hoping this will help in solving a most revolting crime. I remain yours, a [illegible] Mplis January 4- 38.[10]

Once again, detectives were offered a provocative story asserting that Ruth Munson's Black friends were a factor in her death. The challenge, of course, was how to verify the sensational claims. The team of Detectives Donald Kampmann and Cecil Stowe had already secured a list of five female patients with Minneapolis addresses who had been discharged from Miller Hospital since December 9. Detectives Schmidt and Schroeder were able to locate and interview three of them. "None of these three, we are convinced, was the patient referred to in this letter," they concluded. "We made several attempts to see [the other two], but they were not home. We will contact them tomorrow 1–15–38 if possible."[11]

No surviving record shows that the detectives made contact with the other two women. Nor is there any record that the sensational details of the letter were further investigated. Assistant Chief Tierney may not have thought it necessary. In the days immediately following the murder, detectives had talked to numerous Miller employees who knew Ruth Munson personally. Though these interviews were with a different group of Miller employees—cafeteria workers as opposed to nurses—it is likely that sensational rumors about who murdered Ruth Munson would have been shared widely in the hospital's hallways and lounges and eventually relayed to police.

While this particular story was never verified, the persistence of stories about Ruth Munson's connections to Black men could not and would not be ignored.

As Friday wound down and people looked forward to the weekend, at 10:15 P.M. Detective Lieutenant Ray McCarthy sent Detectives Carrier and Kennedy and Patrolman Cook to 313 Laurel Avenue, where they interviewed Mrs. Arthur Stevenson, whose first name was not recorded. She told the officers that her husband had been staying out all night and that he was a drunk. On the night of the Ruth Munson murder, he hadn't come home. In the afternoon, he had telephoned home—something he never did—and told her he had stayed overnight at the Union Depot, Ruth Munson's workplace. The officers made arrangements for Mrs. Stevenson to be at the station at 9:00 A.M. the next morning to see Assistant Chief Tierney.[12]

The three officers visited Mrs. Stevenson again the next morning. They also picked up Arthur Stevenson and took him to headquarters for further investigation. The officers placed enough stock in Mrs. Stevenson's account of her husband's behavior to jot down the license number and description of the car he drove, a Plymouth coupe, so both details would be handy should they investigate his movements on the night of the murder.[13]

At 12:05 P.M. on Saturday, January 15, Mrs. Stevenson gave her statement to Det. Lt. Smith. She painted a picture of an unhappy marriage. She was twenty-five years old. Arthur Stevenson, thirty-two, was a truck driver for Baldwin Transfer Company. He made approximately $25 a week, giving her $10 to pay all the household expenses. He often stayed out several nights a week, "without giving any plausible reason." Recently she had learned that her husband had taken up with Lucille McDonough, age eighteen, and was said to be staying with her in a rented room. On the night of December 8, he had not come home.

"Is this night, December 8, the only night that your husband told you where he stayed when he did not come home?" Smith asked.

"Yes sir—that was the only night."

"Have you ever had any conversation with your husband in regards the Munson murder?"

"Yes sir. . . . After I found out about that murder . . . I asked him where he had been and he said he had been out drinking and then stayed at the Union Depot for the rest of the night—and I told him that was rather peculiar because he never called me before. . . . I asked him if he knew anything about the crime and he said he did."

"And what did he say he knew about it?"

"He said that he knew her well or something to that extent but of course he was only joking at the time."

"Do you know for sure whether or not he knew Ruth Munson?"

"No I really couldn't say."

"Did he ever tell you just how much about the murder he knew?"

"No sir just one time he remarked to me—he said he had done it and asked me if I wasn't afraid that the same thing would happen to me but he said it as a joke."[14]

Whether it was a joke or not, Stevenson's remark was enough to make him a potential suspect.

The arrest of Charles Moore had given the press its first new information on the Munson case in weeks. Moore had confessed to robbing and beating the druggist Stephen Conger on January 9 and attempting to rob five women in downtown St. Paul on December 15. These events, however, almost took a back seat to the Munson case in the *Pioneer Press*'s January 15 coverage. MOORE QUIZZED IN MUNSON CASE read the headline of the paper's page five article. After briefly noting his confessions, the paper reported that "continued questioning" of Moore "was being carried on Friday night in the hope of throwing some light on the Ruth Munson murder," and that "Police questioned Moore concerning his whereabouts the night of December 8 and morning of December 9."[15]

Assistant Chief Tierney was clearly dissatisfied with Charles Moore's January 13 statement—in particular his evasive answers to questions about the Aberdeen Hotel and Ruth Munson. Moore's cagey replies suggested he was hiding something important. He had beaten the druggist Conger brutally and unnecessarily, and he was unable to explain why. For this reason, police assumed he was capable of Ruth Munson's murder. If only there was some way to get past his evasiveness.[16]

The police department had recently acquired a new piece of tech-

Dr. John Dalton, the St. Paul Police Department's criminologist, with the department's polygraph machine, 1936. *MNHS*

nology known as a polygraph, or lie detector. The device measured and recorded various physiological indicators, including blood pressure, pulse, and respiration. Truthful answers usually produced different readings from deceptive answers. A trained operator could study the readings recorded as a suspect answered a series of questions, see where the readings suddenly changed, and thus distinguish the difference between truthful answers and lies.

By Saturday, January 15, Tierney had decided to question Moore again, this time while he was hooked up to the lie detector. "This will be the first time such a machine has been used in St. Paul on any case of importance," Tierney told a *Pioneer Press* reporter that evening. "It has been used in other cases here, but only experimentally. We hope from the success of its use in other cities it will aid in our search for the murderer of Ruth Munson."[17]

The *Pioneer Press* duly noted the development in a short article printed January 16—on page five of the paper's fourth section. This placement suggested the paper's reporters and editors were, like the police, frustrated, even fatigued, with the case. Gone were the blaring headlines above the fold on the front page. Increasingly, articles about the case were fewer in number, shorter, and placed on later pages, as if the paper's editors no longer expected a quick solution.

At 10:30 A.M. on January 17, Detective Thomas Grace finally got around to taking Arthur Stevenson's statement, two days after he had been picked up. Grace had clearly read the statement Mrs. Stevenson had given Det. Lt. Smith. Stevenson denied he had been having "some trouble" with his wife, or "any trouble with anybody elses [sic] wife." "The only trouble we ever have," he said, "is when I don't show up—go out and get drunk." He acknowledged that he had been out on the night of December 8 and that he had said he stayed at the Union Depot, but in reality, did not. He said he had told Mrs. Stevenson that "because I couldn't think of anywhere else I could tell her where I stayed." He admitted that he had "been running around" with Lucille McDonough, but denied he had "any immoral relations with her."

Detective Grace was more interested in the Ruth Munson case than in the Stevensons' domestic troubles.

"And didn't your wife ask you if you knew anything about that crime and you said you did, is that the truth?" he asked.

"No, she said I bet you are the one that did that and I said 'Why certainly that is just my type,' because that was in a joking way which she knew."

"Did you tell your wife that you knew the Munson girl well?"

"I told her that as a joke too which she understood was a joke."

"Did you ever explain how you killed the Munson girl to your wife and your mother?"

"Well they were up to the house one night and they were joking about it—talking about it and I said I was the one that did that; that was all I said about that."

"Did you kill the Munson girl?"

"No I didn't."

"Why did you make such a statement that you did if you didn't?"

"Well it was all on account of they were passing things my way and I was going to make a joke out of it; both of them understood that as a joke."

Stevenson agreed to read and sign his statement, even though Detective Grace added the phrase "knowing that what you have stated can be used against you in Court."[18]

Between Saturday evening, January 15, and the following Monday, Assistant Chief Tierney and Chief Hackert had second thoughts about relying solely on the lie detector to break their suspect. On Monday, January 17, the afternoon *Dispatch* reported on page one that, according to Tierney, "a lie detector was to be used on Moore this afternoon." But there was an addition to the plan. The paper also reported that Moore "will be taken Tuesday to the Aberdeen hotel, where the charred body of Ruth Munson was found on December 9." The plan, Tierney told the paper, was to show Charles Moore the room in the hotel where Ruth Munson was murdered and have detectives watch his reaction closely.[19]

On Tuesday morning, the *Pioneer Press* announced that day's pending trip to the Aberdeen. No mention was made of the lie detector test. The paper reported that Stephen Conger had identified Moore as the man who beat him while holding up his drugstore. Across the river, the morning *Minneapolis Tribune* also mentioned the planned trip to the Aberdeen, noting, "Afterwards the suspect will be questioned with the aid of a lie-detector."[20]

On Tuesday morning, detectives led by Chief Hackert took Moore in handcuffs "through the corridors of the vacant Aberdeen to view the scene of the crime," the *Dispatch* reported. "Police took various means to see whether the prisoner would betray familiarity with the building. His curiosity as to where the fire which burned Munson had started looked natural to casual observers who watched the test."

Moore denied any knowledge of the crime. "I had nothing to do with that," he exclaimed, "half crying" when taken to the burned-out rooms on the second floor of the building. "Before I'd do anything like that I'd blow my brains out."

From the Aberdeen, Moore was taken back to jail. The lie detector test tentatively planned for that afternoon was "probably postponed," pending further adjustment of the machine. There is no record that the test was ever administered. Moore was prosecuted for the robbery of Conger. He was never charged in connection to the murder of Ruth Munson.[21]

Charles Moore was one of the few murder suspects whose name appeared in the press. In the general absence of credible hypotheses about who murdered Ruth Munson and why, citizens spun their own theories, which they eagerly shared with each other. During the same two-day period detectives were questioning Moore, two stories about the case that originated on the streets were documented in police reports. Like the anonymous letter about Ruth's "mulatto boyfriend," the theories touched on a secret life.

On the same morning detectives walked Charles Moore through the Aberdeen, Senior Clerk Frank O'Heron took a statement at headquarters from D. E. Olson, who lived at 292 South Griggs Street. Back on December 15, Olson's mother had taken a bus from Minneapolis to Brainerd. During the long ride, she sat next to a chatty young woman who said she was a chambermaid at a St. Paul hotel. The woman said she had quit her job to take care of her sister and a new baby on a farm near Little Falls, Minnesota. When the Munson case came up during their conversation, Mrs. Olson expressed the popular opinion that the two women with Ruth on December 8 should come forward and tell what they knew. According to O'Heron's report, the young woman said, "the Munson girl is connected with a dope ring and this was the only way out as they were afraid she would squeal on them." Mrs. Olson responded, "they will find them," referring to the two women, and her seatmate replied, "they will never find them."

Olson reported that all during the conversation, the young woman was knitting and constantly smoking. At least a dozen times, she mentioned she was nervous, but didn't say why. She left the bus at Little Falls. The woman was described as being twenty-five to thirty years old, husky, possibly blond, wearing a brown suit and brown oxfords. Mrs. Olson was not sure if she could identify the woman if she saw her again.[22]

The woman's story that Ruth Munson was connected to a dope ring was worthy of a follow-up effort. Over the next couple of days, detectives would speak to the bus driver. The only new thing they learned was that he had turned in "a practically completed pair of childs [sic] mittens" to the Minneapolis depot's lost and found. There is no record that detectives located the young woman.[23]

The next day, January 19, Detective Earl Harken filed a report detailing an account of an incident that a streetcar passenger had given him. On the previous morning, the passenger, riding the Merriam Park line, had engaged in conversation with the conductor. When the streetcar passed the Aberdeen, the conductor commented that the police "were working on the wrong angle . . . regarding the negro Moore, who was to be subjected to the Lie Detectors." The conductor allowed that "Ruth

Munson, with two girls who are now missing, was working undercover for a Federal man in an effort to get a line on a dope ring, which is supposed to be working in this town, and that she was put out of the way because she knew too much." Detective Harken concluded his report with the observation that "the above appears to be the topic of conversation at the Snelling Car Barns."[24]

That same day, Detectives Robert Murnane and Herbert Olson added a handwritten note to Harken's report. They had interviewed the conductor, who remembered the conversation with the passenger. He informed the detectives that a St. Paul fireman assigned to Station Number 1 at Ninth and Main had told him about the "dope angle." The conductor added that he had shared his information with a woman whose husband was a member of the police department, but he could not remember her name.[25]

Working the streets, detectives may have heard the same rumors described in O'Heron's and Harken's reports. There is just one document on file mentioning narcotics in direct connection to the Munson case: the January 7 report noting that Robert Brown was rumored to have visited the Union Depot in the wee hours of the night to meet a train and pick up a package of "dope" from a train porter. And that report went only to Chief Tierney.[26]

Theoretically, it could be argued that Ruth Munson was friendly with Robert Brown and other porters as part of her undercover assignment. If the rumor that she was working undercover for a "Federal man" was true, it is not likely the St. Paul police would have been informed of such an arrangement as a courtesy. While the St. Paul Police Department occasionally worked in tandem with the Federal Bureau of Investigation, the department's own legacy of corruption hung like a cloud over any joint effort. The FBI was still hesitant to trust the department.

On the morning of January 19, "on information received," the team of Carrier, Kennedy, and Cook drove to 815 Iglehart Avenue to talk to Charles Sands. The team had learned that he had two sisters "that were supposed to have been with Ruth Munson at the Ace Café the night she was killed." One sister, Florence Sands, was seventeen years old and employed as a domestic. She never knew Ruth Munson. Her sister, Maria, worked as a cashier at the Golden Rule "and never knew of or heard of Ruth Munson until her death."[27]

That same afternoon, Detective Lieutenant Jack Walsh met with Mr. J. H. Johnson, who came to the station to claim that a man named Grant Ward had made "forceful advances" to his wife and "also attempted to rape a Mrs. Greening, a widow." Mrs. Greening was positive her assailant was the same man who forced himself upon Mrs. Johnson. Johnson believed Ward might be connected to the Munson murder case, as he was well acquainted with the neighborhood surrounding the Aberdeen. According to Det. Lt. Walsh's report, "Both he (Johnson) and his wife have been thinking seriously about the Munson case and up to now he was reluctant to say anything but feels that an investigation should be made regarding the habits of Ward." Ward was described as "37 or 38 years old, about 5′8″ or 9″ tall, with a very stocky build and medium complexion."[28]

In filing his report, Det. Lt. Walsh tossed one more name into the long list of potential suspects in the Ruth Munson murder case.

January 20–February 12, 1938

In late January, Police Chief Clinton Hackert announced that "fourteen picked detectives had been assigned permanently" to work on the case until it was solved. Any frustration Assistant Chief Charles J. Tierney and Hackert may have felt about the investigation's failures they kept to themselves. "These men already have made remarkable progress in the case," Hackert prudently told the *Minneapolis Tribune*, adding that "their findings lead me to believe that case is far from hopeless." For the *Minneapolis Star*, he even sounded optimistic: "Findings promise solution of the case."[1]

In spite of this display of optimism, the investigation's leaders must have chafed at a *Tribune* news report about a completely different case. Charles S. Ross, a wealthy Chicago businessman, had been kidnapped on September 27, 1937, by John Henry Seadlund, alias Peter Anders, and James Atwood Gray. The kidnapping had gone wrong, and Seadlund had killed both Ross and Gray on October 10, burying them in northwestern Wisconsin. Seadlund was captured in Los Angeles by the FBI on January 14. Three days later, he was flown to St. Paul. The bureau's St. Paul office became the staging point for a search for the bodies of Ross and Gray, led personally by FBI Director J. Edgar Hoover. The *Tribune* reported on January 20 that an older man, identified only as Mr. Olson, "got into the FBI offices in St. Paul [and] said he wanted to talk with agents about [a] possible connection of Anders with the Ruth Munson murder in St. Paul on December 9."

If Olson had information about the Munson case, why did he choose to go to the FBI instead of the St. Paul police? Was this the "Mr. Olson" who weeks earlier had reported his mother's conversation with the knitter on the bus to Brainerd? If so, was Olson upset that St. Paul police had not been aggressive enough in pursing the "dope ring" lead? Did he think the FBI was better equipped than local police to handle the case? Olson's background and his motives remained a mystery. According to the newspaper, "He refused to say what he told the agents." No reports documenting an interview with Olson were placed in the Munson file.[2]

The investigation continued to focus on the one piece of physical evidence at hand. In an effort to secure more information about the shear pins, Dr. John B. Dalton and H. H. Goetzinger, who worked for the Minnesota Bureau of Criminal Apprehension, showed the pins to representatives of eight different businesses around the city. The shear pins, they learned, may have come from an outboard boat motor, an automatic switchboard, or some type of generator. The general consensus among the representatives was that they were from a Neptune single or light twin outboard boat motor. From several of these businesses, the duo purchased sample metal rods from which shear pins are fashioned. They created a chart organizing nineteen different samples by their material composition, diameter and length, and—most importantly—what tool had been used to cut each sample. The chart also included the same details on the three shear pins retrieved from the Aberdeen. Hopefully, this comparative data, in particular the method of cutting, would help trace the Aberdeen shear pins to their owner.[3]

The investigation's efforts were not helped by the sudden appearance of another note requesting money in exchange for information about the case. The text outlined terms similar to those recorded by Detective Lieutenant Roy Coffey and Patrolman Lewis Schultz in their December 31 report on the earlier note. "I know where the slayer of RM is Pay $500 to Lewis at Frederick Hotel Lay Off Tierney," the new message read. The note had been composed with letters, words, and symbols cut from magazines and newspapers and pasted on a sheet of paper. It resembled the "ransom note" from the 1934 movie *The Man Who Knew Too Much*. Once again, the amount of $500 was to be delivered to the Frederick Hotel, this time to the attention of "Lewis." The requested amount matched the $500 reward offered by the *St. Paul Daily News* shortly after the murder. That reward had expired, reducing the official reward to the $200 originally authorized by the Ramsey County Board of Commissioners.[4]

The meaning of the phrase "Lay Off Tierney" was puzzling. Was the phrase directed at perceived critics of the investigation, and thus defending Tierney? Or was it an admonition to Tierney himself, as in "stop what you're doing"—or a suggestion he be removed from his job?

Inspector of Detectives William McMullin interviewed John Hildebrandt, owner of the Frederick Hotel, and determined there were no employees there named Lewis. According to the night clerk, the only current guest bearing that name arrived on January 4, 1938, registering as E. E. Lewis of Indianapolis, Indiana. He had taken Room 306 the first night and then changed to Room 1, where he still resided. He generally left for work about 7:00 A.M. in a Dodge coupe. When Inspector McMullin visited the hotel at 7:30 P.M., Lewis was not in, so he was not questioned. Inspector McMullin did not check further on Robert Blum, the perceived creator of the December 31 message who had not been located; it is possible McMullin was unaware of the earlier message.[5]

The investigation had been unsuccessful in advancing the case through visits to the Friendship Club in Minneapolis and the Ace Bar in St. Paul. On January 24, potential new information about Ruth Munson at the Ace came to light. Once again, it was secondhand. Chief Hackert himself brought Paul Morgan to the station to recount information about the case that had originated from Morgan's brother Phil. He was interviewed by Detective Lieutenant Ray McCarthy. Sometime in August or September, McCarthy learned, Phil Morgan had gone over to the Ace, where he met Chester Hull. Hull was drinking with another man. Phil then drove the two men and two women, one being Ruth Munson, to a flat over Esslinger's Saloon at Prior and University "or some other building in this vicinity." Morgan let the men and two women out of his car and then went home. "The chief," McCarthy noted in his report, "thought this ought to be checked a little further."[6]

The task fell to the team of Detectives Boyd Carrier and Frank Kennedy and Patrolman James Cook. Two days later, Detective Carrier added a postscript to McCarthy's report. The trio had determined that Chester Hull, age twenty, had moved to California in early August. They identified the other man as John Hetherton. Hetherton told the officers he had met "these two girls" at the Ace and they wanted to go to "White Bear," but he declined. At that point, Morgan came into the Ace and Hull asked Hetherton to drive them as far as University and Prior, which he did. There, they separated. Hetherton did not remember the names of the two women, but he thought one worked as a maid on Hague Avenue and the other worked on Snelling Avenue south of University Avenue. He promised to try to get their names.[7]

Whether Hetherton ever delivered on his promise is unknown. By his description of the locations where the two women worked, neither of them could have been Ruth Munson. Like other leads involving the Ace, checking out this one "a little further" had turned it into a dead end.

In late January and early February, detectives investigated a number of leads that in one way or another touched on the relationship between the white waitress originally from Grantsburg and Black men from

Rondo. Some of these leads were from citizens who continued to follow the case in the newspapers and talk about it in the bars and cafés. Other leads were the result of detectives' own legwork.

On January 24, the team of Carrier, Kennedy, and Cook investigated a lead regarding the robbery and murder suspect Charles Moore. Through Mrs. Florence Johnson, who lived at 580 Robert Street, they learned that Ruth Green, 157 Valley Street, "knew something about Moore being implicated in [the] Munson murder." The lead must have sounded intriguing. The trio located Ruth Green and interviewed her. She acknowledged talking about the murder. Any hope the team had in linking Moore to the crime quickly evaporated. "She thought a colored man may have done it," the trio wrote in their report, "and when she saw Moore's picture in [the] paper she said that he might have been the one."[8]

A week later, on January 31, Patrolmen Robert Williams and Robert Turpin arrested a Black man, William Lawrence, 382 Rondo, in a bar at 318 Rondo "on information he knows something regarding the Ruth Munson case." (This was the same William Lawrence Patrolman Williams had arrested on December 17—for a similar reason.) Exactly where their information came from is unknown, but as Black officers, Patrolmen Williams and Turpin may well have heard stories about Lawrence while on duty, or they might have plucked a leaf off the Rondo neighborhood's grapevine during their off-duty hours. Assistant Chief Tierney ordered that Lawrence be put on the holdbook. It would be a week before Lawrence was questioned; it is unclear whether he was held in the Public Safety Building for that time or released and brought back for the interview.[9]

In the meantime, on February 5, Charles Moore waived examination in municipal court on charges of beating and kicking the druggist Stephen Conger. He was scheduled to stand trial in district court on Monday, February 7. Conger was continuing his recovery, and the latest report indicated he would not lose sight in one eye, as was feared.[10]

On the day Moore went to trial, Detective Lieutenant Nate Smith finally interviewed William Lawrence. A widower at the age of twenty-seven, Lawrence was unemployed. Smith got right down to business, asking not about the Ruth Munson case directly, but about Clifford Jefferson. Jefferson was a Black man, a former patient of the Minnesota State Hospital for the Insane in St. Peter, where mentally ill patients considered dangerous were sent.

"Are you acquainted with a Clifford Jefferson?" Smith asked.

"Yes sir."

"Under what circumstances did you first meet him?"

Lawrence had encountered Jefferson the previous fall through a fellow named Mozelle Howard in the Keystone Hotel. At a later date, he and Jefferson had bumped into each other at the Keystone or the C & G Bar. After leaving the bar, the two had stopped off at Jefferson's residence on their way to Lawrence's place. Jefferson's mother fixed them a lunch. At some point, Jefferson left the kitchen and went down to the basement. When he returned to the kitchen, the two men headed for Lawrence's place.

"I started up toward Dale Street," Lawrence continued, "and after we got up that way, that is when he produced this, I imagine, poker. I imagine that is what he got when he went down in the basement of his home. My mind was kind of bleary then; I had been drinking before I met him and I walked with him to clear my mind for about ten to fifteen minutes and left him and went back home, went to bed."

"Did he tell you at that time why he had that poker with him?"

"Yes he made mention of a fact that he was out looking for some women or something, at least that is what he said he was going to do."

"Well just what did he say that he was going to do?"

"Use that poker to hit some women in the head."

"Did he tell you for what purpose he was going to hit her in the head—to rob her or attack her?"

"Attack her."

"Did he ever tell you whether or not he had ever attacked any women since he got out of St. Peter?"

"No sir."

"Where did he carry this poker in reference to his person?"

"Under his coat."

"Did you meet any women the night you were in company with him?"

"No sir."

"Has Jefferson at any time told you about any woman he has ever attacked?"

"Just at the asylum, he attempted, I don't know if he succeeded or not."

"Have you any idea about what day of what month it was that you were with Jefferson when he had this poker?"

Lawrence was not sure of an exact date but guessed it was late October or November.

"Are you positive in your statement that you do not know of any women, either colored or white, who have been attacked by Clifford Jefferson?"

"No sir"—meaning he knew of no one.

"On the particular night that you were out with Jefferson and he had this poker, did he tell you in what way he was going to use it on these women he proposed to attack?"

"Not as I remember."[11]

What Det. Lt. Smith did with the information he collected on Clifford Jefferson and how it influenced the Ruth Munson investigation is not known.

On February 10, a third ransom-style note surfaced, again offering to trade information about the Munson case for money. At 5:15 A.M. Superintendent Frank J. Hetznecker filed a report saying the note had been handed to him by Frank Gross, a night watchman. Gross, a brother-in-law of Hetznecker, had found the note about midnight on the front porch of the house located at 1034 Summit Avenue.[12]

Like its predecessors from December 31 and January 22, the note had been "written"—devoid of punctuation—by pasting cut-out letters and words onto a sheet of paper: "I know where the Slayer of RM is Pay $25 to Smith at Frederick Hotel Layoff Tierney." As with the December 31 version, "Smith" was to receive the money, but the amount mysteriously had been reduced from $500 to $25.

Four days later, Patrolman Louis Schultz, who had investigated the December 31 message, filed a report stating that "[Blum] is believed to have written the anonymous letters regarding the Ruth Munson case and a Mr. Smith, a porter at the Frederick Hotel." Patrolman Shultz also noted that Blum had been arrested previously "for assault on a woman in the Daytons Bluff district." "See Lt. Nate Smith about [Blum]," he advised.[13]

With Charles Moore eliminated as a suspect, Willard Wolf had become the investigation's prime focus. He had reported the story about the mysterious man who had entered his garage on the eve of the fire wanting to purchase gasoline; numerous citizen tips had labeled him as a womanizer; and his profession as garage owner and mechanic circumstantially linked him to the three shear pins found in the ashes on the Aberdeen's second floor. Chief Hackert and Assistant Chief Tierney decided to question Wolf again. Rather than connect him to a lie detector, they decided to question him while he was under the influence of sodium amytal, one of numerous drugs popularly known as "truth serum." The belief was that injection of the drug would reduce Wolf's ability under questioning to withhold information about the murder and any role he played in it. It is not known if Wolf willingly agreed to undergo the injection and questioning—or if the procedure was forced upon him.

On February 12, Dr. Gordon Kamman administered the drug at St. Paul's Bethesda Hospital, located just north of the Minnesota State Capitol. Present at the session were Police Chief Hackert, Assistant Chief Tierney, Detective Lieutenant Frank R. Cullen, Detective Thomas Grace, and Detective Lieutenant Ray Doenges, as well as police criminologist Dr. John B. Dalton and physician Dr. R. B. J. Schoch.[14]

Dr. Kamman administered the injection at 5:11 P.M., at the rate of 1 cubic centimeter (cc) per minute. After 5 cc Wolf "became talkative and joked with officers discussing various phases of the investigation," according to Dr. Kamman. He "referred particularly to certain tools which had been taken by police."

"I played ball with you fellows," Wolf rambled, "and I played 100%—if this is on the up and up I am not licked—so is my own statement that I gave you. I see your point—sure, a man married a number of times—work day and night next door—the only reason I work day and night is to feed my wife and baby."

Dr. Kamman asked Wolf how he felt and if he knew where he was. Wolf replied that he felt drowsy and he was at Bethesda Hospital. As the drug was administered, Dr. Kamman and Wolf engaged in incidental conversation. According to Dr. Kamman, after 12 cc, Wolf was "talkative" and "somewhat restless." At 22 cc, his speech became "thick." At 26 cc, his speech was "very confused and blurred and subject asked for water, promising to marry nurse if she would give him some." At 35 cc, Wolf was "very sombulent [sic]."

"Do you know where you are?" Kamman asked.

"Bethesda Hospital."

"What are you here for?"

"I'm here to have the lie detector on me."

"Mr. Tierney wants to ask you some questions—you know what it is about."

After some preliminary questions, Tierney got to the point. "How did you find out Ruth Munson was in the hotel?" he asked.

"The firemen came in and used my phone—newspaper men in and out all morning."

"Was she living when she went to the hotel?"

"How should I know? I figure she got knocked out when the firemen came in."

In answer to Tierney's questions, Wolf described accompanying "a bunch of Dicks" up to see Ruth Munson's body in the wake of the fire.

"What floor was the fire on?"

"I couldn't tell whether it was the 2nd or 3rd."

"In relation to your garage what is even with your roof, the 2nd or 3rd floor?"

"You can get on the roof from my garage—on the roof at the end where the laundry was."

"After you get on the roof of the laundry is there any way to get to the 2nd floor?"

"If you get a ladder."

After a few more questions about ladders, Tierney abruptly shifted his line of questions. "Did you ever own a outboard motor?"

"2 of them."

"What kind?"

"A Johnson and seahorse."

"You are sure you never had a Neptune?"

Wolf was sure that he had never owned, borrowed, or worked on a Neptune motor for anyone.

"Did you ever cut any shear pins?"

"No."

"Have you any tools at your garage that could be used to cut them?"

"I could cut them with hand pliers."

Tierney quizzed Wolf about shear pins and the cordial visit to his garage a month ago by Hackert and McMullin.

"Did you ever carry any shear pins in your pocket?" he asked.

"I did when I had a motor."

"How long ago was that?"

"I sold my motor in the fall of [19]33–35."

"You mean to tell me you haven't carried any shear pins since that time?"

"Yes."

Tierney shifted gears, asking Wolf what day the murder had occurred and repeating earlier questions about Wolf's trip to the Aberdeen to see the body. When Wolf went over to the hotel on the morning of the fire, Tierney asked, how did he know to use the back staircase? Wolf replied that he had simply followed someone else.

"Didn't you go up first?" Tierney asked.

"I didn't know where she was," Wolf countered, then described the condition of the body in some detail.

"What caused the fire—what was used to start the fire?" Tierney asked.

"I don't know."

Tierney asked questions about Wolf's past experience with fire. Wolf talked about a fire that broke out at his business and a long-ago fire at a farm in which livestock was burned.

"Do you keep any gas in your garage?" Tierney asked.

"I have a little." Wolf explained that when he stored cars for the winter, he siphoned the gas from the gas tanks and poured it into a sixty-gallon barrel.

Next, Tierney asked Wolf a series of questions about a recent attack on a woman on Kent Street. Wolf acknowledged that he had discussed the attack with others, not in the garage, but at Curt's, a hamburger shop nearby.

"Did you ever eat there any time that Ruth Munson ate there?"

"I don't know—I might have seen her but I didn't know who she was."

"Did you ever see her in a place on Western Ave.?"

"No."

"Did you ever tell anyone you said you saw her?"

"I never saw her on Western or on Selby."

Tierney asked a few more questions, then shifted back to Ruth Munson.

"Did you ever tell any theory of what happened the night before?"

"The only thing was I didn't think any woman ever walked into that hotel. No woman would be damn fool enough to walk into that hotel."

"What idea did you have as to how she got in?"

In a rambling answer, Wolf said that other people thought she went through the basement door.

"How did she get up the back stairs?"

"Whoever helped her must have carried her up."

"When you expressed your opinion how did you tell them she got in?"

"It was my opinion that the fellow carried her up the fire escape over the engine room."

Later, Wolf repeated a belief expressed by his tenant, Jim McGinley, that a woman committed the crime. McGinley, he explained, had heard from a friend that residents of Grantsburg, Ruth Munson's hometown, believed she was killed by a woman.

"Is it your opinion some woman carried her into the hotel?"

"I told McGinley a woman wouldn't be that strong to do it—he claimed a woman hit her in the back seat of a car and had her boy friend carry her in and dispose of her."

"Where do you think that happened?"

"I don't know—it might have happened the night before."

Tierney asked Wolf why he had not mentioned the theory about a woman being responsible for Ruth Munson's death in previous conversations between them. Wolf said he hadn't been asked any questions about women. Tierney abruptly switched to questions about when Wolf had sold his boat motor, and the difference between a Johnson and Neptune motor.

"Can you tell me or account for any shear pins that would be found on the 2nd floor of the hotel, or how they would get there?"

"I don't know."

"How many did you lose?"

"I don't remember—those I had were discarded—I had one in my pocket that I gave to the detectives when they came up—I know I didn't buy over 24."

"How did those shear pins get into the Aberdeen Hotel on the 2nd floor?"

"I don't know."

"If you didn't want to answer a question truthfully you could lie as well as not—isn't that the truth?"

"They say I can't lie."

"There's no reason why you shouldn't tell me the truth."

"There is no reason."

"Did you ever have trouble with a woman in your garage?"

"Never."

Tierney asked several questions about women who visited the garage and Wolf's interactions with them. His questions seemed to be based on information detectives had gathered about Wolf. Without actually mentioning Ruth Munson by name, Tierney seemed to be indirectly asking about Wolf's interaction with her prior to her death. Each answer Wolf gave generated a new question and an equally indirect answer. Suddenly, Tierney returned to the topic of shear pins.

"Do you think you can tell me any reason you would have for shear pins in your garage?"

"That is for an outboard motor."

"What other uses would you have for them?" Wolf described a number of alternate uses for shear pins.

"How did the shear pins get over in the Aberdeen Hotel?"

"The pins I have I haven't seen for over two years—it is two years that I put them away—I carried a pocketbook full of ignition wrenches and when I didn't use the outboard motor I put the shear pins away— that one dropped out of the pocketbook because one of the ends was ripped."

Once again, Tierney opened a line of questions seemingly unrelated to the case. Then:

"You have quite a reputation among your friends as a 'ladies man' isn't that correct?"

"You got that after I came out of Anchor [sic] Hospital in the Spring of 1933. My wife was a nurse . . . the last time I took any of them out from Ancker was when she went down to St. Peter on Thanksgiving Day, 1933—"

"How do you know where I got my idea from?"

"That is the reason."

"How do you know?"

"It is the only place I have chased around with any women."

Tierney asked more questions about Wolf's relationship with women before zeroing in on his treatment of them.

"You wouldn't hit a woman, would you?"

"No, I never struck a woman in my life."

"Would you hit anybody?"

Wolf admitted hitting someone at the age of fifteen, a boy who had stolen his bicycle.

"Does your wife know what you are down here for?"

"She doesn't know it is down here—she thought it was at the Public Safety Building."

At 7:10 P.M. Tierney's formal questions ended. Afterward, Dr. Kamman asked Wolf a number of questions.

"What happened to you this afternoon?" he asked.

"I just went to sleep," Wolf replied.

"What is the last thing you remember before you went to sleep?"

"When I mentioned about wanting to get my chain tools back."

"What followed that?"

"I don't know what he said after that."

"Then you think you fell asleep. Do you remember the first question Mr. Tierney asked you?"

"The first one I recall distinctly was the one about what door I took Ruth Munson in."

"What were some of the other questions?"

"He asked me if I discussed it with anybody and if I had shear pins. I told him we had discussed it—I told him about this woman (man) [*sic*] from her home town who saw Mr. McGinley this man was under the impression that the talk in her home town was that she was killed by a woman."

"How do you feel?

"I have a big head."

It appears that when William Wolf had recovered from his "big head," he was released from Bethesda Hospital and allowed to return to the Dayton Avenue Garage or go home. After the session, stenographer Theo J. Hall typed up a sixteen-page transcript of Tierney's interrogation. If Hackert, Tierney, and the other men in attendance were looking for confirmation of Wolf's involvement in Ruth Munson's murder or, under the influence of the truth serum, an outright confession to the crime, they were disappointed. From Tierney's line of questions, it seemed obvious he was trying to establish that Wolf was carrying shear pins in his pocket that he accidentally dropped when he took Ruth Munson to the second floor. The typed transcript does not include any police assessment of Wolf's answers to Tierney's questions. It is possible the men conferred after the session with Wolf and determined he had not been involved in the murder. It is equally possible they believed him guilty, but the interrogation had not produced enough evidence to secure a murder conviction in a court of law.

Willard Wolf was never charged in connection to the Ruth Munson murder case. With the exception of his brief story about the mysterious man buying gasoline, the press never mentioned Wolf in its extensive coverage. The general public was never aware that Wolf was considered a prime suspect. In respect to the Ruth Munson murder case, the bad penny was out of circulation.

February 14–June 30, 1938

By the middle of February, the investigation was running out of steam. Promising leads had come up empty: Ruth Munson's companions, the shear pins, tips on Ruth's known friends and activities. Complaints about suspicious men prowling the city's streets and reports of past sexual attacks had also decreased. What new leads there were fell into the same basic focus areas that had characterized the early days of the investigation. With no new developments in the investigation to report, the press had moved on.

Detectives had not made public what little they knew about Ruth Munson's connections with Black men, and reliable details about her activities and the people with whom she associated remained elusive. This lack of publicity all but closed the door to new tips.

On February 18, the investigation took a tentative step forward in the exploration of Ruth's secret life. Detective Lieutenant Nate Smith, Dr. John B. Dalton, Detective James Mitchell, and H. H. Goetzinger from the State Crime Bureau journeyed to St. Cloud, Minnesota, to interview Eugene Dickerson, an inmate of the St. Cloud State Reformatory. Why Dickerson was incarcerated there and how the four men had learned about him is unknown.

Dickerson told the four men that "shortly after midnight on December 9" he entered an alley near "Sylvester Oliver's place" in Minneapolis, where he was staying. The report filed by the men noted that "as he was going to his room . . . using the alley entrance, he had stepped aside to urinate." A car drove into the alley, and two women got out. "Why doesn't Blackie blow town?" one asked. The other woman "said that it would be better that he stay here so as not to create suspicion; that the woman they were talking about knew too much and that Blackie had to do away with her." (Because race is not mentioned, it is reasonable to assume that Dickerson and the two women were all white.) Dickerson followed the two women into Oliver's place. One of the women asked the night watchman, known to Dickerson as "Sarge," who he, Dickerson, was. The woman said he had overheard them talking in the alley "and he had heard too much." According to what Dickerson observed, the two women were "frequenters of Oliver's place" and one of them was "the woman of a negro whose name is Prather who also lives at Oliver's place."[1]

From what the women had said, Dickerson believed Blackie planned to place the woman they had been talking about "in a house [of prostitution] in Minneapolis and that in attempting to convince her how safe it was[,] he had exposed his connections too clearly to her and evidently she had refused to go any further, thereby making it necessary to do away with her because she knew too much on him." Dickerson said the two women talking in the alley did not mention Ruth Munson by name, but "as it was immediately after the Munson murder[,] he felt that they were talking about her." Dickerson described Blackie as "being 31 years, 6 ft. 1, 200 to 210 lbs., olive complexion, black curly hair, wears [a] hat and is a neat dresser." He passed as a white man. According to Dickerson, the "Prather woman" was "an inmate of Jew Ethel's place" and he believed Blackie had intended to place "the girl that the two women were talking about in Ethel's house[,] which is someplace on Washington Ave[nue]" in Minneapolis.[2]

According to Dickerson, Blackie was a "friend and visitor at Dehlia's place at 296 Chestnut" Street, presumably a house of prostitution in St. Paul. The woman who was with "the Prather woman" was described as being twenty-six years old, five feet eight inches in height, 130 pounds, with a light complexion, black hair, and glasses.[3]

The police report summarizing Dickerson's interview did not assess the quality or the value of the information he related. Numerous names could be checked out. More importantly, Dickerson's account also gave the investigation a potential suspect—Blackie, who had a clear motive for murder. And there was something else: though it was only Dickerson's assumption that the two women in the alley were talking about Ruth Munson, for the first time in the investigation, someone had alleged that she was directly linked to the world of prostitution.

Dickerson's information sounded solid, but the man was a convict and the veracity of his story needed to be checked out. That task fell to Detective Mitchell, whose regular assignment was in the Morals Division. An experienced detective, he was well suited for the task. As a Black man, he could work his deep connections to the Black community. Potential Black witnesses were more likely to trust him and share information they would never give to a white detective.

On February 23, five days after the trip to St. Cloud, Detective Mitchell filed a solo report. "Information given by Eugene Dickerson an inmate of St. Cloud reformatory, has been checked," he wrote. "Sylvester Oliver's place" was, in fact, the Serville Hotel at 346½ Fourth Avenue South in Minneapolis. Mitchell determined that "The woman known as Jew Ethel was said to be at present in Winona." William Prather was in Chicago. As for Blackie, "I could not find anyone in St. Paul or Minneapolis who knows him," Mitchell wrote. Dickerson had described Blackie as "a friend and visitor of Dehlias [sic] place." Dehlia Richardson, Mitchell determined, "did not know at any time a man white or negro by that name."

Over the five-day period, Mitchell personally tracked down information on two men who might have been Blackie, but both had left the Twin Cities several years before. He noted, "I contacted a good many of the negro pimps in Minneapolis who live with white women, and none of them know anything of Blackie."

While adding details to the information Dickerson had given them on February 18, Mitchell also found some inconsistencies between his account and details shared by others. Sarge, the night watchman at the Serville, told Mitchell "he did not have any conversation with Dickerson prior to Dec. 9 or after Dec. 10 relative to the Prather woman's conversation in the alley concerning Blackie." Mitchell also uncovered a contradiction in Dickerson's account of how he entered the Serville from the alley. Mrs. Oliver, the wife of Serville owner Sylvester Oliver, told him that the "doors to the fire escape are all bolted from the inside at all times and that it would have been impossible for Dickerson to enter the hotel by the fire escape as he had said." (The February 18 report did not specify how Dickerson entered the building, but Mrs. Oliver's statement suggests he claimed to have used the fire escape, a detail the report's author missed.)

"It appears," Mitchell concluded, "that Dickerson did not have the connections he mentioned," and "he did not have a conversation between the Prather woman and Helen in the alley near the Serville Hotel on the morning of Dec. 10, and that he did not enter the hotel by the fire escape." (Curiously, no one named Helen was mentioned in the original February 18 report or elsewhere in Mitchell's own report.)[4]

Mitchell's report apparently discredited Dickerson's story among his superiors. Having stepped forward to investigate Ruth Munson's secret life, the investigation now stepped back from further exploration of Dickerson's story. No reports were filed documenting further investigation into Blackie as identified by Dickerson on February 18, or in follow-up to Mitchell's detective work over the subsequent five days.

Although Mitchell could not find anyone in St. Paul or Minneapolis who knew Blackie, at least one other police file documented a "Blacky" in the Munson case. In a statement given January 13, 1938, robbery and Ruth Munson murder suspect Charles Moore admitted under questioning that he had purchased a gun from a Black man known as Blacky "on Rondo St." who "worked on the road," meaning the railroad. It is possible Mitchell had not read the Moore statement and was therefore unaware of this piece of information, but someone else associated with the St. Cloud trip was aware of it. Det. Lt. Smith was in the room when Assistant Chief Charles J. Tierney questioned Charles Moore, and he was at St. Cloud when Dickerson told his story.[5]

If Blackie really had "done away" with another person "who knew too much," at some point the crime should have surfaced in the form of a missing person report or a murder case in a neighboring community. There is no record that detectives reached out to law enforcement officials in nearby communities to enquire about missing person or unsolved murder cases.

Whether the lack of further investigation was the result of a deliberate decision by the investigation's director Tierney or the lead was simply overlooked, the outcome was the same: a lead on a potential suspect with a motive for murder was not fully explored. Similarly, no reports were filed by detectives indicating further investigation of William Prather, "the Prather woman," Helen, or Dehlia Richardson and any possible connection these individuals may have had to Ruth Munson.

After the St. Cloud trip, the investigation was all but at a standstill. Within the department, detectives seemed to have run out of ideas about how to move the investigation forward. Over the next three months, most of the sporadic activity in the case was generated by a handful of outside tips from various sources.

Among those tips was a new lead concerning Ruth Munson's companions at the Ace. On February 25, the trio of Detective Boyd Carrier, Detective Frank Kennedy, and Patrolman James Cook drove to Chisago City, Minnesota, to follow up on an anonymous letter mailed from that community on February 17. The writer had enclosed an undated clipping from the local newspaper which reported that "Mr. and Mrs. G. C. Mattson attended the funeral of their niece Ruth Munson in Grantsburg, Wisconsin." According to the clipping, their daughter, Mildred Mattson, had also attended the funeral. The letter writer noted that Mr. and Mrs. Mattson had two daughters. "The people around here are of the opinion that those two girls were the ones that were with Ruth

Munson the night of the murder," the writer declared, adding, "The statement that someone had seen those two girls who were with Ruth board a bus for White Bear may very well have been correct." The writer claimed the three women "were in the habit of visiting beer parlors and other drinking places wherever they have been and have been associated with men of the same type."[6]

Once in Chisago City, the trio of officers interviewed the Mattsons. They learned that the couple's two daughters, Mildred and Ruby, both lived in Minneapolis. The next day, February 26, the three officers interviewed Ruby and Mildred at their respective Minneapolis addresses. Ruby said she had not seen Ruth Munson in about five years. She and her sister had gone home to Chisago City on Friday, December 10, 1937, but she returned to Minneapolis right away. Mildred Mattson had stayed in Chisago City and attended the funeral with her parents on December 12, which meant she could not have caught a bus from St. Paul to White Bear Lake late that night. It was another a dead end.[7]

A second tip came from the Ramsey County Sheriff's Office. On February 27, Sheriff Thomas J. Gibbons sent a letter to Assistant Chief Tierney. "Dear Charley," Gibbons wrote, "in conversation at the Ramsey County Jail with Frank Androef and his manager, Tommy O'Laughlin, the following is some of the information received." Androef was being held in connection with some burglaries or robberies for which Benjamin Gravelle was under investigation. According to Gibbons's summary of Androef's account, Androef, a twenty-three-year-old prizefighter, and Benjamin Gravelle, a former convict, were bar hopping on February 8. They had spent the day in Minneapolis and eventually stopped at the Ace on University Avenue. Later, they stepped into the 38 Club on St. Peter Street. On their way to the Chatterbox Bar, 389 Selby Avenue, Gravelle had pointed out the Aberdeen Hotel to Androef, saying, "There is the hotel where Ruth Munson was killed, you remember her, don't you?" At the Chatterbox, Gravelle had tried to pick up two girls who rebuffed him. "You know the Munson girl that was murdered round the block, well, I am the one that did that," he told one of the girls.

And Gibbons brought a fresh element of racism to the case. Gravelle, he noted, "had gone out with Ruth Munson at least once before her murder," and he was "3/16ths Indian, reported to be vicious character in sluggings, very nervous, mean, a reputation for beating up women."[8]

On the morning of March 2, the *Minneapolis Tribune* reported Androef's account of the Chatterbox incident under the sensational headline: PAL NAMES SLUGGER AS MUNSON SLAYER. Gravelle was not mentioned by name, perhaps because he had not been officially charged with a crime. The article noted that the unnamed suspect "boasted of killing of St. Paul girl" and was now "under arrest," but it did not specify what crime had resulted in his arrest. Androef, the article noted, "was to be turned over to St. Paul police for further questioning."[9]

At noon that day, Detective Lieutenant Frank Cullen took Androef's statement. Under Cullen's questioning, Androef told the same story about visiting the Chatterbox.

"There was no other mention of the Munson case other than what you told us?" Cullen asked.

"No, only what I just said." Androef insisted he had not been involved in any crimes. He had seen Gravelle one other time, about a week after the Chatterbox visit.

"Did you have any conversation with him at that time in reference to this occurrence?" Cullen asked, referring to the Chatterbox incident.

"No I didn't[,] that was the last time I ever talked to him because I imagined he was kidding and it didn't enter my mind any more."

Cullen asked if Androef was willing to sign his statement after it was typed up. Androef refused.

"I am not willing to sign anything yet. I want to see Tommy O'Loughlin first," the prizefighter declared, referring to his manager.[10]

On March 3, the *Tribune* noted that Gravelle, identified only as "the suspect," was questioned by St. Paul police. He denied he had murdered Ruth Munson.[11]

If Gravelle was questioned by St. Paul police about his boasting that he had killed Ruth Munson, they did not include any documentation of that interrogation in the Munson file. No further reports were added to the Munson file regarding any other crimes in which Androef and Gravelle were involved.

Yet another ransom-style note offering information about the Munson case in exchange for money appeared on February 28. This note was discovered by a Shirley Bloom in downtown St. Paul, on St. Peter Street between Fourth and Fifth Streets. "I know where the slayer of RM is," the note declared, "Pay $25 to Nick at Frederick Hotel Lay Off Tierney." Once again, the amount requested for the information was just $25, a figure written in by hand.[12]

Having checked out its predecessors, the detectives brushed off the note. Nevertheless, the note, along with Gravelle's invocation of the

Munson case in the Chatterbox, suggested the case was still fresh in the minds of the citizens.

At the same time the Androef saga unfolded, detectives doggedly investigated three tips involving suspicious men that had, at best, only tangential connection to Ruth Munson herself or the murder case. A neighbor of William Wicker, owner of a secondhand store, reported that Wicker knew Ruth Munson and should be investigated. Floyd Patten, a roomer who attempted suicide and then tried to set fire to his bedding, evoked thoughts of the fire at the Aberdeen. I. J. Bakken, who worked for Minnesota Transfer as a switchman, was reported to be a sex pervert who frequented the Friendship Club. All were checked out, all were dismissed.[13]

Following the truth serum interview of William Wolf on February 12, the investigation's one piece of physical evidence remained unconnected to any suspect. General consensus among area marine experts was that the three shear pins were from a Neptune outboard motor. If detectives could find someone who owned a Neptune motor, or find the tool that was used to cut the pins in someone's possession, they would have a suspect. This is why Police Chief Clinton Hackert had written to Albert M. Pett in Miami asking if he had "made a sale to or purchase[d] a used out-board motor, make unknown, from Willard or Bill Wolfe."[14]

At some point, on the bottom of the chief's letter, Det. Lt. Smith noted that through the efforts of Squad 7 "Mr. Pett was brought to station and turned over to Dr. Dalton." On March 12, a month to the day after the Wolf interview, criminologist Dr. John B. Dalton filed a report describing his work with Pett. First, he noted that Pett had "at one time or another, cut a number of shear pins for Neptune outboard motors." Next, he addressed Pett's methods: "For cutting pins he used either a hacksaw, a pair of end cutters or a chisel and vise. Specimen cuts were made using these tools." Then, Dr. Dalton delivered the bad news: "These cuts do not correspond with the cuts on the pins found at the Aberdeen," meaning they still did not know what tool was used to cut the pins.[15]

Pett had supplied the investigation with a list of ten Neptune owners who lived in the area. He also noted that city fireman F. J. Singewald, 489 Rondo Avenue, "was attempting to buy [a] Johnson outboard shortly after Dec. 9, 1937." Singewald had made remarks around the neighborhood that "he was working on the Munson investigation." A check of fire department records indicated he was working the day shift on December 9, "and probably was not at the fire." In other words, it was unlikely Singewald had accidentally dropped the pins while fighting the fire.[16]

The logical next step in the investigation was to check out each of the ten Neptune owners Pett had identified, but it is not clear that this happened. While the chances of nabbing a suspect were slight, over the course of three months, wild goose chases had become a hallmark of the Munson investigation.

Ten days after filing his report about the shear pins, Dr. Dalton was called upon to examine possible evidence found inside the Aberdeen Hotel. On the evening of March 22, 1938, Detectives Frank Martin and Edward Harkness along with Detectives Patrick Lannon and John McGowan were dispatched to the Aberdeen to investigate a report of a light burning inside the still-vacant building.

They were met at the door by officers from Squad 7, who kept watch outside while the team investigated. "Upon entering hotel from [the] rear[,] found a electric light lit in room adjoining hall where Ruth Munson was found," Martin and Harkness wrote in their report. In that room, they found "two Montgomery Ward flashlight batteries and a piece of a wrapper off a roll of film." They determined that the intruder had used a homemade stepladder found nearby to screw the bulb into the socket. The team searched the rest of the hotel but "could not find anyone." In the rooms where the lights were working "nothing seemed to be touched." The detectives learned from the Squad 7 officers that they had received a call to the hotel two nights earlier, but upon their arrival saw no lights burning.

The officers carefully unscrewed the bulb from the socket. The light bulb, the flashlight batteries, and the wrapping paper were taken to headquarters and turned over to Dr. Dalton. If the four detectives and Squad 7 officers speculated on the identities and motives of the intruders whose prowling they had interrupted, their conclusions were left out of the report Martin and Harkness filed.[17]

The next morning, Dr. Dalton filed a one-sentence report detailing his examination of the evidence: "I examined a light globe, flashlight batteries and a tab from a film pack camera. No Fingerprints Obtained."[18]

It is unknown how many residents and business owners had seen the light burning in the hotel. But as March ebbed away and April crept in, people started talking about the future of the vacant hotel. Long regarded as an eyesore in the neighborhood, the structure seemed cursed, ravaged by fire, and saddled with a macabre legacy. Pedestrians crossed the street to avoid walking past the building. Motorists driving on Dayton Avenue or Virginia Street frequently pointed to it as the site of the grisly murder. On April 7, the *Tribune* reported that the Selby District Commercial Club had determined the Aberdeen to be "a fire hazard" and passed a resolution asking the St. Paul City Council to raze the structure. The newspaper was quick to remind its readers that the Aberdeen was the "scene of the torch slaying of Ruth Munson."[19]

On April 8, one day shy of four months after Ruth Munson's murder was discovered, Police Chief Clinton Hackert penned an interoffice communication to Assistant Chief Tierney. That morning, the chief had received a telephone call from Reverend Grant of Faith Lutheran Church, who reported that he had met with Thorvald Blakstad, 437 Dayton Avenue. Blakstad "claimed that the [government] Relief had not properly taken care of him and his family." He received a dollar from Reverend Grant to buy food for his family. Grant followed up on Blakstad and "found that he did not go home, but stayed out all night." He also learned that Blakstad "has gotten money from other ministers in the same way" and that he "hangs around taverns and 'plays' women."[20]

In his note to Tierney, Hackert suggested Blakstad "Might be a suspect in attacks and the Munson case, as he is out every night until 2 or 3 A.M. He refused to work, claiming he has sick headaches." Hackert enclosed a mug shot of Blakstad taken in April 1937. Hackert's suggestion offered a rare glimpse into the process of how decisions were made on whom to investigate. Hackert's conclusion that Blakstad was a potential suspect apparently was based on an assessment of Blakstad's honesty and on his tendency to stay out late and to "play" women. The fact that he had been arrested at least once prior to the murder also may have influenced the decision.[21]

The note also offered insight into the chain of command within the investigation. Tierney passed the note to Detective Lieutenant Ray McCarthy, who routinely assigned detectives to follow up on leads. McCarthy assigned the task of investigating Blakstad to Detectives John Baum and John Schroeder. "Check out his letter, but don't arrest this man, and leave a detailed report of your findings," McCarthy instructed the pair in a handwritten note.[22]

At 7:00 P.M., Detectives Baum and Schroeder drove to Blakstad's address. He was not at home, and his wife told the detectives she "did not know when he would come home, if at all." The detectives instructed her to tell Blakstad to "report to Asst. Chief Tierney's office, Monday morning, 4–11–38." Mrs. Blakstad said her husband "goes out with other women but he has never struck her during an argument."[23]

It is unknown whether Blakstad showed up at Chief Tierney's office, as instructed. Three weeks later, on April 28, Detectives Baum and Schroeder filed a follow-up report summarizing their efforts to connect Blakstad to the Munson murder. The detectives had interviewed caretakers and landladies at four addresses where Blakstad had lived or taken meals, but learned nothing they did not already know. "We also checked various beer parlors, showed them a picture of Thorvald, but found no place where he was known. None of these people could give any information which might connect Blakstad with any criminal offense."[24]

With no connection to "any criminal offense," Blakstad was no longer pursued as a suspect in the Munson murder case.

The day after Baum and Schroeder filed their report, the investigation received another citizen tip about a suspicious man in the neighborhood where the murder occurred. Willis Mason, who lived at 286 Marshall Avenue, came to the station to report on Mark Fitzpatrick, who lived across the alley on Dayton Avenue. C. H. Hoffman took his report. Mason maintained that Fitzgerald was "continually entertaining girls of about 16 yrs. of age at his house." Mason complained that the girls cut through his yard to go to Fitzpatrick's home, usually in the afternoon after school. If Fitzpatrick did not answer the door, two of the girls retreated to their home and sat on the porch until he waved them over. Fitzpatrick had a room full of antiques. He would show visitors only the room with antiques, but "there are beds in the other rooms which appear to have been used continually." Mason believed Fitzgerald should be checked out. He expressed his willingness to let detectives watch Fitzpatrick's house from his window.[25]

Mark Fitzpatrick's name had first popped up in the investigation on December 9, the day the murder was discovered. On that hectic first day, Detectives Carrier, Kennedy, and Ralph Merrill followed up on a call received by Chief Hackert that a woman at 280 Dayton "was afraid to go out nights for fear of being molested by a degenerate living in the neighborhood." The three detectives did not find the woman at home, but in checking out the six apartments at that address they learned there was "general talk in the building about Mark Fitzpatrick who lives alone on the north side of Dayton in this block. He has many young girls come to the house where he lives." At that time, no further action had been taken regarding Fitzpatrick's activities.[26]

Detectives Erwin Whalen and Alfred Jakobson checked into Mason's complaint on May 5. Upon their arrival at 286 Marshall Avenue, they learned that Willis Mason had moved out that morning. He had been asked to leave after hosting a noisy party the previous Saturday night. Nevertheless, the landlady, Mrs. Paul Cory, was more than willing to talk about Fitzpatrick and his young visitors. "According to her," Detective Jakobson wrote on the back of C. H. Hoffman's April 29 report, "the girls acted wild, dancing and smoking cigarettes as if they had been drinking." Like Willis Mason, Mrs. Cole offered the detectives use of her house to watch the goings-on at Fitzpatrick's home. "The above information was given us relative to the Fitzpatrick premises by Mrs. Cory without any suggestion on our part as to the reason we wanted to contact Mason," Jakobson noted in his report.[27]

It does not appear that detectives took advantage of Mrs. Cory's offer to set up watch on Mark Fitzpatrick from her house. No new suspects or other leads were identified and pursued by detectives. No new tips came in from citizens or other law enforcement agencies. For the remainder of May and all of June 1938, the investigation into the murder of Ruth Munson was at a complete standstill.

July 1–September 30, 1938

After nearly two months of stagnation, the Ruth Munson murder case suddenly took on new life again. On July 7, 1938, Detective Thomas Grace took the first of a series of statements in an effort to verify a claim that Guadalupe (Wally) Yniguez, proprietor of the Tunnel Hamburger Shop where Ruth took many meals, had confessed either to killing her or otherwise having something to do with her death.

Any individual claiming to be the murderer needed to be checked out thoroughly. Several factors made Yniguez worthy of further investigation. He fit an early theory about the case—that the killer was an acquaintance. Yniguez was the proprietor of the Tunnel Hamburger Shop at 215 Selby Avenue, where Ruth Munson frequently ate breakfast or supper. It was possible that Yniguez had developed a crush on her. He lived at 278 Dayton, next door to Ruth's building, increasing the chances of their bumping into each other. And his wife, from whom he was separated, had told detectives he had a fascination with fire.[1]

In his statement of December 14, 1937, Yniguez described Ruth Munson as a frequent customer who always ate alone. She had, to his knowledge, last visited the restaurant for breakfast on Tuesday, December 7. Several Tunnel waitresses had made similar statements, including Aylene Stivers, who worked the evening of December 8 and said she did not see Ruth that night.

The origin of the claim about Yniguez's rumored confession was not documented, but Grace clearly was aware of it when he began the first of three interviews on July 7 and 8. At 11:10 A.M. on the first day, he interviewed a twenty-two-year-old woman who identified herself as Mrs. Leo Gifford. She had been married for three years but was separated from her husband. She lived below the Summit Avenue bluff at 219 Pleasant Avenue, the same address as her longtime acquaintance, Margaret (Marge) Yost. For the previous week and a half, Mrs. Gifford had been a waitress at Tunnel Hamburger Shop. She had known Yniguez for "about a month."

Grace wasted no time in addressing the issue at hand. "Did you at any time when you were talking with Marge Yost tell her that the proprietor of the Tunnel [Hamburger Shop] made the remark that he, Wally, had something to do or did away with Ruth Munson, or words to that effect?"

"I did not," Mrs. Gifford replied.

"Have you at any time ever heard Wally, the proprietor, make any remark similar to the one just mentioned above."

"I did not."

"Did you see Marge Yost this morning."

"Yes sir."

"About what time?"

"About 9:30 on my watch."

"What was the conversation between you two this morning about bringing Marge Yost down to the station?"

In a rambling answer, Mrs. Gifford said she had asked Marge Yost "what it was all about as long as we didn't know anything about the Ruth Munson case." Wally, who roomed with Marge Yost's boyfriend, Lloyd Johnson, "had told her (Marge) that he was the last one to serve [Ruth] breakfast and he talked to her (Ruth) and he also said that they investigated up there and that was all. He didn't say anything about having anything to do with the murder case."

"In your conversation with Marge Yost this morning," Grace asked, "did Marge Yost tell you that Wally had made the remark that he had something to do with the Munson murder but that she, Marge Yost, did not know whether it was you that told her or who it was?"

"She said she was mistaken about it. That I did not say that. The day that Marge and I were talking about it we were both drinking beer at the Villa Venice."

"Who is Lloyd Johnson?"

Lloyd Johnson, Mrs. Gifford said, was a painter, divorced from his wife. He and Marge had been going together "for some time" and had planned to get married in August, but broke up on July 4. "What the trouble was I don't know," Mrs. Gifford insisted, "but to get even with me she's supposed to have said that I had something to say about Wally." She had never heard Lloyd Johnson say anything about the Munson murder.[2]

The next day, July 8, Grace interviewed Marge Yost at 10:40 A.M. She acknowledged that she had known Mrs. Gifford for about eight years.

"Have you and Mrs. Gifford ever discussed the Ruth Munson case?" Grace asked.

"Yes I have."

"Will you tell just exactly [the] conversation you and Mrs. Gifford have had on the Munson Murder case?"

"The conversation we had was in the Villa Venice and she said that she was out with this Wally, I don't know his last name, and that he was supposed to be the one that told her that he killed the Munson girl—I was drinking at the time and never paid any more attention to it at the time. She was supposed to have said that the Munson girl was in Wally's that morning for breakfast. That's all I know about it."

"Well did Mrs. Gifford actually tell you that Wally had passed a remark that he killed the Munson girl," Grace pressed.

"She said she didn't pass that remark and I must have misunderstood her," Yost replied. In response to further questions, she said she didn't know Ruth Munson, she had never worked at Tunnel, and she had known Wally for about a year, "but only about four months I have talked to him." She had never gone out with him.

"Isn't it a fact that you and Lloyd Johnson and Wally and Mrs. Gifford have all been out together?" Grace asked, displaying his advance knowledge of the situation.

"Yes we were riding in the same car the four of us." Four or five different times, she admitted under further questioning.[3]

At 11:00 A.M., Grace interviewed Yost's boyfriend, Lloyd Johnson. Johnson had lived at 278 Dayton Avenue, next door to Ruth Munson's building, since September 1937. He had known Ruth only "when I saw her." Wally Yniguez had been his roommate since February. Johnson had known Mrs. Gifford for four months, Margaret Yost for about a year and a half. He had been going out with her for four months. He confirmed that the two couples had gone driving together four or five times.

"Has the Munson murder case ever been discussed by you, Margaret Yost and Mrs. Gifford and Wally at any time?" Grace asked.

"No."

"Have you ever heard Wally make a statement that he did away with the Munson girl or words to that effect?"

"No."

"Have you ever heard Mrs. Gifford or Margaret Yost ever make a statement that Wally had said such a thing?"

"We were drinking one night in the Walnut Café . . . and Margaret Yost said that Mrs. Gifford said that Wally was implicated in that Munson deal."

"Did Margaret Yost say in what way that Wally was implicated."

"No."

"But Mrs. Gifford was supposed to have made that statement to Margaret Yost, is that right?"

"That I don't know."

"But you got your information from Margaret Yost?"

"That is correct."

"Have you ever seen Ruth Munson in the Tunnel Hamburger shop, run by Wally?"

"I saw her the night before she was murdered; I saw her in the hamburger shop."

"Was she alone at that time?"

"I think she was, I am not sure because there was other people in there."

"And to the best of your recollection, what time do you think that was?"

"It must have been around supper time, around 6 or 7 o'clock."

"Have you ever seen Ruth Munson in the apartment of Wally visiting at any time?" Grace asked.

"No."[4]

Ruth's landlady had told Grace on December 13 that Ruth had left her room between 6:00 and 7:00 P.M. If Johnson was correct, he had just introduced a new location into the places Ruth Munson was known to have been before the murder. But waitress Aylene Stivers had told Detective Lieutenant Frank R. Cullen on December 14 that she had not seen Ruth come into the restaurant that night. It would be up to the detectives to figure out which statement was accurate. No record exists that efforts were made to verify the veracity of Lloyd Johnson's assertion that he had seen Ruth at the Tunnel Hamburger Shop on the eve of her murder.

Sifting through the three interviews offered Detective Grace a microcosm of the neighborhood: men and women in their twenties and thirties, single, separated, or divorced. In these hard times, both men and women lived in single rooms, the women working as waitresses or housekeepers, the men as laborers. They spent evenings in taverns and bars, drinking their troubles away. Ruth Munson easily fit into the general lifestyle of the neighborhood and was connected through the Tunnel Hamburger Shop to these two couples. But Grace was unable to verify the claim that Wally Yniguez had killed Ruth Munson or was implicated in her death. In similar wording, both Gifford and Yost had said that the latter had misinterpreted the former's actual statement— that Wally had said Ruth had eaten breakfast at the Tunnel Hamburger Shop on Tuesday, December 7. With Gifford and Yost in agreement, the matter seemed to have been laid to rest. No record exists of further questioning of Yniguez himself.

If Grace thought he was finished with the issue, he was mistaken. Five weeks later Margaret Yost would return to headquarters with a different story.

In the meantime, detectives working the case spent the rest of July investigating a sparse handful of miscellaneous leads. One sworn officer reported rumors of a woman, presumably white, taking pictures of "colored" people, and her father, who was somehow connected to the Munson case. The rumor intrigued Detective Lieutenant Nate Smith to the point that he ordered Antone Brinks, fifty-six years old, and his daughter Astrid, twenty-five years old, to be brought from their home at 1895 West Minnehaha Avenue to Assistant Chief Charles J. Tierney's office for questioning. Smith soon learned that Astrid was an amateur photographer. Later, he viewed "in the neighborhood of 500 pictures and snapshots" the younger Brinks had taken. "In regard to pictures of colored people," Smith concluded, "the pictures are colored and not the people." The elder Brinks, Smith learned, was a heavy drinker, and in an intoxicated state made comments about the Munson case mingled with comments about his daughter's hobby, giving rise to the sworn officer's assumption. "I am sure in my investigation," Smith wrote in his report, "that neither Mr. Brinks or his daughter Astrid know anything about the Munson case."[5]

On July 22 and 24, detectives addressed two incidents involving assaults on women. Clarence Jeffers, who had lived near the Aberdeen Hotel for the last four years, was arrested and placed on the holdbook for investigation of assault. And two days later, Alice Langewin reported that about 11:15 P.M. she was walking up the hill on Kellogg Boulevard between College Street and Summit Avenue when a man grabbed her and then ran into the alley between the Cathedral School and the Park Court Apartments. Because the incidents involved assaults and occurred in the neighborhood of the Munson murder, the reports were added to the Ruth Munson file for further reference.[6]

Empty and forlorn, the Aberdeen Hotel was a magnet for scavengers and adventurers. On the morning of July 23, Emergency Car 4, Squad 7, and Cruiser 3 were dispatched to the vacant hotel to investigate a report that a man was in the hotel's basement talking to women as they passed. According to Detectives Fred Nielsen and Alfred Jakobson, Mrs. L. Renner told Jim McGinley, the hotel's former caretaker, about the man. McGinley went over to the window, saw the man, and spoke to him. The man disappeared into the recesses of the building. "We borrowed search lanterns and made [a search] basement to roof," Nielsen and Jakobson wrote in their report, "but were unable to locate anyone."[7]

Later, Mrs. Renner told Patrolmen Joseph McDonnell and Frederick Schimmel of Squad 7 that she was walking past the hotel on Dayton Avenue and saw the man in the basement. Street cleaners working in front of the building also saw him. "We were first told that man in basement tried to coax Mrs. Renner into basement," McDonnel and Schimmel wrote in their report, "but Mrs. Renner stated he did not." According to descriptions McDonnel and Schimmel received, the man was about forty years old and stocky, with either light- or medium-dark hair. He wore a wine-colored shirt.[8]

The following day, Patrolmen Schimmel and McDonnell filed a more optimistic report about the troubled hotel. Mr. McQuillan "would be in [the] Hotel for the purpose of giving plumbing estimates today and possibly for a week or two other contractors would be there," they reported. McQuillan had secured the keys for the building from police headquarters. "This building may be converted into an apartment house," the patrolmen concluded. It was not clear whether this prediction was McQuillan's or their own.[9]

On August 13, Margaret Yost was back in police headquarters. It is unknown whether she was summoned or made the effort on her own initiative. As before, Detective Grace interviewed her.

"Now on July 8, 1938 you gave me a statement regarding a conversation that took place between you and Mrs. Gifford, did you not?" Grace began.

"Yes, I did."

"Now today, August 13, 1938 do you [wish] to change that statement?"

"Yes, I do."

"Now will you relate in your own words what the true statement is that you wish to make regarding the conversation previously held between you and Mrs. Gifford."

"It happened at her house," Yost said, "she went out with Wally Yniguez on Friday night and Saturday morning after I got through work I went up to her house. . . . She said that she was out with Wally Friday night and that they were talking about this Ruth Munson girl and Wally told her that he was the one that killed the Munson girl and if she pulled any dirty tricks he would to [sic] the same thing to her. He didn't like to stay in the apartment he lived in cause whenever he went to bed up there he would see this Munson girl standing before him. That's all I can say right now."

This unsettling conversation, Yost told the detective, had occurred back in May or maybe June.

"Now when you came to the Station on July 8, 1938 there was an understanding between you and Mrs. Gifford that you were both to tell the same story," Grace said.

"Yes."

"And that story was to the effect that you misunderstood what Mrs. Gifford said, is that correct?"

"Yes."

"And at this time you are telling the exact truth of the conversation between you and Mrs. Gifford."

"Yes."

In answer to Grace's questions, Yost admitted she had been in the Tunnel Hamburger Shop "last Thursday," August 11. Gifford was there, but before Yost could talk to her, Wally Yniguez had ordered her to leave.

"I was going to talk to her on account of her accusing me of going out with her brother," Yost explained. "He is married. I went up to the tavern to meet Lloyd Johnson." Yost insisted she hadn't seen Gifford's brother for two years.

"Now is there anything else that you want to tell me at this time?" Grace asked.

"Mrs. Gifford told me about a week ago that Wally wanted to leave town and after he left he would send her some money to come after him."

"Did Mrs. Gifford tell you why Wally wanted to leave?"

"No, she just said that he had a guilty conscience about something." He had moved out of his Dayton Avenue apartment with Lloyd Johnson, and according to Mrs. Gifford, he was "sleeping in his car" for a week or two.[10]

Whether Grace felt Yost was finally telling the truth or was fabricating a story to get back at Mrs. Gifford and Wally Yniguez is unknown. There is no record that Wally Yniguez was interviewed again after Yost's declaration that "he was the one that killed the Munson girl." No attempt appears to have been made to determine why Yniguez had a guilty conscience.

Dr. John B. Dalton had not given up on using the shear pins to track down those responsible for Ruth Munson's murder. In the latter part of August, the criminologist made a trip to Washington, DC, taking one of the shear pins with him. While in the nation's capital, he visited the

Federal Bureau of Investigation's Technical Laboratory and turned the shear pin over to the technicians for analysis.

On September 8, FBI Director J. Edgar Hoover sent a letter on official letterhead to Police Chief Clinton Hackert. "My dear chief," Hoover wrote, "Reference is made to this Bureau's Technical Laboratory on August 20, 1938 of Officer Dalton at which time he delivered for examination a small rod recovered in connection with the case entitled, Ruth Munson, Victim; Murder." Summarizing the research by the technicians, the FBI director concluded that the brass rod "Is therefore commercial 5/32 diameter stock and not a fragment of brass wire." There was a "remote" possibility that the "brass rod is #22 wire." Director Hoover suggested that the "rod was probably used as a pin though a shaft or other object 1 1/32" in diameter," but "no opinion can be given as to the exact purpose for which the brass rod may have been produced."

In its precise wording, Hoover's letter did nothing more that confirm what Dr. Dalton already knew. Having delivered the technicians' conclusions, Hoover noted, "The original piece of rod submitted for examination is being returned herewith, it being noted that a small wedge shaped section was removed from the center of the rod for analytical purposes."[11]

Hoover's letter marked the last documented reference to the investigation's one piece of physical evidence.

September 1938. It had been almost nine months since the murder of Ruth Munson. Although the investigation was stalled, the case had not been forgotten. On September 14, an anonymous citizen wrote a note to Police Chief Hackert: "Chief, I think that you can locate the murderer of Ruth Munson by looking for a special watchman that comes in a hamburger shop on Selby at Farrington. He wears a uniform of dark blue." The note was signed "A Friend." Detective Grace assigned the task of tracking down the watchman to Patrolman James Cook and Detective Frank Kennedy, the latter having been on the case since the morning the murder was discovered. It would take a week for the pair to locate the watchman and file a report concluding, "There is no foundation to contents of this letter."[12]

In the meantime, by accident, Patrolman Robert Williams stumbled upon information that provided another glimpse into Ruth Munson's secret life. At the time, the Black patrolman was assigned to the morals squad and not working on the Munson case. Exactly what case he was working is unclear, but on September 21 his investigation took him to 394 Dayton Avenue, where he inquired about the resident of Apartment 3, Mrs. G. C. Bergstrom. Hazel Bohen and Ruth Willmar, he would learn, also lived in Apartment 3. Presumably, all three were white.

Mrs. Grace Tull, who lived in Apartment 1, was generous with her comments about her neighbors. She told Williams that Bergstrom had been "put out of her flat on account of the number of suspicious looking men that visited her apartment." She had moved to Apartment 7 at 272 Dayton. "The woman occupying Apartment 3 Hazel Bohen is a known prostitute," Williams wrote. It is unclear whether he was quoting Grace Tull or adding his own information to his report. Hazel Bohen had been "ordered out of this apartment and is supposed to vacate by Saturday." "Her man" was one J. R. Washington, whom Williams described as "colored" and living upstairs at 262 Rondo. A porter for the railroad, Washington would be back in town the following day, September 22.

Hazel Bohen and Ruth Willmar, according to Tull, were known to "visit with Bergstrom at 272 Dayton Avenue." Further, Williams noted in his report, Tull "identified the pictures of Ruth Munson as a woman she saw hanging around Western and Dayton Ave., but [she] never saw her talking to any one." Tull thought it was possible Ruth may have known Bergstrom. At 272 Dayton "suspicious men" were always hanging around, but "As to whether some of these men were Negro's [sic] she (Mrs. Tull) could not say." That detail, Williams observed, coincided with "Information [that has] come to me from time to time that a flat in the 200 block on Dayton have colored men visiting an apartment. This may be the Bergstrom Apt."

In the report, Patrolman Williams included a detail that had the potential to unlock the Munson case. "When this murder occurred there," he wrote, "Hazel and Ruth [Willmar] left the city." Anyone reading his report would wonder if Hazel Bohen and Ruth Willmar might have been the two mysterious women who accompanied Ruth Munson to the Ace the night before the murder. "We will not have anything definite until we have a talk with Washington," Williams observed. Williams concluded his report with the note that he had not yet interviewed individuals who were living at 394 Dayton Avenue when the murder occurred.[13]

On September 23, Patrolman Williams, working with Detective George Failes, filed an update regarding his investigation at 394 Dayton Avenue. Whether they had talked to Washington upon his return to the city is unclear. But the pair had interviewed Grace Tull a second time. Tull stated that when Ruth Munson was murdered, detectives did not contact Mrs. G. C. Bergstrom, who now lived at 272 Dayton Avenue. "Every time she talked with Mrs. Bergstrom," the officers noted, "she always told her something new regarding the Munson murder. . . . One thing she remembers in particular, is that she (Ruth) was hanging out at a colored tavern at Western and Rondo St. Ruth Munson hanging out on Rondo St. was supposed to be known only to the police. So how did Mrs. Bergstrom get this information[?]." Failes and Williams didn't take into account the fact that everyone else in the "colored tavern" probably knew Ruth was there. But Bergstrom was white, and thus shouldn't know. They thought Bergstrom "should be questioned regarding her source of information."

The two officers made another suggestion to help establish a deeper connection between the Munson case and 394 Dayton Avenue. According to their information, Mrs. Carl Stokes, a Black woman living at 543 Mississippi Street, "alleges that she saw a man and three [white] women in the beer parlor at Western & Rondo St. We would like to have her view Mrs. Bergstrom, Hazel Bohen and Ruth Willmar to see if she can identify them as being the women she alleges that she saw with Ruth Munson."[14]

The officers' question about how Mrs. Bergstrom got her information about Ruth Munson's activities pointed out the difficulties of effectively managing such a sprawling investigation, so important connections could be made. Patrolman Williams's observation that Ruth Munson's presence on Western and Rondo was "known only to the police" confirmed that the department withheld information about her contacts with members of the Black community from the public and suggests that Mrs. Bergstrom's knowledge came from the street. Contrary to Tull's claim, Bergstrom had been interviewed as part of the neighborhood canvass by Detective Alfred Jakobson on December 29, 1937. It appears Williams and Failes were unaware that Bergstrom had been interviewed a year earlier. Since Jakobson filed no follow-up report about Bergstrom, it is likely she was not forthcoming during their conversation. Had the officers known of this earlier interview, they might have pushed harder for Bergstrom to be interviewed. And since Hazel Bohem and Ruth Willmar left town after the murder, the officers may have wondered if they were the two women who accompanied Ruth Munson to the Ace.[15]

Williams's September 21 and 23 reports were handwritten. They were never formally typed up with copies distributed to Chief Hackert,

Assistant Chief Tierney, and Public Safety Commissioner Gustave H. Barfuss. Was it possible that Tierney, the investigation's director, remained unaware of these developments?

There is no record that the Ruth Munson murder investigation took the information recorded in Patrolman Williams's reports of September 21 and 23 any further. If Mrs. Bergstrom, Hazel Bohen, and Ruth Willmar were ever questioned, perhaps while being investigated for another case, it is possible that reports about them were filed in a different case file. In such instances, however, it was common practice for copies to be placed in Offense File 33436. How extensively the three women were questioned about the Munson case—or any case—remains unknown.

18   "The Cat Out of the Water"

October 1, 1938–December 31, 1938

In October and November 1938 detectives working the streets were not necessarily documenting the full scope of what they learned. The content and tone of their reports, along with the questions interviewers asked while taking witness statements, indicate the investigation had uncovered additional information that is not documented in other reports. Detectives were now working to confirm what they had learned.

In October, detectives heard a remarkable story that someone claimed to be in possession of Ruth Munson's underwear. On October 13, Detective Frank Kennedy, who usually worked the street, questioned Wilfred Van Danacker at police headquarters in an effort to verify the details.

Van Danacker and his wife lived at 226 Western Avenue. In the latter part of April or early May of 1938, the couple had been at Marge's Chicken Shack.

"She left before I did," Van Danacker explained, "and when she left[,] I asked her to let me have a jit (nickel) and she gave me fifty cents, so I stayed until I spent the fifty cents." When he arrived home, he asked his wife for another quarter to "get three bottles of beer," which she gave to him. She implored him to "hurry right back," but he did not return home until 4:00 in the morning.

"What kind of conversation did you have with your wife after you returned home?" Kennedy asked.

"I didn't know what to tell her where I had been all this time so I makes this story up about being in the apartment."

"What was the story?"

In a wandering response, Van Danacker explained that he told her he had been drinking in an apartment with a strange man whom he had never seen before.

"Did you tell her that this man had underclothing belonging to Ruth Munson in his drawer and that he showed it to you?" Kennedy pressed.

"I told her something to that effect but I didn't word it that way exactly. I told her he was raving and acting foolish. I told her that when

I went for the beer I met this fellow and we went to his apartment to drink the beer[,] then I told her that he was nutty and acted goofy and had a gun and a knife and he started to rave about Ruth Munson, he mentioned Ruth Munson and said that he had some underwear belonging to Ruth Munson and showed it to me in the drawer, but I didn't get a chance to examine the garments. I told my wife that he was virtually holding me as a prisoner."

"You also told this story to Al Vickery?"

"Yes."

"Lt. Talbot before we talked to you?"

"No."

"You also gave the same story to Detectives Cook and Kennedy?" Kennedy was referring to himself and Patrolman James Cook.

"Yes."

"Since you have told this story, you have decided to tell the truth about this matter."

"Yes.

"And what is the truth?"

"That this story is false and that I just made it up to protect myself from my wife."[1]

With Van Danacker's admission, a sensational clue and a potential murder suspect disappeared in an instant.

About two weeks later, detectives took another look at a suspect questioned early in the investigation. On October 29, acting under orders from Assistant Chief Charles J. Tierney, Detective Alfred Jakobson and Officer Blade arrested Lee Len, aka Charles Lee. The pair noted Lee as "Chinese" in their report and placed him on the holdbook "for inv[estigation] on Munson Murder." What prompted Tierney to order this arrest ten months after Lee was initially questioned is unknown, as no statement by Lee was recorded. According to the *Minneapolis Tribune*, the suspect was to be questioned by immigration authorities about illegal entry into the United States. Lee was never charged in the Munson case.[2]

From the earliest days of the investigation, detectives had carefully noted Ruth Munson's interactions with Black men: her friendships with porters at the depot, the beer-drinking event at Rossini's, the word that she was well known around the intersection of Rondo and Western Avenues and the Keystone Hotel, and her personal relationships with Robert Brown, who admitted to wanting to have intercourse with her, and Daniel Faulkner, who asked a fortune teller if Ruth would marry him. Added to this, in the wee hours of the night during the week before the murder, Black men had taken taxis from downtown locations to her Dayton Avenue address.

Ruth Munson kept these relationships secret from her friends and family. On the one hand, as the daughter of a small Wisconsin town, she may have privately embraced a progressive attitude about working and socializing with Black folks but publicly bowed to the cultural mores that demanded segregation.

On the other hand, it was possible she was engaged in some unknown illegal activity. Prostitution immediately came to mind. Police had interviewed many white men with whom she had had short-term relationships, but most denied ever having intercourse with her. Detectives did not record suspicions that Ruth Munson exchanged sex for money and that the practice had in some way led to her death. But the investigation's continuous exploration of her relationships with men and the potential links between her and known prostitutes suggested that at a minimum they considered the possibility she was a prostitute. While they continued to pursue any leads that pointed at white men, detectives also appeared to believe her activities involved individuals living in the Black community.

The St. Paul Police Department had purposely withheld every detail detectives had discovered connected to Ruth Munson's secret life. They had a practical reason to do so: this secret life was likely a factor in her death. Any information released to the public could tip off those responsible for the crime and send them into flight.

Late in November, detectives brought six Black residents of the Rondo community to police headquarters for questioning. Charles Williams and his wife, Eva, lived at 597 Rondo Avenue. Williams's father, Henry Williams, had been living with them, but six weeks earlier had moved to 416 Carroll Avenue, where William (Willie) Fields and his wife lived (Mrs. Fields's first name never appeared in police reports). The two couples were well acquainted. Mrs. Fields's adopted brother, John Warren, lived at 754 St. Anthony, one block north of Rondo Avenue, and often was a guest in the Fields home.

The interviews show that detectives had somehow assembled a cache of information they were seeking to confirm. It pertained to a gathering, in either the Williams home or the Fields home, of two Black men and one or two white women that took place around 4:00 or 5:00 on the morning of the Munson murder.

Exactly how detectives assembled this cache of information remains unclear. It is likely Detective James Mitchell secured some of this information by working his contacts in the Rondo community. At 5:00 P.M. on November 23, Detective Mitchell arrested seventy-nine-year-old Henry Williams at 422 Carroll Avenue "on suspicion of window peeping" and placed him on the holdbook for Detective Lieutenant Thomas Grace, who had been promoted from detective on November 19. It is not clear what Mitchell may have learned from Henry Williams at this time—or what he knew before he made the arrest. Two days later, on November 25, Grace dispatched the team of Cook and Kennedy to pick up Willie Fields and put him on the holdbook—also for "window peeping." For two men who knew each other and would soon be questioned along with the other four individuals, the arrests for the identical offense hardly seemed coincidental.[3]

The next day, November 26, Grace questioned the three younger men, then the two women. Henry Williams was questioned on November 28.

Grace interviewed Charles Williams at 8:35 A.M. Williams was forty-four years old and worked for the Works Progress Administration (WPA) at Hidden Falls. He had been married for "about six years" and had lived at 597 Rondo Avenue for a year. A native of Shreveport, Louisiana, he had lived in St. Paul since 1929.

"Now," Grace said, "Do you know Mr. and Mrs. Willie Fields?"

"Yes sir."

"Do you know a man by the name of John Warren?"

"Yes sir."

"Do you know a man by the name of Henry Williams?"

"That's my father."

"Have you and your wife ever been over to the Fields home on Carroll?"

"No sir."

"Have they been at your home?"

"Not together; he has been there several times by himself. About Christmas last year he and his wife came in for a short stay."

"Now was there ever at any time either at [the] Fields home on Carroll Avenue or at your home on Rondo Street where you and your wife, Fields and his wife, and John Warren, ever discussed the Ruth Munson murder case?"

"No sir."

"Was there at any time since you have lived on Rondo Street any white people visited at your house?"

"No sir, I'll take a death oath on that."

"Isn't it a fact," Grace pressed, "that at one time there was two men and one white woman, possibly two white women, were there at your home in the early hours of the morning and some liquor was consumed and the Ruth Munson case was discussed?"

"No sir, that's another thing I'll take a death oath on."

"Isn't it a fact that when these people left there around about four or five o'clock in the morning that the remark was passed that Ruth Munson talked too much and by this time she was probably burned?"

"No sir, no white people were at my house. There was no discussion like that and nobody left there at that hour of the morning."

"Has there ever been any colored men and white women visiting at your house?"

"No sir."

"Was there ever any company at your house that consisted of all colored people who discussed the Munson murder case?"

"No sir."

"At the time mentioned above when these people were supposed to have been at your home early in the morning drinking, isn't it a fact that upon leaving they shook hands with you and said good bye and we don't know whether we'll see you again or not?"

"No sir, no one ever left my house at that time in the morning because I can recall where I was that morning."

"You can recall where you were what morning and what night?"

"Well that was on December 8; I was home all night because I got up on that morning and got in my own car and drove out to the end of the Rice Street car line and that's where my assignment was as to go out to Lake Vadnais; that was on the 9th of December."

"Let me understand you correctly. On December 8 you state that you went to the Court House and got your assignment?"

"Yes sir."

"How is it that you remember the 8th of December so plainly?"

"Because we spoke about it yesterday."

"You mentioned the 8th of December, not me, isn't that correct?"

"That's what you told me but I probably misunderstood you."

Grace questioned Williams about other work assignments he had been given, but he was less clear on remembering the dates. He suddenly switched gears, as if trying to catch Williams off guard.

"Did you know Ruth Munson?"

"No sir, I did not."

"Did you visit any of those colored beer spots in the Rondo district?"

"Yes sir."

"Have you ever seen her in any of these places?"

"I don't know her; I wouldn't know her if she walked in here right now."

Grace asked a series of questions about Williams's wife, Eva, and his father, Henry. Did he, Williams, have any troubles with them? Williams claimed he did not.

"Have you cut any newspaper clippings out of the papers regarding the Munson case?"

"Yes sir."

"Have you still got those clippings."

"No sir I have not."

"What became of them."

"Burned them up."

"Why were these clippings taken out of the newspapers?"

"Like a clue came today and then we would let the paper lay around three or four days and read it over like that."

"Have you cut other clippings out of the newspapers also?"

"Yes sir, like some of the colored folks who have had trouble, some people getting married and some people having babies, etc."

Williams agreed that he had made his statement of his own free will, that no threats or promises had been made, and that he would sign it after reading it and finding it to be correct. The interview finished at 8:55 A.M.[4]

At 9:05 A.M. Grace questioned Willie Fields. Fields, thirty-four, lived at 416 Carroll Avenue and had been married for six years. He worked for the WPA at the Como Park Golf Course. He acknowledged that he knew Charles Williams and his father, Henry, as well as John Warren and Adolph Perry, who were his brothers-in-law. Grace ignored Fields's recent arrest for window peeping and concentrated on the Munson case.

"Now," Grace said, "have these people that I have just mentioned ever been at your house and discussed the Ruth Munson case?"

"No sir, not that I know of; if they did, I didn't hear it."

"Now about a week ago, was Henry Williams the old man, John Warren and Adolf Berry [sic] at your house?"

"Yes sir." They had all been there nine days earlier, about 9:30 in the morning on Thursday, November 17. But Fields insisted when asked a second time that he "didn't even hear a word" of discussion about the Ruth Munson case.

"Did you ever hear Henry Williams state at any time that he had something on his son Charley?" Grace asked.

"Yes sir."

"What did Charley's father say that he had on his son?"

"He didn't say to me."

"But the old man did make a statement that he had something on his son; is that correct?"

"Yes sir, that's right."

"Has there ever been any white women with colored men visiting at your house at any time?"

"No sir."

"Have you ever seen any colored men and white women visiting at Charley Williams' house on Rondo Street."

"No sir I haven't."

"Did you ever hear anyone [sic] of the people whose names I have mentioned state they knew anything or had any information about the Ruth Munson case?"

"No sir."[5]

Fields read and signed his statement.

Grace interviewed John Warren at 9:30 A.M. The thirty-one-year-old Warren lived with his brother-in-law Adolph Perry at 754 St. Anthony Avenue. He had moved to St. Paul in March of 1937 from Blytheville, Arkansas. He knew William Fields and his wife, as well as Charles Williams and his wife and Henry Williams.

"Now about two weeks ago in the morning," Grace began, "were you at the home of Willie Fields and his wife at 416 Carroll Ave., and the time you were there, Henry Williams who is Charlie Williams' father was there, and Adolph Perry was there, is that correct[?]."

"Adolph wasn't there that morning," Warren replied, contradicting Fields's statement from a half hour earlier.

"Now while you people were all together in the Fields home," Grace continued, "did Henry Williams make the statement that he had something on his son Charlie?"

"He did."

"Now will you state as closely as you can just what the statement of Henry Williams, the old man, was?"

"Henry Williams said that he knows something on his son, Charlie and his wife Eva that he didn't care to tell—he had something under cover that he didn't care to tell but if they fooled with him he would let the cat out of the water. That was the explanation he gave me—I asked Henry Williams the old man just what he meant by letting the cat out of the water and he said he didn't care to tell what it was and he kept saying never mind . . . [that] I'll find out later. . . . I got ready to leave and

Mrs. Fields asked me did I know what he was talking about and I said no and she explained the Munson girl's murder case and then I left."

"The old man, Henry Williams did not state just what he knew about the Munson case did he?" Grace pressed.

"No sir, not to me in my presence."

"Do you know under what circumstances, the old man, Henry Williams came into possession of the information of the Munson murder case?"

"No sir I don't."

"Have you ever been at the home of Charlie Williams at 597 Rondo St?"

"I have." He had been there one time, on Christmas Day, 1937, with Willie Fields.

"Do you know if the old man Henry Williams visited the Fields home quite often?" Grace asked.

"Yes."

"And you visit there nearly every day yourself?"

"That's right."

Grace confirmed that when Henry mentioned he had something on his son, only Willie Fields, his wife, and Henry Williams were there besides Warren himself.

"At any time you were at the Charles Williams home on Rondo St. were there any colored men and white women there?"

"No sir."

"Have you ever seen colored men and white women at the Fields home?"

"No sir."[6]

Like Charles Williams and Willie Fields, John Warren read his statement after it was prepared and signed it.

Having interviewed the three young men, Grace turned his attention to the two women. At 11:45, he interviewed Eva Williams, who was forty-one. She and Charles had been married for seven years; she was his second wife. She had lived in St. Paul since 1931. Clara Parker, Clara's daughters Delores and Gloria, and Roy Stewart also lived with them. Until the second week of October, Henry Williams had occupied the back bedroom, near the kitchen and bathroom.

"Now," Grace said, getting down to business, "was there at any time while you lived on Rondo St., any colored man and white women visited at your house?"

"No."

"Has there any time during the early morning hours any colored men and white women come to your house?"

"No."

"At any time at your home on Rondo St., has there been any drinking during the early hours of the morning?"

"No."

"Has there been at your home on Rondo St. anybody visiting there from outside of the city who might have called on you and your husband and spent the evening there and which ran into the early hours of the morning?"

"No."

"Do you recall anybody being at your home visiting there and at the time leaving everybody shook hands and said Goodbye and the parties said, we don't know when we'll see you again?"

"No—I don't remember anything like that."

"Has there [been] at any time at your home on Rondo St., any company there that discussed the Ruth Munson murder case and stated that Ruth Munson talked too much and that probably by this time she was all burned?"

"No."

"Has there [been a time] since you have lived on Rondo St., [that] a colored fellow named Roy Stewart and yourself and white women (2) were [sic] together in a back bedroom?"

"No."

"Did any conversation take place in your home about such a thing taking place?"

"No."

"Isn't it a fact that Henry Williams, your husband's father told your husband that you and Roy Stewart and 2 white women were in the back bedroom."

"He did tell my husband that."

"Was it the truth?"

"No."

"Have you ever been in a bedroom at any time with Roy Stewart?"

"No."

"Why did your father-in-law, Henry Williams[,] make such a statement as that?"

Mrs. Williams said that she didn't understand why, that her husband said his father was "a big liar and kept up a disturbance wherever he lived." She got along with Henry "considering" he was her father-in-law.

"You are absolutely sure that there has been no white women and colored men congregating at your home at the early hours of the morning discussing the Munson case?"

"I am."

"Do you know anything about the Munson case yourself?"

"No sir."

In answer to Grace's questions, Eva Williams acknowledged that Roy Stewart had roomed at their home from the middle of December 1937 until the second week of March. He had left because of disagreements with Henry. She acknowledged that Clara Parker and her two daughters were "colored people."[7]

At 12:15 P.M., Grace began to question Mrs. Willie Fields. Grace did not ask for her first name and she did not offer it. She and her husband had been married since 1933 and were the parents of six-year-old twins, a three-year-old girl, and a three-month-old baby. She acknowledged that John Warren was her adopted brother and that Henry Williams was a frequent visitor.

"Now do you recollect about two weeks ago of the old man, Henry Williams, and John Warren being at your home on Carroll St.[?]"

"Yes."

"Was there anybody else there other than who I mentioned?"

"Not at the present."

"Now did the old man, Henry Williams, make any complaint in his conversation about his son, Charlie Williams, and Charlie's wife?" Grace seemed purposefully vague, as if trying to draw a particular statement from Mrs. Fields.

"Well," Mrs. Fields answered, "he said his son wasn't treating him right."

"What else did the old man say?" Grace pressed.

"There wasn't anything else said, he was talking but I didn't understand him."

"Did the old man pass this remark and which referred to his son, Charlie, and Charlie's wife that: 'If they don't quit messing around with me that he, the old man, would let the cat out of the water'?"

"Yes, he said if Charlie didn't quit fooling with him he would let the cat out of the water."

"And did you ask the old man, Henry Williams, what he meant by 'letting the cat out of the water'[?]."

"Yes, I did."

"And what answer did the old man give to you?"

"He said about this Munson case."

"Did he mention anything else about the Munson case?"

"No, he didn't. Not to me."

"Did he mention it to anyone else that you know of?"

"No, not in my house."

"Well, John Warren was there wasn't he?"

"Yes, at the time he and I was the ones in there."

"Did the old gentleman, Henry Williams, tell you just exactly what he had on his mind about his son regarding the Munson case?"

"No, he didn't—not to me."

"Did you hear the old gentleman make the remark that there were some colored people and some white women at his son's house drinking until the early hours of the morning?"

"No I didn't hear him say it myself."

"Did you hear any remark of that kind made by anybody?"

"No, nobody made remarks but him."

"But the old man."

"Yes."

"Now is there anything you know of that the old man spoke about and that you haven't told me?"

"No."[8]

Two days later, on November 28, Det. Lt. Grace interviewed Henry Williams. Williams, seventy-nine, had lived with the Fields at 416 Carroll Avenue for the previous six weeks, after leaving his son's home. Originally from Natchitoches, Louisiana, he had been in St. Paul for a year and three months. Married once, he was the father of fourteen children. Once again, Grace skipped over the window peeping and concentrated on the recent meeting at the Fields home.

"Do you remember about two weeks ago, that you were visiting at Fields' house, that there were Mr. and Mrs. Fields, John Warren and a man by the name of Perry there?"

"Yes I do."

"And while all you folks were there, did you say that you had something on your son Charlie and his wife?"

"I said I had something on his wife," Henry Williams corrected.

"Did you pass this remark while you were at Fields' home 'that if Charlie and his wife don't quit messing around with you' you would 'let the cat out of the water'?"

"No."

"What remark did you make?"

"The remark I made was that if Charlie's wife don't let me alone I am going to tell Charlie what she does."

216 | PART 1. THE INVESTIGATION

"What does Charlie's wife do that you were going to tell on her?"

"That she's got a man."

"What do you mean by that?"

"When Charlie leaves a man comes and stays and lives with her."

"What do you mean when you say 'this man lives with her'?"

"He keeps her and has her."

"Who is this man that comes there when Charlie is gone to work?"

"I don't know him at all."

"How often have you seen him at Charlie's house?"

"Four or five times a week when she's not working."

"When you were at Fields' house with the people that I mentioned above, did you say something about the Munson murder case?"

"No I didn't."

"And did you at any time tell anybody that while you were in your bedroom while you were living with your son Charlie on Rondo Street that there were some colored men and white women in the kitchen at Charlie's house and that they were drinking till early in the morning, such as, four or five A.M. and that they were talking about the Munson Case and that someone said that Ruth Munson talked too much and that by this time that she was probably burned[?]. Did you hear anybody make that remark?"

"No."

"Did you tell anybody at Fields' house at any time while you were visiting there that you heard such a remark as this?"

"No."

"As I understand this matter," Grace summarized, "it amounts to this, that you were talking about when you were at Fields, was that you knew that someone was visiting Charlie's wife and that's what you were going to tell?"

"Yes, that's it."

"And that's the truth is it?"

"Yes, that's the truth."

"Do you remember passing a remark that you were 'going to let the cat out of the water'?"

"Yes, I said that."

"And when you said that you were 'going to let the cat out of the water,' what did you mean?"

"I meant that I was going to tell Charlie what his wife is doing."

Grace asked Henry Williams about his relationship with his son. He had come up from Louisiana to visit his son, intending to stay for only six months, but decided to remain in St. Paul.

"Do you know anything about the Munson Case?" Grace asked, returning to the subject at hand.

"No sir, I don't know anything about that."

"Can you read and write English?"

"No."

"You understand all the questions that I asked you though?"

"Yes, I understand every question you asked me."

"You have made this statement of your own free will, no threats or promises were made to you and when written up, if you could read it you would sign it. Is that correct?"

"Yes."[9]

Det. Lt. Grace had begun the six interviews hoping to confirm and expand on a set of allegations that police had assembled. He found little new information to show for his efforts. No one had acknowledged that someone within the group or from "outside of the city" had said that "Ruth Munson talked too much and by this time she was probably burned."

All six had firmly denied that Black men and white women had congregated at either the Williams or the Fields homes early on the morning of the Munson murder—or at any other time. Recognizing the gravity of the situation, Charles Williams had even claimed he would take "a death oath" while making his denial.

Were these six individuals telling the truth? There is always the possibility that the uniformity of their answers to Grace's questions was simply a byproduct of the truth. The uniformity of their testimonies could also be interpreted as a sign that they had coordinated their stories prior to the interviews.

The nature and tone of some of Grace's questions indicated he had suspicions that his witnesses were not always speaking truthfully about what they knew regarding the Munson case. "Isn't it a fact," he asked Eva Williams pointedly, "that Henry Williams, your husband's father told your husband that you and Roy Stewart and 2 white women were in the back bedroom?" While she acknowledged the accusation had been made, she denied it was true. "You are absolutely sure that there has been no white women and colored men congregating at your home at the early hours of the morning discussing the Munson case," he asked her a moment later. "I am," was the answer.

While questioning John Warren, Grace did uncover one piece of information suggesting a link to the Munson case. Warren had acknowledged that nine days before the interviews were conducted, Henry Williams had made a statement at the Fields home about having something on his son in regard to the Munson case, and that if further provoked, he would "let the cat out of the water." Warren had cited his adopted sister, Mrs. Fields, as the source of his information. In her own interview, Mrs. Fields had also acknowledged Henry Williams as the statement's author. When questioned, Henry Williams first denied then acknowledged making the comment, but he claimed it referenced Mrs. Williams "having a man" rather than it having anything to do with the Munson murder case.

Although no clear-cut evidence had been established, Warren's statement was enough for detectives to contemplate the possibility that if none of the six was actually complicit in Munson's death, at least some of them may have known something about the individuals who were.

In the wake of the interviews, no arrests were made and no charges were filed against any of the six individuals Grace questioned. But seven months later, Charles Williams would be sought in connection with another crime. The detectives who made that investigation would note on their reports an assertion by Detective James Mitchell about Charles Williams's complicity in the Munson case.

On the same day that Henry Williams was interviewed by Thomas Grace, Detectives John Baum and Darwin Morse picked up R. L. Peterson at the Sperry Realty Company and took him to the Aberdeen Hotel. The previous evening, two squads had been dispatched to investigate reports of a lantern burning on the vacant hotel's fourth floor. They found the lantern, but a search of all floors had failed to locate its owner. Two officers had noticed that on "one place on the second floor there was a small pile of plumbing fixtures that obviously had been taken from bathrooms." The lantern had been turned over to Dr. John B. Dalton to check for fingerprints. Now in the fading light of the day, Baum, Morse, and Peterson looked the place over. Peterson, the real estate agent, had no idea who had left the lantern the night before. According to him "the place looked about the same as it did about 6 weeks ago," including the pile of plumbing fixtures on the second floor. Broken windows on the upper floors were broken when he lasted visited the building, he told Baum and Morse.[10]

December arrived. On December 9, a full year had passed since Ruth Munson was murdered. Although police had made several arrests over the course of the year, no one had been charged in the case. On December 15, an anonymous citizen wrote a postcard addressed to the police department. "Dear sir," the citizen wrote. "Maybe Louis Kaufman can tell you something about the lighted lantern that was found in the Aberdeen Hotel. I seen him coming out of there. Louis Kaufman is a janitor in the State Office Building. He is a short man smooth face. I won't give my name because I don't want to mix up with the Police."[11]

This postcard—the only documented activity in the case for the month of December—also represented the last entry in Offense File 33436 for the year 1938.

19 Death Threats and Silverware

January 1–December 31, 1939

As St. Paulites prepared to ring in the new year of 1939, the stagnation of the Ruth Munson murder case and the desire to leave no stone unturned may have factored into Assistant Chief Charles J. Tierney's decision to spend New Year's weekend in Spokane, Washington, where he planned to question James Leo Smith. Smith, described as a "transient," had confessed to murdering eighteen-year-old Laura Kruse in Minneapolis in the spring of 1937. The Kruse case bore striking similarities to the murder of Ruth Munson. Minneapolis Police Captain James Mullen also made the trip to Spokane. While Mullen was questioning Smith about the Kruse murder, the suspect recanted his confession and signed a statement to that effect. His explanation for the false confession was that he did not feel safe at large, and he believed he would feel safer in an institution. Tierney fared no better when he questioned Smith about the Munson murder. Disappointed, the two men began their long train ride home from Spokane on January 3.[1]

On February 16, Police Chief Clinton Hackert received an offbeat tip in the form of a letter. The writer, Mary Connelly, claimed to have been in touch with Ruth Munson's spirit. The letter, written in a stream of consciousness and largely devoid of punctuation and capitalization, hinted at knowledge of detectives' plans to go to Duluth and the opportunities that awaited them there—according to what Ruth Munson's spirit had told her. "This is what Ruth Munson said," Connelly wrote, "you are thinking of going to Duluth to find the red haired girl—she is still at the Spaulding Hotel and you will find her there—she is afraid of that man—tell her you are a friend of mine and then she will talk— then tell her they have the man in jail—and she must come and identify him."[2]

Connelly continued; she seemed to be saying that the man in question was also responsible for the Laura Kruse murder. Additionally, she made reference to "another woman," a beauty operator, and, finally, the attack on a woman who had escaped her assailant by hiding in a cornfield. The Munson murder, the search for a redheaded woman as one of her two companions, the Kruse murder, and the case of the woman who escaped to the cornfield had all been covered extensively by the daily newspapers. Mary Connelly wrote more, but the jumble of words amounted to gibberish.

Unfortunately, Ruth Munson's spirit had neglected to tell Mary Connelly who had murdered her, but Connelly indicated that the spirit would tell her more later. Unwilling to wait, Ray Doenges, now inspector of police, dispatched Sergeant Alvin Johnson, Detective Harry O'Keefe, Patrolman Thomas Shanley, and Detective Michael Sauro to Mary Connelly's residence at 524 Ashland Avenue to investigate.

"We gave her a lot of attention and consideration," the officers' report noted, "but she refused to talk any more saying the information she had was in this letter. Miss Connelly states she would connect with the spiritual world later on and should she receive any more information that will help the police she will be glad to give it to us." The report concluded with a rare assessment: "We are of the opinion that she is slightly demented."[3]

A year and four months into the investigation, it was rare for a new suspect to emerge. In early April 1939, Olaf Anderson, Ruth Munson's old boyfriend, informed Officer Quinn that Knute Sabo had been "a former suitor or sweetheart of Ruth Munson." The assignment of investigating Sabo was given to Detectives LeRoy Tynan and Oscar Enebak. After several interviews, they learned Sabo might have left the city. They spoke to the landlady at the rooming house where Sabo had once stayed. She told the detectives that two years earlier, a former roomer had received a Christmas card Sabo had mailed from Detroit. She had heard he was now in California. "We are satisfied that Sabo was not in St. Paul at the time of Munson murder," the detectives concluded, closing the door on a potential suspect.[4]

On the morning of June 8, 1939, police received a call from Mrs. H. J. Henley, who lived in the city's prosperous Macalester-Groveland neighborhood at 1346 Goodrich Avenue. Detectives Adelard Goodrow and Axel Soderberg were dispatched to that address in answer to Mrs. Henley's complaint. The Henleys employed a maid, Eva Williams, who was separated from her husband, Charles, both of whom had been interviewed the previous November. Williams had telephoned the Henley residence at various times early in the morning and threatened Eva's life. About 9:30 A.M., he declared "he was on his way to 1346 Goodrich to do occupants bodily harm and that Mrs. Henley better not be there."

Six months had passed since Detective Lieutenant Thomas Grace questioned Eva and Charles Williams, along with four others. Williams's threats against his wife and Mrs. Henley suggested to police that he was capable of violence. Motorcycle Officer Eickhoff was dispatched to 1346 Goodrich in case Williams actually showed up. Eva Williams told Goodrow and Soderberg that she would "appear in court if needed."

At this time, Williams was a porter in a barbershop in South St. Paul. Goodrow and Soderberg contacted the South St. Paul police, and officers were dispatched to detain him. At 1:03 P.M., Goodrow and Soderberg drove to South St. Paul, picked up Williams, and transported him to St. Paul headquarters. Detective Lieutenant Ray McCarthy ordered him to be placed on the holdbook for suspicion of a threat.

When Soderberg wrote up the duo's report about their day's work, almost as an afterthought he added a cryptic comment at the bottom: "According to Det. Mitchell, Ruth Munson was supposed to be at this Charles Williams' house the night she was murdered."[5]

Like an iceberg whose bulk lies beneath the surface, Soderberg's enigmatic comment hints that many important details about the Munson case lie below the surface and out of sight, never recorded in police reports or reported in the daily newspapers. Detective James Mitchell was the Black detective whose investigative efforts had debunked Eugene Dickerson's tale about overhearing two women say that another woman, assumed by Dickerson to be Ruth Munson, had "heard too much" and "Blackie" had to do away with her. The previous November, Mitchell had arrested Henry Williams for window peeping, possibly touching off the investigation of the Williams and Fields households. (Ironically, he was not involved in questioning the six individuals who were subsequently brought to police headquarters for interrogation.)[6]

What else did Mitchell know about the Munson case? Was he the source of the allegation about the early morning meeting where the participants said Ruth Munson knew too much and by this time she was probably burned? Common sense indicated that Ruth wasn't present for that alleged conversation. How did Mitchell reach the extraordinary conclusion that Ruth Munson was in the Williams home the night she was murdered? That meant she would have been at the Williams house earlier, but when? Was it before she went to the Ace with her two friends, or was it afterward—sometime in the early part of the seven-hour time gap?

Mitchell was plugged into daily life in St. Paul's Black community. While checking out Dickerson's story, he had talked to the Black pimps in St. Paul and Minneapolis, suggesting that in addition to his street knowledge, his work on the morals squad brought him familiarity with the underworld where prostitution thrived. Was his assertion about

Ruth's presence in Charles Williams's house a product of his ability to work his connections in the Rondo community? Or did he somehow arrive at this conclusion as a result of the statements given by Charles Williams and the five others in November of 1938?

The fact that Grace never asked any of the six people he questioned about Ruth's presence in the Williams home suggests Mitchell had yet to make his assertion when those interviews occurred.

Mitchell himself never committed his claim to writing. Among the rank and file, at least Soderberg and Woodrow were aware of Mitchell's claim. It remains unclear how widely known Mitchell's assertion was among the police department's leadership—and how much credibility they gave it. A copy of Soderberg's report containing his comment about Mitchell's assertion went to Chief Hackert. Two copies went to Assistant Chief Tierney. Additional copies were distributed to other departments. No report documenting further action taken by police against Charles Williams after he threatened his wife and Mrs. Henley was added to the Ruth Munson file. It is possible that further action taken against Williams was detailed in a different offense file.

Charles Williams was never charged in relation to the Ruth Munson murder case. Detective James Mitchell retired from the force on August 22, 1939, at the age of sixty-two.

In late October 1939, Patrolmen Stanley Pehoski and Rueben Halvorson investigated three separate leads, reporting their findings to Det. Lt. Thomas Grace, who in recent months appeared to be the point person of the investigation. Pehoski and Halvorson, new to the Munson investigation, alternated writing up their reports. Halvorson had a tendency to substitute a plus sign for the word "and." Pehoski habitually misspelled his partner's last name as "Halvarson."[7]

The first lead the two patrolmen investigated touched on Ruth's secret life: a rumor that a Black man had purchased a set of silverware at the Emporium department store to give to Ruth Munson. If it checked out, establishing the identity of the man who made the purchase might lead police to her killer.

Sometime around October 23 or 24, the two patrolmen went to the Emporium. "Checking the sale of silver ware at the Emporium to Ruth Munson, we found it (the silverware) was purchased Feb. 9, 1935 on a contract + paid up June 20, 1935." At the time of purchase, the address for Ruth Munson was listed as 535 Ashland Avenue, an apartment building previously not associated with her. "Munson's signature was at the bottom of the contract," Patrolman Halvorson wrote in his report, a fact which seems to contradict the rumor that the purchase was made by a Black man.[8]

The silverware was not taken out of the store until September 5, 1936. The delivery address was listed as 265 Dayton Avenue, where Ruth lived prior to moving to 276 Dayton. The officers determined that she had rented an apartment at 265 Dayton Avenue on September 4, 1935, and moved May 1, 1936, leaving no forwarding address.

Emporium clerks working at the time of the sale and subsequent delivery of the silverware were unable to recall any details about the transactions. "We were informed late this evening that we could contact Mrs. Messer through 'George' who can be reached in a drug store at Rice + Summit," Halvorson wrote. Halvorson did not mention what Mrs. Messer's connection was to the issue at hand, but it later became obvious she had repeated the rumor, and perhaps even started it.[9]

On or about October 25, 1939, Pehoski and Halvorson interviewed Messer at her home at 255 Iglehart Avenue. "We questioned Mrs. Messer closely on the statement that she made in effect, that a woman clerk at the Emporium had sold a set of silverware to a negro man," Pehoski wrote in a follow-up report, noting the silverware "was to be sent to Ruth Munson 276 Dayton." "Mrs. Messer denied ever having made such a statement to anyone," Pehoski noted. "She said she had heard rumors that Ruth had been out with Negros but that was all."

Under further questioning, Messer said she had seen Ruth Munson at a dance hall on West Seventh Street "a great many times." She had also seen her at the Dutch House "in the company of three girls." For about a year, she had seen Ruth at dances "in the company of the same man." When asked for a description of the man, she was "vague and rather elusive," Pehoski noted. Messer conceded that she had danced with the man several times and thought his name was "Billy" or "Bergland." She described the man as "28 years, 6 feet 160# slender build, very blond. Neat dresser spoke with foreign accent. Probably Scandinavian." Throughout the interview, Pehoski observed, Messer was "very nervous" and "seemed reluctant to give information which would reveal this man's whereabouts, if he was wanted." Unsatisfied with Messer's answers, the patrolmen made arrangements to talk with Pearl Bacigalupo, who, the officers discovered, had heard Messer make the statement about the silverware purchase.[10]

About October 26 or 27, Pehoski and Halvorson returned to the Emporium, hoping to view shipping records to gain additional information about the silverware purchase, but Miss Freize, who headed the silverware department, had not completed her records check. The two men drove to the home of Pearl and Louie Bacigalupo. Both Pearl and her husband had heard Messer say she had danced with Ruth Munson, something she had denied when she was initially questioned. Pearl Bacigalupo also said that "Mrs. Messer told her distinctly that a negro had purchased a set of silverware at the Emporium, placing the order for delivery to Ruth Munson on Dayton Ave."

According to the Bacigalupos, after Pehoski and Halvorson had questioned Mrs. Messer on or about October 25, she came over to their home "very excited over being questioned by police and tried to figure out how the police had gotten her name." At the end of this report, Pehoski noted they had not yet contacted Mrs. Messer for further questioning. He also attached to his report a picture of a spoon showing the silverware pattern.[11]

Sometime after visiting the Bacigalupo home, Pehoski and Halvorson returned to 255 Iglehart to question Mrs. Messer further. Her story was different. During her first interview on October 25, there had been no question that she had seen Ruth Munson at dances. Now she said "she didn't think it was the same girl." Later she changed her story again, saying it *was* Ruth. In the first interview, she said she had seen Ruth about four months before the murder. Now she said she hadn't seen her since about 1930 at the Dutch House, which, according to Pehoski, didn't have a rathskeller for women until 1933 or 1934. Throughout the interview, Mrs. Messer's husband continuously interrupted the officers, anxious to end the interview and send them on their way.

"It is our belief," Pehoski concluded, "that regardless of whether this woman really has any information of value to this case, she evidently seems to fear that she has talked to[o] much or said something which she should not have."[12]

Pehoski and Halvorson returned to the Emporium on October 27. They checked again with the shipping department, and also the auditing and credit departments, for a sales slip documenting the silverware purchase. "We were finally informed that a Mrs. Barnes has charge of a vault in which original sales slip are kept for a period of six years," Halvorson wrote in their report. "Mrs. Barnes is ill + is not expected to return to work until sometime next week."[13]

Thwarted once again, the officers began to check out a second lead about two women, Irene Hammer and Myrtle Simonson, believed to be acquaintances of Ruth Munson. They interviewed Adeline Moen, twenty-one years old, a beauty operator on St. Paul's East Side. Moen knew the two women well, but she was not sure how well they knew Ruth Munson. She was quite sure, however, that Hammer and Simonson were "steppers." "Myrtle Simonson went out with married men + Irene Hammer would go out with anyone that would ask her," Halvorson noted. "Irene would monkey around the negro porters at the bus depot. One negro named 'George' in particular." When the officers asked Moen if the two women "would go out with negros," her answer was "she wouldn't put it past them." Both women were believed to frequent the Friendship Club.

Shortly after the murder of Ruth Munson, the two women had left town. Myrtle Simonson returned to her hometown of Coral, Wisconsin, "to stay." Irene Hammer left St. Paul about the same time. She was believed to be in Ironwood, Minnesota, staying with a sister.[14]

Pehoski and Halverson were unfamiliar with the investigation's countless details, which may be the reason they missed a potential opportunity to advance the case. The two women's departure from the city shortly after the murder should have made them candidates for further investigation. Were these the women who had accompanied Ruth to the Ace on the last night of her life? If the two officers further investigated Myrtle Simonson and Irene Hammer, they failed to record their findings.

Around the time Pehoski and Halvorson were investigating these two leads, they took up a third one. Sometime before October 30, Halvorson and Pehoski interviewed Bernice Berglund. They learned she was a pupil of Ruth Munson's when Munson taught school at Trade Lake, Wisconsin. At Trade Lake, Ruth had become friends with Edla Peterson, now Mrs. Floyd Fleming. Both of these women later moved to the Twin Cities in search of new opportunities. Bernice Berglund took a position at St. Luke's Hospital in St. Paul.[15]

Why Pehoski and Halvorson undertook an investigation of Bernice Berglund and Edla Peterson and what they hoped to learn from them in respect to the Munson investigation was not addressed in their report, but they soon abandoned their effort. Perhaps they had learned that it duplicated information established in January 1938 by Detectives Boyd Carrier and Frank Kennedy. Their interest in Bernice Berglund (they spelled her first name Vernice) was related to the fact that she was a redhead, something Pehoski and Halvorson seemed to have missed.[16]

Pehoski and Halvorson did no further work on the case. If they ever returned to the Emporium and secured a sales slip or shipping document confirming the silverware transaction and shipment to Ruth Munson, they did not mention it in their reports. None of their reports contained information that confirmed a Black man had purchased silverware at the Emporium or who that individual was. All six of the reports they made addressing the three leads they investigated were handwritten, usually directed to Det. Lt. Grace. No copies appear to have been made to distribute to Chief Hackert and Assistant Chief Tierney, suggesting that after almost two years of dead ends, the investigation had taken a back seat to other police work. For the rest of the year, the Ruth Munson case was dormant.

January 1, 1940–September 4, 1953

When the minute hand on the clock clicked to 12:01 A.M. on January 1, 1940, the unsolved Ruth Munson case extended into a second decade. Detectives remained unable to unravel the mysteries of motive, means, and opportunity in such a way that identified her killer. Motive remained a mystery. Had she been randomly attacked on the street as she walked home in the dark hours of the night? Had someone killed her as an act of revenge? Had she been silenced because she knew too much? It was generally believed she had been killed by an acquaintance. The destruction of the crime scene by an intentionally set fire and the efforts of the firemen to extinguish the blaze made it difficult to determine the means of her death, but it was believed she was bludgeoned. Quite probably she had also received a postmortem blow to the head from a fireman's implement. The lateness of the hour and darkness had provided the killer or killers an opportunity to escort, force, or carry her into the Aberdeen and up to the second floor without being seen.

The theory that Ruth Munson had died at the hands of an acquaintance was most likely in Police Chauffeur Arthur Stattman's mind when he drafted a note to Assistant Chief Charles J. Tierney on February 15, 1940. Stattman had been to the hospital the previous evening to visit another officer who "gave me the following information to give to you in regard to the Munson murder." A man with worker tag number 713 at Ford Motor Company "lived at 242 or 246 Dayton next door to where Ruth Munson lived before the crime." The unidentified man had formerly lived in Grantsburg, Wisconsin, Ruth's hometown, but "denies that he knows her. Some time after the crime he was supposed to have made a trip to that town and during the time he was there he traded in his Ford car for a Buick."[1]

A hometown in common and a car traded off shortly after the murder was enough to make the man a potential suspect. But it took more than a month for anyone to investigate. When they did, they were thorough. Patrolman Louis Schultz and Detectives Fred Nielsen and James Mathiesen researched the tip extensively. They tracked down the identify of Ford employee number 713, Benjamin Branstad, and learned that he worked day shifts on December 8 and 9, 1937. They traced his apartments through fourteen years of St. Paul city directories, then visited six different addresses to see what information they could dig up. They learned of his marriage and divorce, located his nephew, and checked out his automobile, a light brown 1937 Ford Delux touring sedan. It appeared Stattman's information that Branstad had traded a Ford for a Buick shortly after the murder was incorrect. They checked for records of his wife Alice Branstad with the Ramsey County Welfare Board, the Works Progress Administration, the St. Paul postal inspector, and the Ramsey County Recorder's Office.[2]

Why Nielsen and Mathiesen were so interested in Benjamin and Alice Branstad is unclear. Throughout their investigation, they do not appear to have talked directly to either one of them. Other than some discord in their marriage, investigators had failed to uncover any suspicious information about the couple. They had not exposed any links between either of the Branstads and Ruth Munson that could be considered a motive to commit murder.

No further reports were filed on the Munson case over the remaining nine months of the year. The year 1940 closed on a sad note. Detective Lieutenant Bertram Talbot, age sixty-five, died December 28, without seeing a solution to the Munson case.[3]

On April 2, 1941, the Ramsey County Board of Commissioners announced they were withdrawing their $200 reward. Three years and four months had passed since the murder. The announcement appeared to have little impact at police headquarters. For all practical purposes, the case was dormant.[4]

One person who had not abandoned the case was the man directing the investigation, Assistant Police Chief Charles J. Tierney. Along with Police Chief Clinton Hackert, Tierney had been key in reforming the police department back in 1936. Under his watch, the investigation had not succeeded in identifying Munson's killer, a failure he no doubt took personally. On increasingly rare occasions, law enforcement officials from other districts forwarded information to St. Paul authorities about a man in their custody who might be a suspect in the Munson case. It was Tierney who either made the trip to the other jurisdiction to question the suspect or questioned the suspect if he was transferred to St. Paul.

Such was the case on two occasions in 1941. In mid-May, from a Hennepin County jail cell, thirty-year-old Willis Huntsberger confessed to the July 13, 1940, murder of fourteen-year-old Mary Jane Massey at

Fort Snelling. His confession came after he was convicted of attacking a different woman in the restroom of a Minneapolis theater. Prior to that, Huntsberger had been jailed in relation to a dozen cases in Minnesota and other states. In Hennepin County's custody, he had cut his wrists with a broken light bulb.

On Wednesday, May 14, Tierney along with a Minneapolis detective and an FBI agent questioned Huntsberger for two hours "about the torch murder of pretty Ruth Munson in St. Paul more than three years ago," as the *St. Paul Pioneer Press* put it. When showed a picture of the Aberdeen, the suspect admitted he recognized the building by its fire escape, a perceived entry point of the killer. According to the paper, "Tierney and the other officers were not satisfied with the results of the questioning."[5]

Despite his confession, Hennepin County authorities were skeptical of Huntsberger's guilt in the Massey murder. Huntsberger's "mania for sex crime literature," authorities believed, caused him "to concoct stories involving himself in such crimes." There was equal skepticism about Huntsberger being Ruth Munson's slayer. Nevertheless, Tierney made plans to take Huntsberger to the Aberdeen Hotel and monitor his reaction, as he had done with Charles Moore.[6]

Whether Tierney followed through on his plan to walk his suspect through the Aberdeen is unknown, but his inclination to do so indicated the assistant chief was still dedicated to solving the case. It also suggested that no decision had been reached about the guilt of any previously questioned suspect who had not been charged for lack of proof that would stand up in court.

Six months later, Tierney made a trip to Balsam Lake in Polk County, Wisconsin, to question yet another suspect. A twenty-four-year-old filling station attendant had been arrested on November 25, 1941, in connection with the kidnapping and beating of a young woman in the nearby town of Amery, Wisconsin. The next day, Tierney and Ramsey County Attorney James F. Lynch joined Polk County Sheriff James Moore in questioning the suspect about both the Amery and Munson cases. The three men questioned the suspect "for several hours." He confessed to the Amery attack, but denied that he knew Ruth Munson or had anything to do with her death. He admitted, however, that he had been working in Minneapolis around the time of the murder.[7]

The new suspect revived press interest in the nearly four-year-old Munson case. Once again, the dailies emphasized the sensational aspect of the case. TORCH MURDER SUSPECT MET ST. PAUL GIRL VIC-

TIM, POLICE SAY blared the headline in the *Minneapolis Star-Journal.* According to the paper, Police Chief Hackert "asserted the man met Miss Munson while she lived at Grantsburg, Wis., before she came to St. Paul to work as a waitress in the union depot." This probably was a bit of exaggeration on Hackert's part. Ruth had left Grantsburg about 1928, when she was twenty-two. That year, the suspect would have been about twelve. Hackert also claimed the suspect had been under surveillance since the Munson slaying, though he offered no details. That, too, may have been an exaggeration. Coincidentally, Ruth's sister, Helen, was a schoolteacher in Amery. After carefully questioning the suspect, Tierney "was satisfied" that he "had no connection with the torch slaying of Ruth Munson."[8]

Two weeks after the Balsam Lake suspect was questioned, Japanese planes attacked the US naval base at Pearl Harbor and the United States was drawn into the global war. Although the Munson investigation remained dormant, the unsolved murder came to mind with each new case where a woman was the victim. Each new suspect in those cases was viewed as a potential suspect in the Munson murder case. In October 1942, George Schubert Knapp, a former inmate of the St. Peter State Hospital, was arrested and charged with murder in Bastrop, Texas. The Knapp family home was in Stillwater, Minnesota. During the time he was an army private at Fort Snelling, Knapp was involved in the theft of an airplane at nearby Wold-Chamberlain Field. Knapp's Texas arrest and his St. Paul area connections made him a potential suspect in the murder of Ruth Munson, as well as the murders of Laura Kruse and Mary Jane Massey. How extensively Knapp was investigated for these murders is unknown.[9]

On July 30, 1943, Police Chief Clinton Hackert died at the age of forty-six. He had been in ill health for about three months. A sixteen-year veteran of the force at the time of his appointment, Hackert had been chief for seven years. He had led the department through an extraordinary period of transformation. In announcing his death, the *St. Paul Pioneer Press* noted, "He was given much of the credit for cleaning up St. Paul and for bringing its police force to its present high standard of efficiency and courtesy." Public Safety Commissioner Gustave H. Barfuss, who had appointed Hackert, cited the "national recognition" Hackert had brought to the department, noting that "his sincere and untiring efforts . . . will remain a monument to him for years to come."

Hackert himself credited his success to "freedom from politics in the police department." Unfortunately, the department's "high standard of efficiency and courtesy" had not brought about a resolution of the Munson case. But Hackert's passing was a time for lauding his considerable accomplishments, and there was no mention of the painful fact that Ruth Munson's murder remained unsolved. Assistant Chief Charles J. Tierney was appointed acting chief and given the position permanently on September 1, 1943.[10]

Demolition of the Aberdeen Hotel, "once a fashionable St. Paul apartment hotel and home of Minnesota governors and supreme court justices," began on February 1, 1944. In marking the occasion, the *Minneapolis Morning Tribune* reminded readers that the hotel "was the scene in 1937 of the still unsolved slaying of Miss Ruth Munson."[11]

During the demolition, the "Aberdeen Hotel Jinx" claimed two more victims. On August 17, as demolition crews worked on the sixth floor, workman Leo Christianson was buried "in a cavein [sic] of old bricks and plaster." Christianson was freed from the rubble, but possible fractures of his left hip and left leg prevented rescue workers from moving him until his injuries were stabilized. The sixth floor could only be reached by ladders. Police Surgeon Dr. George Crossette began climbing to apply the splints, but when he reached the second floor, he fell and landed on a pile of bricks. Crossette suffered a back injury and was transported to St. Luke's Hospital. Dr. Maurice Weisberg was summoned and successfully made the climb to the sixth floor, where he treated Christianson. With considerable difficulty, rescue crews were finally able to lower Christianson's stretcher to the ground. Immediately following the incident, hospital attendants described the condition of Crossette and Christianson as "only fair." In reporting on the incident, the *Morning Tribune* reminded readers for a final time that the hotel "was the scene of one of St. Paul's most brutal murders." In lurid detail, the paper once again described how the "pretty waitress" had been "bludgeoned to death" and her body found "under a heap of blazing rubbish," the victim of an unsolved crime. The demolition of the hotel continued without further incident.[12]

Two officers who logged many hours on the case died in 1945. On March 21, Detective Lieutenant Nate Smith, who had taken statements from many witnesses and suspects at police headquarters and later out in the field, died at the age of forty-seven. Smith had been in ill health for about two years, but he had remained active on the force. On October 8, Detective Frank Kennedy died after suffering a heart attack. At the time of his death, he was forty-eight years old and served as vice commander of the city's fourth district. Beginning with the report on the discovery of Ruth Munson's body in the Aberdeen, he and his partner Detective Boyd Carrier had filed at least forty-nine investigative reports connected to the case. With Patrolman James Cook, the team had filed an additional fourteen reports. Kennedy had also filed solo reports and a handful of reports with other officers. The loss of Smith and Kennedy robbed the investigation of a warehouse of knowledge about the case.[13]

On December 10, 1946, the Minneapolis Police Department forwarded on its letterhead a retyped letter, dated December 6, that had been sent to the department by the Richland County Attorney's Office in Sidney, Montana. "We have in custody in Richland County, Montana at Sidney, a man by the name of George (Goldie) Adams," wrote Milton C. Anderson, the county attorney. "We picked him up on a second degree assault charge [and] I write to you to find out whether you have within your knowledge or the records of your office the unsolved murder of a blond woman, who might have been murdered in a Minneapolis hotel or rooming house six or seven years ago, in 1939 or 1940." While in "an intoxicated condition" the suspect had "made remarks suggesting that he possibly had been implicated in some such affair in Minneapolis."

The suspect, Anderson wrote, denied ever having been in trouble in Minneapolis. He admitted to working in a lumber camp near Rice Lake, but Anderson did not specify whether it was Rice Lake, Minnesota, or Rice Lake, Wisconsin. While in custody, Adams had attempted suicide and "almost succeeded." Milton wondered why one would attempt suicide for second-degree assault and then answered his own question: "We have come to the conclusion that there must be something else in his past from which he is attempting to escape."

"This inquiry is strictly a shot-in-the-dark," Anderson acknowledged, "but we felt that the hearsay information which we heard regarding so serious an offense would, I am sure, warrant bringing the matter to your attention." He closed the letter with a request that Minneapolis authorities forward any information they may have "on the above suggested matter."[14]

On the same day Tierney received the retyped letter from the Minneapolis Police Department—nine years and one day after the murder of

Ruth Munson was discovered—the police chief wrote a letter to Anderson. He noted that the Minneapolis Police Department had forwarded a copy of the letter to the St. Paul department. He described the vacant Aberdeen Hotel, the fire, and the discovery of "a body of a woman who had been murdered by a fiend." Tierney described Ruth Munson as "a blond who was employed as a waitress at our Union Depot Restaurant and spent most of her nights dancing in various public dance halls." In point of fact, pictures of Ruth Munson showed that she was dark haired, and none of the investigation's documents mention that she had dyed her hair.

Summing up years of frustration with the case, Tierney conceded, "Although we have investigated hundreds of leads and clues, this murder is unsolved." He ended his letter with an appeal: "I would be grateful if you would question George Adams to determine whether or not he is implicated in this murder, and wire me the results of your endeavors."[15]

As a matter of professional courtesy, it is likely the Richland County Attorney's Office or the Sidney police carried out Tierney's request, questioned Adams, and later reported the results. Any reply Tierney may have received was not placed in the Munson file.

As the years passed, the press evoked the unsolved Ruth Munson case while covering similar cases involving vulnerable women on St. Paul's streets. On August 9, 1948, thirteen-year-old Juanita Wendel disappeared after leaving her home in the West Seventh Street neighborhood. The very next day, August 10, Geraldine Mingo, seventeen years old, was raped and murdered in the Highland Park neighborhood, where she worked as a domestic. There was immediate speculation but no evidence that the murders of these two young women were related. In reporting the Geraldine Mingo story, the *Minneapolis Star* noted that the vicious murder resembled both the unsolved Ruth Munson and Laura Kruse murders. Immediately following the Mingo murder, the *St. Paul Pioneer Press* and *St. Paul Dispatch* offered a $1,000 reward for information leading to "the arrest and conviction of the slayer." A month after Wendel disappeared, her body was discovered in Dakota County. Like the Munson case, neither of these cases were solved.[16]

In 1949, veteran detective Boyd Carrier died. Carrier had partnered with Frank Kennedy in the first few months of the case, later adding Patrolman James Cook to their team. After the Ruth Munson murder, Carrier had also worked on other murder cases involving young women. On April 16, 1948, he had resigned from the department to go on pension. Carrier died on May 26, 1949, one month shy of his fifty-seventh birthday.[17]

On May 30, 1952, Memorial Day, Police Chief Charles J. Tierney suffered a heart attack at home and died at the age of fifty-five. He had directed the Munson investigation from its beginning. Appointed in 1943 to succeed Clinton Hackert, Tierney served nine years as chief. Often during those years, he had questioned potential Munson suspects himself, indicating that the lack of a solution in the case troubled him. Although Tierney "had an occasionally stormy career," noted the *Morning Tribune*, he was "highly regarded as a law enforcement official." Ramsey County Sheriff Thomas J. Gibbons described Tierney as "one of the world's greatest detectives and a great chief of police. His cooperation with my sheriff's department and with other communities made St. Paul and the Northwest a greater place in which to live."[18]

A year and three months after Tierney's death, the Ruth Munson murder case surfaced again. In the late afternoon on September 2, Detectives Oran Stutzman and Melvin Plummer were dispatched to a downtown location to meet Officer Biagi. Biagi was holding fifty-nine-year-old Albert Legrand, who had been detained by citizens. Legrand had written "Ger. Mingo. I killed her" on the deodorizer in the men's room at the Roundup Bar. On the urinal he had written "Ruth Monson [sic] I killed her." According to Detective Plummer's report, "Legrand had a paper bag in his possession with writing in ink [saying] Ruth Monson, I killed her and that awful girl, I was in love with."

Any confession to a murder merited investigation. The detectives took Legrand to headquarters and questioned him. Legrand claimed the writing on the urinal, the deodorizer, and the bag were doodles. Legrand admitted, Plummer wrote, that he might "have wrote Geraldine Mingo or some of our other girl murders as well as Munson." Legrand said he was a reader of *True Detective Stories* and the magazine may have given him "ideas."

The detectives determined that Legrand had lived in St. Paul since 1915, originally working as a railroad fireman. He later hired out in the harvest fields of Minnesota and North Dakota. In 1944, he started working as a pinsetter and at the time of his arrest worked at Harkins Bowling. When Ruth Munson was murdered, Legrand was living at the St. Regis Hotel on West Kellogg Boulevard. He remembered the Ruth Munson murder because of the "talk of cab drivers in [the] Venice Café at the time."

The detectives put Legrand on the holdbook for suspicion of murder. Pictures of the writing on the urinal, the bag, and the pens he used were tagged and turned into the Bureau of Records. Copies of Plummer's report were sent to Police Chief Neal McMahon, Inspector Mondike, the Homicide Division, the Identification Division, the Property Room, and Records.[19]

Two days later, Dr. Leo O. Burr questioned Legrand about writing on restroom walls. Legrand admitted he wrote on walls when he was under the influence of liquor. "In view of evidence of inmate's writing abnormal things [I] believe psychitric [sic] consultation would be advisable," Dr. Burr concluded.[20]

The two reports about Albert Legrand dated September 2 and September 4, 1953, were the last reports filed in Offense File 33436.

At some point in the years that followed, the records associated with Offense 33436 were gathered together in a single box large enough to fill most of a file drawer. It contains multiple copies of police reports—115 statements made by suspects, witnesses, and Ruth Munson's acquaintances, plus over 500 miscellaneous reports—filed between December 9, 1937, and September 4, 1953. It contains photos of the crime scene and other locations associated with the crime, various lists that detectives consulted, letters bearing tips sent by citizens and other law enforcement agencies, and a few newspaper clippings. And it contains Ruth Munson's personal materials: her gold-embossed five-year diary, her green address book, some letters she wrote, and some letters she had received.

The box was kept in the Records Division at the Public Safety Building at 100 East Eleventh Street until 2003, when it was moved to the St. Paul Police Department's new headquarters at 376 Grove Street.

Unsolved murder cases are never closed. They only grow cold.

Part 2

Autopsy:
Why the Ruth Munson Case Was Never Solved

21 A Lack of Evidence and a Number of Theories

A surprising amount of information is embedded in the Munson case file's reports, statements, letters, and other documents. Yet for all that these documents reveal about the case, an equally surprising amount of essential information is missing. It is likely that key aspects of the case were investigated and never recorded in reports, and that individuals were questioned at headquarters and no formal statement taken.

In making these reports, investigators stuck to basic facts. They advanced no theories about the crime in terms of motive, means, and opportunity. Generally, they did not assess in writing the credibility of the people they interviewed. At the administrative level, the men who directed the investigation—including Police Chief Clinton Hackert, Assistant Chief Charles J. Tierney, and those in supervisory roles who gave detectives their daily assignments—seldom filed reports documenting their activities. Though contemporary newspaper accounts on occasion quoted Hackert or Tierney, the papers seldom recorded how and why these men made administrative decisions about what and whom they would investigate.

As a result, the historical record contains many blank spots. A twenty-first-century police investigator reading this account might argue that *of course* the detectives would have checked further into this clue or that one—but we know for sure only what detectives wrote in their reports, and that is what we must use to evaluate the investigation.

Nevertheless, the historical record offers enough information to allow an examination of the reasons why investigators never unraveled the mysteries surrounding Ruth Munson's life and death. No single reason dominates. Like a set of gears, one small reason turns another, larger reason, which rotates yet another. In searching for a motive, for example, detectives encountered a wide range of human behaviors which turned on peoples' emotions—fear for their safety, fear of being caught and punished, embarrassment at being discovered—all emotions that were themselves turned by something even larger—the social and cultural mores of the day, their own racial prejudices. Thus, when interviewed by police, witnesses and suspects withheld information. When one witness directly contradicted another, someone was lying about their activities and their relationship with Ruth Munson.

In the end, everything became connected, and with every gear turning, detectives were unable to answer the fundamental questions about the murder—motive, means, and opportunity—that would lead them to the killer.

From the outset, the investigation was hamstrung by a lack of physical evidence. Both the fire and the work of the firemen wreaked havoc on the body of the victim and the area around it, making it difficult to determine the exact cause of death and to find traces of evidence associated with her killer. Further, doors and windows of the Aberdeen were broken by the firemen, making it impossible to determine for certain how the killer, or killers, entered.

The only physical evidence that emerged from twelve bushels of debris scooped up by detectives were three brass shear bins. It was always assumed by investigators that the shear pins were dropped by the killer. Investigators were unable to link the pins to Willard Wolf or any other suspect. In reality, the pins were a marginal piece of evidence. The hotel had stood vacant for eleven years, and scavengers and adventurers had roamed its rooms and hallways. It was quite possible the pins were dropped by one of these trespassers years before the murder occurred.

Detectives also traced Ruth Munson's activities in the hope that clues would begin to emerge. The logical place to begin was the Ace Box Lunch, where Ruth was last seen alive on Wednesday, December 8. Detectives were faced with the task of closing the approximately seven-hour gap between her departure from the Ace between 11:30 P.M. and midnight and 7:00 the next morning, when the fire alarm for the Aberdeen was called in.

The most likely sources of information, of course, were Ruth Munson's two friends, said by bartenders and patrons to frequently accompany her. At the outset, detectives assumed Ruth's companions were close friends. What happened after the three women left the Ace? Did they split up? If so, where and when? Or did they remain together? Did they take the streetcar or have access to an automobile? Did they catch a ride with someone? Were the three women still together when Ruth encountered her killer? Ultimately, none of these questions were answered because the women were never identified.

Why didn't the women come forward? One witness reported having heard that the two women worked at Miller Hospital and hospital administrators sent them out of town to avoid negative publicity by keeping them from being questioned by police. According to the *Min-*

neapolis Journal, police attributed the women's silence to their concern about their reputations. Mayor Mark E. Gehan and Assistant Chief Tierney, the paper noted, "promised to do all in their power to protect the young women from publicity, if fear of publicity in connection with their presence in a tavern has motivated their silence." In other words, concern for their reputation as respectable women in the community kept them silent.[1]

More likely, after learning about their friend's horrific fate, or possibly even bearing witness to her death, the two women were fearful for their own safety. Were these two women among the white women police believed to have gathered with Black men in the home of Charles Williams or William Fields on the night of the murder? If the murder was a spontaneous crime committed by one individual, then once the killer was caught, he would be off the streets, unable to cause the women harm. The women's silence suggested something larger was afoot.

When the women did not immediately come forward, detectives went looking for them, questioning Ruth Munson's friends and escorting several other women to the Ace for possible identification by bartenders Fred Meyer and Gus Gavanda. On at least one occasion, Meyer accompanied detectives to the Friendship Club in Minneapolis in the hopes that he would spot the two women among the crowd.

Detectives were unable to learn more about the three women enquiring about a room for rent near the Ace, or the three women whose car bumped the parked car of an Ace patron sometime after 11:00 P.M. If, however, the women in the car were this trio, it suggests they left the Ace by car. Ruth did not own an automobile, so if verified, the clue added a facet to detectives' search for the two women: one of the companions owned or had access to an automobile.[2]

In retrospect, it seems incredible that police were never able to identify Ruth's friends. Investigators often withheld key information from the press and the general public. It could be argued that detectives knew who the two women were but withheld the information to protect them and avoid tipping off the killer. But the files indicate this was not the case. For months after the murder, detectives investigated different pairs of women and on occasion individual women, in particular women with red hair—only to determine they had credible alibis, or to hear witnesses say they were not the women they saw. If the identities were known to police, they would not have expended time and resources investigating additional women.

Even without having the identities of Ruth's two companions, detectives uncovered plenty of tantalizing clues about the seven hours between Ruth's departure from the Ace and the discovery of the fire at the Aberdeen. These can be organized in chronological order, although some of the clues overlap in time or crowd the time of known events.

The first of these clues involves the Aberdeen Hotel. Christian Christianson, walking home from work at 12:30 A.M., saw a man near a "new dark coach or sedan" on the Virginia Street side of the Aberdeen. When the man grumbled about having to wait, Christianson laughed and said, "It's kind of cold to have to wait for your girlfriend," and the man snapped at him. If Ruth and her companions left the Ace as early as 11:30, they would have had ample time to arrive near the Aberdeen. In this scenario, Ruth would have already been taken into the Aberdeen, and the man was keeping watch outside. The waiting man was never identified.[3]

Another clue suggested a different scenario. From the Ace, did the three women make their way to the 38 Club in downtown St. Paul, a place mentioned in Ruth's diary? At about 1:00 A.M., three women there allowed three men to buy them drinks. One of the women took a cab driven by "Boss" to 282 Dayton Avenue, near Ruth's building. A man whom the team of Detective Ralph Merrill and Patrolmen Schultz and Stanley baselessly believed fit the description of head porter Robert Brown, a Black man who was a friend of Ruth's, emerged from her building, declined the cabdriver's offer to take him somewhere, and disappeared into the night. In this scenario, the three men may have figured in Ruth's death.[4]

Numerous clues about the time gap involve Dayton Avenue. Several residents of the Ramsey Hill neighborhood told detectives they heard a scream or screams along that street in the middle of the night. Some of the reports originated near 276 Dayton, where Ruth lived. Others were closer to the Aberdeen Hotel, two blocks west. The estimated times varied, but the range approximately covered the period from 1:30 to 4:00 A.M.[5]

Despite multiple leads, detectives were never able to track any reported scream to its source. No other incidents involving a nighttime scream were reported to police or identified by detectives. Though concrete proof is lacking, it is probable these screams are connected to the crime. At 276 Dayton, Ruth could have been abducted and forced into an automobile, accounting for the screams near that address. The screams near the Aberdeen, less than a quarter of a mile away, could be attributed to her being forced into the hotel against her will.

This scenario of abduction by automobile gained credibility through numerous reports of vehicles present at both locations within approximately the same time range as the scream reports. Different witnesses identified different makes, model years, even colors for the cars. Comparing the different car descriptions yielded no standout, detailed description. The files indicate that detectives took the clues about cars very seriously. Unlike the scream that broke the night and was gone in a heartbeat, the car was a physical object that could be traced. Ruth's former boyfriends, her male friends, and the potential suspects were all asked what make, model, and year of car they drove. None of their answers sparked action by detectives when compared to witnesses' descriptions of the cars.

The abduction scenario temporarily gained further credence with the discovery of a broken bracelet lying in the snow in front of 450 Dayton Avenue, a block and a half west of the Aberdeen, but the lead dissolved when a woman in the neighborhood claimed ownership of the bracelet and Ruth Munson's own bracelet was found at her parents' Grantsburg home.[6]

The gates leading to the gardens behind the Aberdeen provided another tantalizing clue to detectives trying to close the seven-hour gap. At 5:14 A.M., paperboy Stephen Westbrook walked by the gates at the beginning of his deliveries and remembered the gates were closed. He remembered the gates being open when he finished his route at 5:45 A.M. A woman walking down Virginia Street on her way to the streetcar stop on Selby Avenue noticed the gates were open at 5:40 A.M. These observations suggested the killers entered the grounds between 5:14 and 5:40 A.M. and secured entry into the hotel from the back of the building. This information established that the gates were open before firemen arrived and compromised the crime scene.[7]

One additional clue fits somewhere near or within the seven-hour timeline, but exactly when is unknown. A year and a half after the murder, Detective Axel Soderberg noted that "According to Det. Mitchell, Ruth Munson was supposed to be at this Charles Williams' house the night she was murdered." Detective James Mitchell himself never made this assertion in writing, and Soderberg did not specify a time. Did this incident occur between 7:00 P.M., when landlady Clara Broughton said Ruth Munson left her room, and approximately 8:30 P.M., when she arrived at the Ace with her friends? Or did it take place sometime after she left the Ace, perhaps just before the time when strange cars were sighted on Dayton Avenue and screams were heard? Did one or both of Ruth's women friends accompany her to the Williams home? What happened there? Was this supposed visit an innocent but culturally

taboo gathering, or did Ruth's death grow out of the gathering, leading police to believe a second gathering at the Williams home occurred
in the early morning hours of December 9, where a remark was made
"that Ruth Munson talked too much and by this time she was probably
burned"?[8]

As tantalizing as all these clues were, detectives were unable to take
them further. Today, the seven-hour time gap remains just as mysterious as it did on the morning of the murder.

Though motive, means, and opportunity are the fundamental aspects
of a criminal investigation, detectives seldom addressed any of these
elements by name in their reports. Similarly, detectives rarely referenced theories about the murder, although the daily newspapers speculated about theories early in the case, usually attributing them to
police. Over the course of the investigation, various theories about the
case surfaced, along with a variety of motives ascribed to the killer.

The possibility that Ruth had been hit by a car and the subsequent
fire set in an attempt to cover up the accident was soon dismissed,
based in part on "the removal of the girdles from the body." No other
type of "accident" was considered.[9]

Almost from the outset, detectives believed the motive behind
Ruth's murder was sexual assault. Initially, every adult male in the city
was a potential suspect. The crime appeared to be one of opportunity.
In this theory, the killer encountered Ruth on the street and—in spite
of the near-zero temperatures—attacked her, resulting in her death.
Dr. John B. Dalton, police criminologist, challenged this idea, main-
taining that no sperm cells were found in a vaginal smear taken during
the autopsy.[10]

And of course, police investigated the idea that Ruth was killed by
an acquaintance. Her former fiancé William Nelson, her ex-boyfriend
Olaf Anderson, her friend Whitey Unglamb, and her current boyfriend
Dick Das, among numerous others, were all investigated and eliminated as suspects. Two Black men, Robert Brown and Daniel Faulkner,
were identified as acquaintances of Ruth's. Brown was investigated
thoroughly but never charged in the Munson case. The claim that he
had picked up a package containing "dope" was never investigated further, suggesting the police did not regard the rumor as credible. A third
Black male, Merton Ewing, was also questioned about the case.

Robbery was indirectly considered as a motive when detectives considered Charles "Big Slim" Moore as a murder suspect. Robbery was
Moore's motive in attacking five women in downtown St. Paul on

December 15 and a University Avenue druggist several days later. His savage beating of the druggist suggested to police that he was capable of murderous violence. Moore stood trial for the robberies, but he was never charged in the Munson case.

Revenge was also considered as a motive. On December 15, six days after the murder, the *Minneapolis Journal* theorized that an acquaintance of Ruth Munson's sought revenge for some transgression: "Hope for the solution lay within this circle, police believed, as they advanced a theory that the young woman's death was plotted and planned in minute detail." The paper did not speculate on why the killer sought revenge. Officers had also heard a rumor that the wife of the "captain of the porters" had hired men to kill Munson.[11]

Ruth's coworker Violet Thoreson told the *St. Paul Pioneer Press* that Ruth had told her she didn't believe she would live until Christmas, which hinted at revenge as a motive. No further information surfaced to substantiate Thoreson's claim. Similarly, detectives taking witness and suspect statements didn't seem to prod suspects on the revenge theory.[12]

Several reports taken by detectives recorded rumors circulating around the city that Ruth Munson was killed "because she knew too much" about something. Two rumors involved drug trafficking—one on each side of the law. One rumor held that Ruth Munson was working undercover for federal agents at the Union Depot and she "was put out of the way because she knew too much"—presumably by the drug dealers. Another rumor, expressed by the unnamed passenger riding a bus from the Twin Cities to Brainerd, held that she was part of a "dope ring" and the killer or killers "were afraid she would squeal on them." If true, this rumor could account for the fact that the two women with Ruth chose to remain anonymous, or they were squirreled away out of town, or they themselves were eliminated—although no reports of the murders of other women emerged during the same period. No reports of in-depth investigations of these rumors made their way into the Munson files.[13]

According to another rumor, Ruth Munson knew too much about a prostitution operation run by a pimp known as "Blackie." More than a year after the murder, Detective Mitchell investigated the story told by St. Cloud State Reformatory inmate Eugene Dickerson that he had overheard two women talking about another woman who "knew too much and that Blackie had to do away with her." Blackie was "to have placed the girl in a house in Minneapolis" but "she had refused to go any further, thereby making it necessary to do away with her." Mitchell was unable to locate a pimp who went by "Blackie" in either Minneapolis or St. Paul. But Mitchell's report only confirmed that *he* didn't find anyone named Blackie. There is no evidence that police ever connected Dickerson's rumors about "Blackie" with Charles Moore's purchase of a gun from "Blacky," leaving open the possibility that Dickerson's story was accurate.[14]

No reports in the Munson file directly link Ruth Munson to prostitution rings or speculate that she sold herself for money. The press did not speculate on the issue either. The fact that several police reports in the files reference prostitution or suspected prostitutes does suggest detectives were probably looking for connections. On one hand, Ruth was known to have "many boyfriends," which no doubt gave detectives pause. She made only nine dollars a week as a waitress, yet she engaged in a very active social life which, according to her diary, took her to restaurants, bars, and dance halls several nights each week. The fact that prostitution was illegal complicated police efforts to unearth facts. Anyone talking about Ruth in this regard exposed themselves to criminal investigation and prosecution. It is also possible that friends and acquaintances withheld such information in an effort to protect her reputation. If police established any credible links between Ruth Munson and prostitution, they were never committed to writing.

In the end, although various theories and motives about the crime were reported in the media, detectives never really established a clearcut motive or theory. Doing so could have helped lead them to the perpetrator.

From the beginning of the investigation, friends and acquaintances offered detectives two contrasting portraits of Ruth Munson. The day after the murder, Mrs. Milton Otto told Detective Paul Hanft and Detective Lieutenant Thomas Jansen that "Ruth Munson was always very quiet about her affairs and very much to herself." Landlady Clara Broughton described Ruth as "very quiet" and one who "stayed in her room with her door closed." On the telephone, she was "very very careful. You would never know what she was talking about." Ruth's friend Gertie Zernhill noted that Ruth "had always been quiet about her outside activities."[1]

In contrast, two days after the murder, the wife of the Friendship Club manager told Detectives Boyd Carrier, Frank Kennedy, and Edward Harkness that she had noticed "a big change in Ruth in the past nine weeks." She "would come late and would show signs of drinking." On one occasion, the manager "had to give her black coffee to try and straighten her out." Martha Fischer, who lived in a nearby building, told Detective Alfred Jakobson that "the character of Ruth Munson was not too good."[2]

Similarly, detectives soon encountered two impressions of Ruth's general state of mind. A few days prior to the murder, Ruth had told coworker Violet Thoreson that "I'll never live to see Christmas." But another coworker and friend offered a very different impression. When asked if she had noticed changes in Ruth's behavior, Joan Pivoran replied that Ruth had "seemed happier during the past month than ever before."[3]

To resolve these contrasting portraits and emotional profiles, detectives could turn to Ruth's own diary. Her short, daily entries chronicled her work schedule, the nightspots she visited, who telephoned her and wrote her letters, along with mundane activities such as ironing and laundry. Reading her diary, one could conclude that she was sentimental about birthdays and anniversaries; that she wrote and received many letters; that she went out dancing or socializing almost every evening; that through her active social life she had developed many acquaintances if not deep friendships; that she was extremely close to her sister Helen; that she followed boxing and the University of Minnesota football team. She belonged to a sewing circle and occasionally went to movies.

One thing she did not do in diary entries was unburden herself of her troubles or write down her innermost thoughts. Nevertheless, detectives carefully mined the diary for names—especially men's names—to investigate.

Ruth's diary did little to establish in her own words her goals in life. She entered the working world as a teacher. By 1929, Ruth had decided that teaching wasn't for her. She moved to St. Paul in search of . . . what? No evidence exists that she was career minded. She worked as a domestic, then a waitress at Miller Hospital, before taking the waitress position at the Union Depot.

In 1937, it was acceptable for a single woman to work. But cultural norms expected women to get married, be a good wife, have children, and run the household. For Ruth, marriage did not appear to be a priority, or at least it was not in the cards. At age thirty-one, she was a full decade beyond the median age for a first marriage for American women. She had had opportunities for marriage. While living in Wisconsin, she was engaged to William Nelson. The engagement lasted for a year and a half before ending because of the Depression, according to Nelson. After a five-year gap, they reconnected as friends. Starting around 1930, Ruth had a five-year, intimate relationship with Olaf Anderson. Anderson told police they were not engaged and the relationship ended when he started going with another woman, whom he later married. Once again, Ruth maintained a friendly relationship after the breakup.[4]

Elmer "Whitey" Unglamb carried on a friendship with Ruth over a period of years. In the statement he gave to Detective Frank Cullen, the exact nature of their relationship was not discussed, but at least one person interviewed by police noted that Whitey wanted to marry Ruth, that Ruth didn't want to marry him, and that she was afraid of him. However, the fact that Ruth visited Whitey when he was hospitalized for gallbladder surgery in November and wrote him in December, just two days before her death, suggests the relationship was cordial.[5]

In early November, Ruth turned down a marriage offer from the recently widowed Dick Das, whom she had met in October, saying in part that she could not be the ideal Christian wife he deserved. Ruth chronicled the doomed but "beautiful" relationship in two letters she wrote to Das a month before her death, which he turned over to the detectives at some unspecified time after they took his statement. "We discussed some delicate subjects last night," she wrote on November 3, "and after that I am convinced that I can not [*sic*] fill the place that Martha once filled. She lead [*sic*] such a beautiful Christian life that I am sure she must have been an ideal wife and mother and you being the type of person you are deserve one equally as good." By referencing Martha's Christian life, Ruth seemed to be indicating she did not compare. Was this an expression of false humility to ease the breakup, or was she guarding a secret? Undaunted, Das continued to court her, telephoning and writing her the next day. On November 5, Ruth tried again to step back from the relationship. "It wasn't because I didn't love you that I wrote you that letter (I think you know that I care for you)," she wrote, "but it was just because I came to the conclusion that I couldn't marry you so out of fairness to you I thought we shouldn't go on."[6]

But go on they did. Their relationship continued until her death. On the last night of her life, she agreed to babysit for Das's two children the following evening.

If career and marriage were not in the cards for Ruth, where did her interests lie? Her diary entries suggest that social activities were the focus of her life, as Adolph (Ade) Hultgren observed: "dances and fellows" appeared to be her key interest. At one point, Ruth told Hultgren "I'll never get married," though it was unclear if her pronouncement was a declaration or a lament.[7]

Her penchant for the night life was not without its risks. Evenings at restaurants, taverns, and dance halls exposed her to many men, any one of whom could have interpreted her interest in "dances and fellows" as a sign that, in the vernacular of the day, she was an "easy" woman. She often traveled late at night, catching a Selby-Lake streetcar home from the Friendship Club in Minneapolis or from the Ace, some four miles west of her apartment, using one of several routes available. Other times she caught a ride with someone.

On a weekly wage of nine dollars (plus whatever tips people might leave, given the strains of the Depression), she must have found it a challenge to pay for going out several nights a week. Police investigated rumors that she had applied for a part-time job at a café and learned that she never reported for work. Was this an abandoned effort to take a second job to finance her social life? As a woman made vulnerable by her choices and her circumstances, did she decide to investigate sex work instead? Such a decision could be one explanation for her having many boyfriends.

Her letters offer hints that her lifestyle choices took an emotional toll and she longed for something more. In her November 3 breakup letter to Dick Das, she wrote, "If I could manage[,] I'd go out West now. Miles may help me to forget but upon second thought it would be very lonesome out there all alone so I guess I'll wait." On December 7, the day before she went to the Ace, she wrote to Whitey Unglamb that "a person gets lonesome and discouraged in the city too."[8]

Although detectives never used the term, they realized as the investigation dragged on that Ruth Munson maintained a secret life her friends seemed to know nothing about. They collected many pieces of information connected to her secret life, seldom fleshed out with details but offering plenty of room for speculation. For example, although her diary notes visits to the Ace Bar on Thursday, November 18, Saturday, November 20, and Tuesday, November 30, she did not identify her companions, as was often her custom when she patronized other nightspots. Detectives learned she was a fan of the Happy Hollow Gang, which played at the Ace on Wednesday nights. Wednesday entries in her diary do not show a pattern of her spending a night out with the same two women, which would offer a clue to the identities of the women who accompanied her to the Ace on Wednesday, December 8. This raises the possibility that these women were from her secret life, which would help explain why the women never came forward.[9]

Collectively, several pieces of information point to Ruth's association with Black men. Ruth was even more secretive about these connections. It was said she was friendly with the Black porters at the Union Depot. She was friendly with head porter Robert Brown, referring to him in her diary and address book in coded terms. Daniel Faulkner asked a fortune teller if Ruth was going to repay him the money he had loaned her to bail a friend out of jail—and if he was going to marry her. There is no mention of Faulkner in her diary. Ruth "was well known at the Keystone Hotel," said a cabdriver, though he provided no details. Numerous cabdrivers confirmed to detectives that they had driven Black men from downtown to 276 Dayton Avenue, Ruth's building, or to nearby buildings, in the days before the murder.[10]

Various sources suggested that as part of her secret life, Ruth knew too much about something. She may have been aware of prostitution activities. One questionable source claimed she was offered a position in a house by the phantom pimp Blackie, which she refused, resulting in her death. Numerous police reports touch on the subject of prostitution. None of the reports in the Munson file link either the Williams house or the Fields house to any prostitution operation.[11]

If, indeed, Black men and white women did gather in either the Williams or the Fields houses, those meetings may have been entirely social or involved intimacy between consenting adults. If nothing illegal was afoot, something considered culturally unacceptable by whites certainly was. Though sex between Black and white folks was not illegal in Minnesota, socially it was considered taboo; marriages between white people and Black people were rare. Black men and women were well aware of the general contempt and fear many whites held against them, especially in matters involving sex. They were also aware of the potential consequences Black men faced at the hands of whites.

In 1937, as reported by the *St. Paul Recorder*, there were eight lynchings in the United States, including three in Florida, two in Mississippi, and one each in Alabama, Georgia, and Tennessee. Minnesota's Black population knew lynching was not necessarily confined to Southern states. In 1919, Black St. Paul police officers James A. Mitchell and James T. Queries (also spelled Quarles) prevented a Black robbery and murder suspect from being lynched in South St. Paul, after he accidentally killed a lodger in a rooming house during a robbery attempt. On June 15, 1920, in downtown Duluth, three Black carnival workers falsely accused of rape by a white woman were dragged from their jail cells by a white mob and lynched from a lamppost on the street. Commenting on Minnesota's "first lynching-bee," an editorial in the Black-owned newspaper *Northwestern Bulletin* asked the question that would haunt Minnesota's Black residents for years to come: "Could there be a repetition of this in Minnesota? Officers of the law say 'No.' But who knows?" The *Bulletin*'s question still carried weight in 1937.[12]

Ruth Munson's knowledge about any prostitution ring or the fraternization between Black people and white people, whether nefarious or innocent, could have resulted in the decision that she needed to be silenced, which became a motive for murder. If this was the case, however logical such a decision may have been in the minds of her killers, it drips with irony. Ruth was secretive about her relationships across the color line. One is left to wonder what evidence her killers saw in her behavior that she had already broken a confidence or would do so in the future. Or was three centuries of oppression at the hands of whites, magnified by their own experiences on the streets of St. Paul, enough to arouse her killers' fears?

The question suggests yet another reason why the Munson case was never solved. If nothing "nefarious" was afoot, racism certainly was.

The Ruth Munson murder investigation was barely forty-eight hours old when cabdriver Walter Lucci walked into the Public Service Building and told police that a colleague had told him that Ruth was "the girl I took two n - - - - - s up to call on" at 276 Dayton Avenue. Ruth Munson, Lucci declared, "goes out of her way to talk to the porters in the Union Depot . . . n - - - - - s in other words." From that moment on, the investigation was influenced and often hampered by racist attitudes and practices exhibited by citizens and police alike. Among the reasons the Munson case was never solved, racism ranks near the top.[1]

After the sensational murder, scores of tips poured in from the general public. Although police never publicized Ruth's connections to the Black community, everyday white citizens were quick to link Black men to the case. Detectives received an abundance of tips about Ruth Munson being seen in the company of Black men; for example, someone reported that Ruth and a Black man spoke after getting off the streetcar at the same Selby Avenue stop. The woman who "thought a colored man may have done it" was quick to say Charles Moore "might have been the one" when she saw his picture in the paper. Numerous tips offered by white women described instances unrelated to the case in which they claimed Black men had followed or harassed them, which, in the women's view, automatically made the men suspects in the Munson case.[2]

White citizens' attitudes about Black citizens, and Black men in particular, were evident in these reports. On December 23, Detective Lieutenant Bertram Talbot and Patrolman Robert Williams took a report from Gertrude Were, twenty-nine years old, who reported that she was approached by a "colored man" at 1:40 A.M. in downtown St. Paul, from whom she fled. She described the man as wearing a "dark overcoat" and being of "medium height, good shoulders, big lips, white teeth." Detectives Alfred Jakobson and Herman Schlichting investigated and quickly cleared the man accused in an anonymous postcard as "the dirty black janitor" at the First National Bank who was "the Cold Bloody slayer of the poor Munson girl," who should be "lynched by sunrise[,] the dirty black cur."[3]

Among many citizens, white and Black, there was a natural tendency to be wary of police. While some people signed their names to tips they mailed in to police and later agreed to be interviewed for the record, many others submitted them anonymously. "I don't want to get mixed up in this" was a common refrain at the bottom of postcards and letters. Citizens' preference for anonymity also may have been influenced by their hesitancy to be associated with such a sensational crime.

While there is no evidence that a Black man or woman voluntarily contacted police with information about the Munson murder, it is possible they may have sent tips anonymously. Black residents well understood—and deplored—the obvious fact that police and the justice system treated Black residents differently from whites. "The black man is singled out," the *Northwestern Bulletin* noted on its editorial page in 1922, summarizing the past and forecasting the future. "His shortcomings and bad deeds are put before the public.... No masks are used to cover up the facts but instead, every effort is made to play upon the least discreditable act a black man commits." The *Bulletin* noted that "the deeds for which a black man would be lynched, a white man may commit and simply be scorned by his friends . . . and given a fair trial in the courts of justice." Fear of being mistreated contributed to a widespread sense of mistrust of both police and the justice system among Black residents. Robbery and murder suspect Charles Moore understood this. As he told police, when he made an attempt to flee arrest, "I figured I would just let him kill me and get it over with."[4]

In short, among members of the Black community, contact with the police was to be avoided if possible. Why step forward and put yourself at risk by offering information that might be turned against you?

At the time of the Munson case, two recent investigations, one federal, the other municipal, were still fresh in the minds of St. Paul's Black citizens. The FBI's so-called "white slavery investigations" in 1937 resulted in arrests of Black men. Federal agents had also compiled a list of several individuals who resided in Apartment 13 at 276 Dayton Avenue, Ruth's address. The agents shared the names of six men and women with the police, all of whom were presumably white. None of the six were ever linked to the Munson case. Nevertheless, the federal investigation and its aftermath made Black folks wary.

In July and August 1937, the St. Paul police had conducted raids on the Rondo neighborhood. Police records show the number of arrests of Black individuals in July (61) and August (65) was nearly double the 35 arrests made in September. While the exact reasons are unknown, it is likely police were raiding after-hours nightspots.[5]

These investigations deepened the long-standing mistrust of police by Black people in St. Paul. Detectives seeking information about the Munson case found the Rondo neighborhood surrounded by a wall of silence. Their attempts to verify tips were met with evasion and denial: Alice Mayes, the Black maid in charge of the women's toilet at Kirsch and Gillis, had supposedly said "she knew who done the job" on Ruth Munson but, when questioned, denied having any knowledge about the case.[6]

Merton Ewing, the Black waiter at the Lowry Hotel dining room whose white coworker reported hearing him say "he knew who Ruth Munson was out with" and "he knew of no reason why he should tell the Police Dept. all he knew," denied he had said words to that effect. Eventually (and reluctantly) he revealed the names of Black waiters at the Lowry who had taken taxis from the hotel "out Rondo." Ewing, who would be serving as the head of the Minneapolis Waiter's Union local by 1943, denied knowing anything about social activities between the Black waiters and white women.[7]

Attempts by police to engage help from members of the Black community met with little success. On December 12, three days after the murder, the team of Detective Lieutenant Joseph Heaton and Patrolman James Cook interviewed Charles Smith, "head red cap, colored," who at their urging agreed to "try and find out some facts," presumably about porters taking taxis from downtown to Ruth's neighborhood. There is no record that Smith ever contacted the department or that Heaton and Cook checked back with him.[8]

Black residents were even hesitant to speak negatively about others in their community to a police officer. Patrolmen Robert Williams and Robert Turpin described the porter Ira Dorsey as "a bitter enemy of Robert Brown, who is Captain over him." Dorsey confirmed to them that he had spoken to Ruth Munson about the football jackpot, but he passed on the golden opportunity to make trouble for his "bitter enemy." He made no comment to police about a fellow Black man talking to Ruth Munson—or to any white woman.[9]

The silence about the Munson case extended to the Black newspapers. In 1937, Black residents turned to the *St. Paul Recorder* and its sister publication, the *Minneapolis Spokesman*, for the community's news. (The city's large daily newspapers generally ignored stories about St. Paul's Black residents, other than arrests and prosecutions.) These weekly papers covered neighborhood news and gossip; publicized upcoming social, club, church, and entertainment events; and carried advertisements for Black-owned businesses. The papers also reported local, state, and national political news that directly affected Black residents.

Neither the *Recorder* nor the *Spokesman* covered the raids on Rondo as a news story. Neither paper treated the federal white slavery investigations as a news story, although both carried stories about Black men facing such charges. While both papers also reported the arrest and prosecution of Black individuals for other crimes, there was never any mention of the Munson case in either paper. People most likely discussed the sensational case informally. When Black suspect Charles Moore was questioned about the Aberdeen Hotel, he noted, "they said something about a n - - - - - being involved."[10]

Exactly why Cecil E. Newman, publisher of the two papers, elected to ignore the Munson case altogether remains a mystery. It is likely the story simply did not fit within his stated mission: "this paper covers thoroughly the Negro market."[11]

Police Chief Clinton Hackert's efforts to reform the St. Paul Police Department and erase its legacy of corruption was lauded by the daily newspapers at the time of his death. One aspect his reforms did not address, however, was the racism that infected the entire department, including detectives who worked the streets and administrators who directed the investigation from the Public Safety Building.

In reports and statements taken, detectives (in keeping with the times) routinely described Black witnesses and potential suspects as "colored" or "negro." The police department's list of men arrested for sex crimes in 1937 singled out Black man by placing "(N)" next to their names. Often the tone of written reports and transcripts of statements subtly revealed officers' racial attitudes. For example, when Detective Thomas Grace questioned Robert Brown about his relationship with Ruth, his tone was condescending: "Now Bob," Grace began, as though he were addressing a child. In some cases, the officer's racism was more obvious, if shielded from others. In one instance, an officer filed a formal report using the then acceptable term "negro" to describe an individual, but in writing his personal notes, he used the N-word.[12]

While conducting investigations, detectives faced an age-old conundrum that plagues police departments to this day: based upon information received, while investigating a person of color, are police merely investigating a suspect who happens to be Black, or are they profiling suspects for investigation because they *are* Black?

Unfortunately, the Ruth Munson file is rife with examples of officers pursuing investigations of men simply because of their skin color. On December 15, 1937, six days after the murder, Patrolman Edmond Kane directed a memo to Assistant Chief Tierney noting that in 1935 "while working in the Rondo district," he had sought "a colored man (young), wanted for rape." If the suspect was still in town, "he might be a suspect in Munson case," Kane concluded. While referrals of white suspects were made to detectives by police and citizens alike, they weren't selected solely because of their skin color. Nearly a month after the murder, Detective Ralph Merrill, Patrolman Louis Schultz, and Patrolman Thomas Shanley ended their description of the man seen exiting 276 Dayton Avenue with "could not tell if white or black." Nevertheless, the trio concluded that "This description fits Robert Brown."[13]

Racism existed at the administrative level as well, particularly in how Black officers were assigned throughout the case. At the time of the murder, there were at least three Black officers on the 361-person force: Detective James Mitchell, Patrolman Robert Williams, and Patrolman Robert Turpin.

Turpin was new to the job, receiving his appointment on April 1, 1937. He was paired with Robert Williams and, at the time of the murder, both were working in the Morals Division under Lieutenant Frank Mondike. In celebrating Turpin's success, the *St. Paul Recorder* noted, "Since his appointment, he has made several important arrests of bootleggers and policy writers."[14]

Williams, fifty-eight years old, had joined the force in 1920 as a patrolman. He lived in the Rondo neighborhood and for many years worked out of the department's Rondo substation. James S. Griffin, a Black officer who joined the force in 1941 and later wrote a history of Black people in the police and fire departments, noted that in the late 1920s, Williams had survived an effort by the commissioner of public safety to "systematically eliminate" Black police officers from the force. The administration "attempted to discharge Robert Williams on the basis that he had been too old when he was appointed." Williams had been forced to go to court to retain his position.[15]

James Mitchell had joined the department as a detective in 1917. His contemporaries viewed him as "a hard man, but a very good detective." On one occasion, Mitchell and two other detectives attempted to arrest a murder suspect in a second-floor apartment on Rondo Avenue. At their knock, the suspect opened fire through the door, then made his escape. Mitchell pursued him and single-handedly captured him about two hours later.[16]

Between them, Williams and Mitchell had thirty-seven years of experience on the force, and Turpin was nearing one year of service. If the leaders in the police department thought the killer was a Black St. Paulite, the three men seemed like the perfect choice to work on the Munson case—even though they may have had other departmental assignments. The three officers' names appear on only ten out of the approximately 500 miscellaneous reports that were filed.

Though James S. Griffin credited Mitchell with working the Munson case, only three reports carry Mitchell's name: the team interview of Eugene Dickerson at the St. Cloud reformatory, the solo report debunking Dickerson's story, and the arrest of Henry Williams for "suspicion of window peeping." Months later, Detective Axel Soderberg noted that Mitchell claimed Ruth Munson was in Charles Williams's house on the night she died. Mitchell may also be the source about the alleged early morning discussion among Charles Williams and others that Ruth knew too much. Mitchell's ability to dig out information suggests he could have contributed to a solution for the case if he had been given a free rein.[17]

Similarly, Patrolman Robert Williams's name appears on only a handful of reports. He filed two solo reports, one when he arrested Black resident William Lawrence for questioning and a second when he interviewed Grace Tull about Mrs. G. C. Bergstrom and rediscovered Hazel Bohen and Ruth Wilmar, women who left town immediately after the murder and whose pictures had been turned over to the investigation a year earlier. "Information comes to me from time to time," Williams noted, "that a flat in the 200 block on Dayton have colored men visiting an apartment. This may be the Bergstrom Apt." Two days later, he and a white detective, George Failes, reinterviewed Tull, who told them about Ruth Munson hanging out at a "colored tavern" at Western and Rondo Street, a fact that "was supposed to be known only to the police."[18]

Williams and Turpin filed two reports together: the interview with Ira Dorsey at the St. Paul Union Depot and the second arrest of William Lawrence, "on information he knew something regarding the Ruth Munson case."[19]

Like James Mitchell's reports, those by Robert Williams suggest he had rooted out information that white detectives working the case had not. It is noteworthy that the bulk of Mitchell's and Williams's reports were filed weeks, sometimes months, after the murder, as though they had worked their sources to ferret out the information they recorded.

Why didn't Tierney reassign Mitchell, Williams, and Turpin to work on the case? Among the three, Mitchell was the only detective.

Williams and Turpin were patrolmen. It was not uncommon, however, for white patrolmen to file reports associated with the case. Tierney and his lieutenants who handed out assignments did recognize the value of a Black officer working in the Rondo community. When Detective Lieutenant Nate Smith first attempted to arrest suspect Charles Moore at 225 Rondo, he had Detective Mitchell accompany him. On December 18, 1937, Patrolman Williams accompanied Det. Lt. Talbot to 607 St. Anthony Avenue in the Rondo neighborhood to bring in Pat White "who runs the place" and two women who lived with her. All three were white women, the officers' report noted, "and associate with negros."[20]

Much of the time, however, Black officers routinely faced discrimination when work assignments were handed out. Police historian James S. Griffin, who eventually rose to the position of deputy chief of police, noted that "Black officers were given the most undesirable and toughest beats, always in the lowest social, economic and educational areas." These assignments were commonly referred to as "shit details." These disagreeable assignments included being a "plant" in a building believed to be a target for burglars. "During the winter, the building might be unheated," Griffin recalled, "there may be rats and other adverse conditions present. This is the most dreaded detail an officer can be given." Throughout the 1930s and 1940s, there was an "unwritten rule that no Black be assigned to squad car duty with any white officer or be assigned motorcycle duty. The only time Black and white officers worked together was on special assignment, the jail or the patrol wagon." As a rookie officer, Griffin noted that he, like Turpin—a four-year veteran by then—got "more than my share" of "shit details."[21]

Such discriminatory treatment of Black people was not unique to the St. Paul Police Department. Racial discrimination in the department mirrored the culture in general. "Blacks were employed in menial jobs such as laborers, bootblacks, coachmen, waiters and porters," Griffin recalled. Black laborers were usually the last to be hired and the first to be fired. White-collar jobs for Black workers in government and industry were few and far between. Outside of the workplace, Black folks were often refused service in hotels, barbershops, and other businesses.[22]

By adhering to the racial prejudices of the era, Tierney, as the investigation's director, failed to take advantage of the community knowledge and trust the department's Black officers had at their command. If Ruth Munson's companions at the Ace were part of her secret life, these officers might have been able to identify them, and their testimony would have helped fill in the seven-hour gap between the time the trio left the Ace and the next morning when Ruth Munson's body was found in the Aberdeen. The officers might have been able to determine if the two mystery women were among the Black men and white women who police believed were in the house of Charles Williams on the night of Ruth's murder. Whether they were directly involved in her murder or not, the way Det. Lt. Grace questioned Williams and the other five individuals associated with him shows that the police believed these witnesses knew something about her death.

In short, along with the lack of evidence, Ruth's own secrecy, and the missed opportunities discussed below, racial prejudices may well have doomed the investigation. They contributed to mistrust of the police among members of the Black community and the underutilization of the Black officers familiar with the community. If, indeed, Ruth Munson's death came at the hands of someone from the Black community, it is ironic that racism prevented the case from being solved.

For its time, the scope of the Munson investigation was huge. More than a hundred officers worked the case, filing hundreds of reports and statements, each containing a litany of names, dates, and details. In Assistant Chief Charles J. Tierney's office, reports were numbered as they came in. At some point, in an effort to bring order to the growing volume of information, officers created an alphabetical list of individuals mentioned in the reports keyed to the numbers of the reports in which they appeared. Since reports often included more than one name, a second list of reports by number included all the names mentioned in each. It is not known if all of these reports and the indexes were available to any detective working on the case. Given the vast amount of information assembled, how could any one individual know everything in the files? Who among the scores of officers working the case was able to read the reports and see connections amid the thousands of details. Who was there, for example, to put "Blackie" and "Blacky" together?

Within the sprawling investigation, detectives missed a number of investigative opportunities, each of which fell within one assumption or another that they made about the case. For example, from the investigation's earliest days, it was assumed Ruth Munson was killed by someone she knew. The reports identify at least two of her acquaintances who deserved deeper investigation than they appear to have received.

The first is Daniel Faulkner, the man said to have offered Jule Miller sexual services and to have asked fortune teller Maud Krenick if Ruth would pay him back the $25 she had borrowed "to bail out a friend" around the time of the "raids on the Rondo Street district." Faulkner also asked the fortune teller "if he was going to marry Ruth Munson." Detectives Boyd Carrier and Frank Kennedy arrested him on December 23 for molesting women, and he was "released for lack of prosecution" the next day. The interview of Maud Krenick took place December 31. Despite Faulkner's sexual proclivities, the fact that Ruth owed him money, and his apparent interest in marrying her, no record exists of Faulkner himself being questioned specifically about his relationship with Ruth Munson, or where he was on the night of December 8. In late October 1939, Patrolmen Stanley Pehoski and Rueben Halvorson, new to the Munson investigation, were searching for the Black man rumored to have purchased a set of silverware for Ruth Munson. Faulkner should have been an obvious candidate for investigation as the purchaser. Yet no record exists that these detectives were even aware of his existence.[1]

Another of Ruth's acquaintances who deserved further investigation was Guadalupe "Wally" Yniguez, the proprietor of the Tunnel Hamburger Shop, where Ruth ate meals "an average of four or five days a week." He claimed not to know her by name, but Margaret Yost, who was allowing Yniguez's girlfriend, Mrs. Leo Gifford, to stay in her apartment, claimed Gifford and Yniguez were "talking about this Ruth Munson girl and Wally told her that he was the one that killed the Munson girl and if she pulled any dirty tricks he would do the same thing to her." In addition, she noted that Yniguez "had a guilty conscience about something" and wanted "to leave town."[2]

It is possible that Yniguez, as others had done, was falsely claiming responsibility for the murder to gain leverage over his girlfriend. Nevertheless, any confession of murder was worthy of further investigation. Yniguez, who was separated from his wife at the time of the murder, could have developed a romantic interest in Ruth. He lived next door to her. Conceivably, he could have met her in front of their buildings during the late hours of December 8 and 9 and made advances that she refused, which led to screams and a scuffle that ended badly. His estranged wife's charge that he had a fascination with fire created a potential link to the conflagration at the Aberdeen. Despite these factors, there is no record that Yniguez was ever re-questioned about the Munson murder case.[3]

Though detectives may have considered revenge as a motive for Ruth Munson's murder, there is only one report or statement that directly addresses this theory. Dorothy Wagner, an employee at Ancker Hospital, had overheard two women talking, one of whom was a woman of color. The detectives noted what she heard: "Ruth Munson was going out with the captain of the porters at the depot and . . . they (the porters) think the wife of the captain hired two men to kill Ruth Munson." The "captain of the porters" was likely Robert Brown, the head porter at the St. Paul Union Depot. By this time, the investigation had already determined that Brown and Ruth Munson had a social relationship. Brown had acknowledged he was interested in having sexual intercourse with her, though he denied they had been intimate.[4]

On its face, gaining revenge on a straying husband by eliminating his love interest would appear to be a motive worthy of investigation. Despite continued interest in Robert Brown as a potential murder suspect, it appears he was never questioned about this rumor. There is no record that detectives questioned any porters at the Union Depot to secure additional information. No record exists of an interview of Robert Brown's wife, or any other woman who may have been the spouse of "the captain of the porters."

Was this lead quietly addressed, with no reports filed to document the outcome? Did this lead simply get lost amid the myriad of tips forwarded to detectives, who at that time were focused on checking out known sex offenders and studying the shear pins found near the body?

What role did race play in the decision? Though the investigation privately pursued leads that pointed to Black men, the subject of race was avoided in public discussions, a proclivity which mirrored society at large—where whites dominated. Was the decision not to pursue this specific lead made in part simply to avoid dealing publicly with the messy issue of race? In a society where Black folks were routinely subjugated to the will of whites, did those directing the investigation discount as ludicrous the possibility that a Black woman would have the temerity to hire someone to kill a white woman? Or, given the era and the racial prejudices that most whites held against Black people, did detectives summarily discount the talk among the porters, most of whom were Black, as nothing more than idle gossip, and not worth their investigative time? Any one of these scenarios is plausible.

Early in the investigation, it was assumed, logically, that the two women who accompanied Ruth Munson to the Ace Bar the night before she was murdered were close friends. As the detectives uncovered evidence of the parts of her life that Ruth kept secret, they may have realized these women were from that secret life. When their efforts to expose Ruth's secrets were unsuccessful, the investigation began to run out of steam. As new detectives were given assignments in the case, less attention was paid to establishing the identity of the two women. This may be the reason two pairs of women possibly connected to Ruth's secret life were never adequately investigated.

Patrolman Robert Williams may have come closest to finding the answers. In September 1938, he investigated Mrs. G. C. Bergstrom, which led him to Hazel Bohen—"a known prostitute"—and Ruth Willmar, acquaintances of Bergstrom who had been ejected from an apartment in the same building. Talking to Bergstrom's neighbor, Grace

Tull, Williams learned that Bergstrom may have known Ruth Munson. From there, it was a logical step to assume Ruth also knew Bohen and Willmar. Williams uncovered several connections between Bergstrom, Bohen, and Willmar and the Black community. According to Tull, shortly after Ruth's murder, Hazel Bohen and Ruth Willmar left town.[5]

Detectives Carrier and Kennedy had been given a picture of Bohen and Willmar on December 15, 1937, although Patrolman Williams appeared unaware of it. No record exists that the detectives investigated the two women or showed the picture to the bartenders at the Ace.[6]

Were Bohen and Willmar the women who accompanied Ruth Munson to the Ace Bar, and could they shed light on what happened that night? Why did the two women leave town after the murder—was their departure coincidental, or were they in hiding, fearful for their lives? Were they sent away by the perpetrators, so they were out of reach of the police? We'll never know.

We'll also never know for sure whether those directing the investigation were ever aware of Williams's investigative work. His reports are handwritten. No record exists that they were typed up, with copies forwarded to Tierney, Police Chief Clinton Hackert, or others for possible action. Nine months into the investigation, it appears that the Ruth Munson case was no longer receiving the careful attention it had received in its early days. And that the work of one of the department's three Black officers may have been disregarded.

A similar case of a missed opportunity can be argued for two other women. Detectives Pehoski and Halvorson interviewed Adeline Moen in late October 1939. She told them about Irene Hammer and Myrtle Simonson, whom she knew well and who she believed knew Ruth Munson. She described the girls as "steppers" and "wouldn't put it past them" to go out with Black men. Both women left St. Paul in the weeks after the murder. During the course of the investigation, detectives checked out multiple pairs of women, but it appears these women were not questioned about the Munson case. Like Williams's reports, those of Pehoski and Halvorson are handwritten, and it is unknown whether the investigation's directors were aware of their findings.[7]

Detectives apparently missed another opportunity to unravel the mystery of Ruth Munson's secret life. Charles and Eva Williams, Mr. and Mrs. William Fields, Henry Williams, and John Warren, interviewed in November 1938, had all denied allegations "about colored men and white women" gathered at either the Williams or Fields home the night of Ruth's murder. Some seven months later, on July 8, 1939, when Charles Williams was arrested by Detectives Adelard Goodrow and Axel Soderberg for threatening the lives of Eva and her employer, Soderberg noted that "According to Det. Mitchell, Ruth Munson was supposed to be at this Charles Williams' house the night she was murdered."[8]

Mitchell himself never committed his assertion to writing. According to Detective Soderberg, Eva Williams agreed to "appear in court if needed." Her husband's threats may have put her in a more cooperative state of mind than when she was previously questioned. If she was questioned about the Munson case again, no record of the conversation made its way into the Munson file.

Daniel Faulkner certainly was part of Ruth Munson's secret life. "Wally" Yniguez fit the profile of an acquaintance who might have seized a late-night opportunity to press his feelings upon Ruth Munson. Whether it was fact or rumor, a wife's desire for revenge against her cheating husband represented the strongest motive for murder to actually be described in the investigation files. Identifying the two women who accompanied Ruth to the Ace Bar would have helped close the seven-hour time gap. Finally, Goodrow's and Soderberg's offhand statement regarding Mitchell's claim about Ruth's presence in the Williams home on the night she was murdered remains the closest the investigation ever came to naming her killer or killers.

If investigated more deeply, any one of these missed opportunities could have helped detectives solve the case.

Did the police know who killed Ruth Munson but find themselves unable to file charges against the killer because they lacked convincing proof of the killer's guilt? There is no evidence of this in Offense File 33436. Chief of Police Charles J. Tierney was following leads as late as 1946. The Munson investigation became inactive in the 1950s.

It was not until the 1970s that the term "cold case" was popularized to describe unsolved murder cases. The Ruth Munson murder case has now been "cold" for more than seventy years, and investigative techniques have evolved. Could modern investigative methods be used to solve the case?

Modern forensic science, the application of scientific methods and techniques in investigating and solving crimes, has evolved dramatically since 1937. Forensics now regularly play a role in solving crimes, along with traditional investigative methods involving the questioning of witnesses and suspects, logic, common sense, and problem-solving. Forensic DNA (deoxyribonucleic acid) analysis, first developed in 1984, is used to profile victims and suspects and to connect them to each other and to the scene of the crime. Similarly, microscopic elements of paint, a host of chemicals, microorganisms, pet hair, even cellular matter from plants have been used to link together suspect, victim, and the scene of the crime. Along with fingerprints, shoe tracks and tire tracks have been found scientifically to be unique to each shoe or tire and are used to link suspects to the crime scene. "People lie; science doesn't" is a popular axiom in the law enforcement community.

Unfortunately, today's sleuths have no real opportunity to employ current forensics in finding a solution to the case. The scene of the crime was destroyed in 1944. No physical evidence from the crime has survived for analysis—including, apparently, the three shear pins. No DNA samples survive from the time of the murder to which new samples—obtained only through monumental efforts—might be matched.

It is unlikely any surviving public records from the period contain clues that have not already been identified and pursued by detectives working the case. To make matters even more challenging, the police files of related cases from the same era, such as the arrest of Charles Williams, have not survived.

Perhaps the best chance for solving the case lies in the remote possibility that new written materials in the form of memoirs will surface. To date, no memoirs written by Police Chief Tierney, who directed the investigation, or Detective James Mitchell, who named the house he believed Ruth Munson visited on the night of her death, have surfaced. Another possibility is a deathbed confession written by the killer, an accomplice, or a silent witness seeking to clear their conscience before passing on.

One source of semipublic records exists that has yet to be explored. Street rumors of the day connected Ruth Munson to drug traffic on both sides of the law. These whispers may have grown out of press coverage of a narcotics case and trial in federal court at the time of the Munson investigation. Involving defendants William (Big Bill) Hildebrandt and Joe (Sixty) Katz, the case was tried in federal court in the first days of January 1938. The press coverage filled the vacuum caused by an absence of new and accurate information about the Munson case.[1]

If, indeed, Ruth Munson was working undercover for a "federal man," internal FBI memos or reports linked to its investigation of the Hildebrandt/Katz case, or even other cases, could conceivably list her name as an informant. That notion isn't as far-fetched as it might seem. St. Paul police investigated a report that head porter Robert Brown was at the depot in the wee hours of the night to receive a package rumored to contain drugs. While no charges were ever made against him, it could be argued that Ruth maintained a friendly relationship with Brown in the hopes of digging out information about drug trafficking. Subsequently being discovered as an informant by someone involved in illicit drug traffic could constitute a motive for her murder.[2]

Assuming Ruth Munson was working undercover, would special agents in the local FBI office have informed the St. Paul police? The two law enforcement agencies occasionally cooperated on operations and shared information, as the bureau did when passing on names of residents at 276 Dayton garnered in their investigation on white slavery. But this sharing of names appears to be the exception, rather than the rule. The only other significant record showing cooperation between the two agencies in regard to the Munson case is FBI Director J. Edgar Hoover's perfunctory letter documenting the bureau's technical analysis of the shear pins. If there was any additional communication between FBI agents and local police, it was conducted orally. That seems unlikely, however. The FBI remained cautious about sharing information with a department whose chief had tipped off gangsters of impending federal raids just three years earlier.[3]

Anyone interested in searching for clues to the Munson case embedded in FBI files faces a daunting task. According to the National Archives and Records Administration, FBI cases are filed by FBI case number, which the bureau assigns. To access relevant files, a researcher would need to figure out the individual case numbers and then request the appropriate files through a Freedom of Information Act request. The process generally takes years.[4]

If new evidence does not emerge, sleuths interested in the case will have to solve it with newspaper reports and the files that have survived at the St. Paul Police Department—files that did not bring resolution in the 1930s or 1940s, and have not in the 2020s.

Why study the Ruth Munson murder case after all these years? The story of this unsolved murder is now often reduced to a sentence or two in articles recounting the history of the luxurious Aberdeen Hotel, one of many buildings razed as the city of St. Paul continuously reinvented itself in the years following the murder.

The fate of the Aberdeen was emblematic of the further deterioration of the Ramsey Hill neighborhood through the 1950s, when white families abandoned their old community in favor of new homes in the city's growing suburbs. By the 1960s, block after block of the neighborhood's once elegant homes were subdivided into apartments, were boarded up, or had turned into empty shells, their windows broken out. Ramsey Hill was considered a high crime area. Drug traffic and prostitution flourished along Selby Avenue. Banks refused to finance mortgages for houses in the neighborhood. Rents were dirt cheap. Increasingly, those who lived in the neighborhood could not afford to live elsewhere.

By the early 1970s, the same cheap rents that helped doom the neighborhood began to attract a new kind of resident. Local artists and young professionals interested in living in an urban setting began moving in, purchasing the old homes one by one and beginning years of restoration work. The American Bicentennial in 1976 fueled interest in preserving America's past, helping to spawn a national re-urbanization movement. That year, the Ramsey Hill neighborhood and an extended portion of Summit Avenue was designated a national historic district. The reclamation of Ramsey Hill continued through the 1980s and 1990s. By the turn of the twenty-first century, Ramsey Hill had regained much of its former elegance and was once again an exclusive residential district.

Ruth Munson's "room on the hill" at 276 Dayton Avenue is still standing, as are two of her earlier places of residence, 251 and 265 Dayton Avenue.

The Rondo neighborhood experienced a much different fate. Though labeled as a "slum" on city maps of the 1930s, Rondo thrived through the 1940s as a vibrant community that was home to 80 percent of the city's Black residents. But national policy and local decision-makers sealed the neighborhood's fate. The Federal-Aid Highway Act of 1956 initiated the construction of an interstate highway system across the country. The state of Minnesota used the act to build a freeway between the downtowns of St. Paul and Minneapolis. Planners and political leaders considered a northern connection following an abandoned railroad line paralleling present-day Pierce Butler Route, but turned instead to a more direct route between the two cities. The chosen pathway obliterated Rondo Avenue and cut the Black neighborhood in two. Black residents did not have the political power or the economic resources to successfully oppose the project. Between 1956 and 1968, an estimated 700 homes were demolished or moved and scores of Black-owned businesses were closed or torn down. Homeowners and business owners alike were given inadequate compensation for their property. The tightly knit Black community was devastated. At the time, many former Rondo residents believed the route that decimated their neighborhood was deliberately chosen to cripple the Black community, a sentiment widely shared among St. Paulites today.[1]

The respective fates of the Ramsey Hill and Rondo neighborhoods reflect how St. Paul—indeed, American culture—has and has not changed in the eighty-five years since the Ruth Munson case first made headlines. Like the city, culture continuously reinvents itself. Unfortunately, the city's cultural reinvention process has never resolved key issues that characterized St. Paul when Ruth Munson was murdered. Interlocking issues that surfaced during the investigation remain with us today, confounding investigators working new cases and negatively impacting residents' daily lives as well.

In 1937, women were vulnerable walking St. Paul's streets and gathering in the city's evening spots. In the year before Ruth Munson's murder, twelve reported or attempted rapes occurred within a mile of her apartment. In the days immediately following the murder, more than a dozen women reported to police that they had recently been harassed on the streets, or they came forward to report a previously undisclosed rape. More than eighty-five years after Ruth Munson's death, women in St. Paul—and in cities and towns across the nation—remain vulnerable to sexual harassment and attack. In 2018, 63 percent of Minnesota women stated they had been sexually harassed. In 2021, 2,213 women in Minnesota reported they were raped. In 762 of those cases, the rapist and victim were acquaintances. Police believed Ruth Munson knew her killer as well. Women's vulnerability extends beyond sexual assault. In 2021, fifty-two women were murdered in Minnesota, an increase of 8.65 percent over the previous year.[2]

As a single woman making nine dollars a week, Ruth was vulnerable economically, which limited her opportunities and influenced her choices. Women are still paid less than men. For every dollar a white male earns, a white female earns $.81, and Black, Latina, Asian, and Native American women earn even lesser comparative amounts. Economists attribute the gender wage gap to a combination of factors, including differences in education, occupational segregation, experience, and gender bias. Poverty disproportionately impacts communities of color and households headed by single females. In 2019, 12 percent of Minnesota women were living below the poverty level, about 1.2 times the poverty rate for men.[3]

Race and racism pervaded the investigation of the Ruth Munson case. St. Paul's white citizenry was quick to point accusing fingers at Black and Asian men, and white detectives profiled Black men for investigation. Mistrust of the police by Black citizens contributed to a wall of silence that detectives were never able to penetrate. Fear that Ruth Munson knew too much about activities involving Black individuals— whether they were illegal or simply culturally taboo—was a plausible if unproven motive for her murder. Despite sweeping reforms initiated by Police Chief Clinton Hackert, the St. Paul Police Department discriminated against Black officers and failed to promote them to positions of authority. The department dismissed the opportunity to fully engage the talents of its officers of color and take advantage of the connections and trust they had within the Black community.

Just as racism in its various manifestations stymied the Ruth Munson investigation, today racism stymies our efforts to, in the efficient words of the US Constitution's preamble, "form a more perfect Union, establish Justice, insure domestic Tranquility, provide for the common defense, promote the general Welfare, and secure the Blessings of Liberty to ourselves and our Posterity." While a legitimate argument can be made that there has been progress in renouncing the cultural taboos between white people and Black people that characterized our nation at the time of the Munson case, unfortunately racism continues to prevail. The murder of George Floyd by a Minneapolis police officer in 2020 ignited a national outcry against racism that still exists within police departments—and in our communities. Communities of color continue to mistrust police, even as police departments—and our nation—struggle to address reforms. Until racism is defeated and all people are treated equally and respectfully, we cannot have "a more perfect Union."

How does the murder of Ruth Munson in 1937 fit into all of this?

Beyond being an intriguing mystery, this case is a snapshot in time that reminds us that issues we struggle with today—the vulnerability of women, economic insecurity, mistrust of the police, police reform, race, and racism—have plagued us for centuries. Studying the Ruth Munson murder case offers us an opportunity to examine the gears of our society, large and small, and to see how one gear turns another, which turns yet another, eventually leading to an encounter that results in a criminal act. At the same time, these turning gears influence investigators' ability to solve the crime. Understanding how and why these various gears turn helps us make new progress toward "a more perfect Union" where everyone, regardless of who they are, feels free to search for their room on the hill.

Acknowledgments

Although only my name appears on the cover, this book could not have been written without the contributions of many people. Since I first became interested in the Ruth Munson case, many present and former members of the St. Paul Police Department have been generous with their assistance. My sincere thanks to former Chief of Police William K. Finney and Public Information Coordinator Michael Jordan for making the Ruth Munson case file available for research. Thanks to former Chief Todd Axtell and Angie Steenberg of the chief's office, who provided support as my research and writing got underway. Thanks also to current Chief of Police Axel Henry and Public Information Officer Sergeant Mike Ernster for their support and assistance during the production phase of this book.

To Sergeant Melvin Carter Jr. (retired): thanks for your interest in the case. Your insight and probing questions often helped me to think like a detective instead of a historian.

The St. Paul Police Historical Society's website contains a wealth of information about the history of the St. Paul Police Department. That information was augmented by the expertise of several members who were generous with their knowledge. Thanks to members Jeff Newberger and Officer Fred D. Kaphingst (retired) for your early assistance during my research.

I owe a deep debt of gratitude to the organization's president, Edward J. "Ed" Steenberg. A former deputy chief of the St. Paul Police Department, Ed retired in 1999 with the rank of senior commander after thirty-five years of service. He generously provided biographical information about most of the more than 100 officers who worked on the Munson case. Throughout the course of this project, Ed answered dozens of questions, large and small, with efficiency and cheerfulness.

Thank you Nieeta Presley for information about the Rondo community in the early and middle years of the twentieth century.

Thank you Pearl Mitchell Jackson for your insightful perspective about your uncle, Detective James Mitchell.

Thanks to early readers Joe and Barb Miska, John Buzza, David Peacock, F. Garvin Davenport, and Leanne Brotsky. Your enthusiasm for the first few chapters convinced me I had found the right voice in which to tell this story and inspired me to keep going.

Thank you to the members of my writing group: Cynthia Kraack, Terrence C. Newby, Loren Taylor, Charles Locks, Ames Sheldon, Kathy Kerr, and Jim Lundy. You read these chapters as they were written and offered praise tempered with constructive criticism that influenced future drafts.

Thanks to the Minnesota Historical Society Press for recognizing that this long-forgotten story is a lens through which we can interpret a small part of Minnesota's history, a story where the whole somehow is greater than the sum of its parts.

To my editor, Ann Regan: thank you for your deep understanding of my vision for the book and your patient and honest editorial work. Your wisdom and graceful touch are evident on every page.

I am indebted to my family, who accepted Ruth Munson as a holiday houseguest and a tagalong on our vacations. Thanks to daughter Ellen and her husband Evan and to son Graham and his partner Leah for listening to endless investigation stories and progress reports.

The most important thank-you I have saved for last. Thank you Kate, my beautiful wife. In addition to pursuing your own extraordinary career, you always found time to be my cheerleader, my anchor, and a great sounding board throughout the creation of this book. Over the course of two years, you tolerated me living in the 1930s, sometimes returning to the present only for meals and to crawl into bed. I can never fully repay you for your love and kindness, but I'll keep trying.

Notes

Author's Note on Sourcing

Aside from newspaper sources, most of the documents cited in these notes can be found in Offense File 33436, housed at the St. Paul Police Department, 376 Grove Street, St. Paul.

Abbreviations used:

MR: Miscellaneous Report, Bureau of Police, City of St. Paul. Miscellaneous Reports were forms police officers filled out to document their work. The blanks were filled in by the reporting officer, who used abbreviations and other shortcuts in completing them. To standardize these references, when listing two officers named as authors of a report, I have used an "and" in place of a comma, dash, or ampersand, followed by the date and time of day the report was filed, if they wrote it down. In some cases, I have placed the typist's name in parentheses to distinguish between reports that would otherwise appear identical.

SPPD: St. Paul Police Department. The unit's official title under the city commission form of government, from 1914 to 1972, was the Bureau of Police, but that title was not commonly used.

Statement: Statement Made at St. Paul Police Headquarters. Formal statements were taken at police headquarters. To standardize these references, following the word "Statement" I have given the name of the individual and the date and time the statement was taken.

Notes to Chapter 1: "There's a Body Here!"

1. MR, Bureau Martin and Welander, December 11, 1937, 4:45 A.M.
2. Statement, Herman James Koroschetz, December 12, 1937, 9:40 A.M.
3. Statement, Stephen Waugh Westbrook, December 12, 1937, 10:00 A.M.
4. MR, Schroeder and Woodhouse, December 10, 1937, 9:45 P.M.
5. Letter from William C. Schroder, fire inspector, to William J. Sudeith, fire chief, St. Paul, undated, regarding Aberdeen Fire on December 9, 1937, 6:59 A.M.
6. MR, T. Jansen, January 3, 1938, 6:00 P.M.–11 P.M.
7. MR, T. Jansen, January 3, 1938, 6:00 P.M.–11 P.M.
8. MR, Kennedy and Carrier, December 9, 1937, morning.
9. MR, McMahon and Fahey, December 9, 1937, 7:30 A.M.
10. MR, Carrier and Kennedy (Hall), December 9, 1937, 7:47 A.M.
11. MR, Carrier and Kennedy (Irish), December 9, 1937, 7:47 A.M.
12. MR, Carrier and Kennedy (Hall), December 9, 1937, 7:47 A.M.

13. MR, Carrier and Kennedy (Irish), December 9, 1937, 7:47 A.M.; MR, Carrier and Kennedy (Hall), December 9, 1937, 7:47 A.M.

14. MR, Carrier and Kennedy (Irish), December 9, 1937, 7:47 A.M.

15. MR, Carrier and Kennedy (Hall), December 9, 1937, 7:47 A.M.

16. MR, Carrier and Kennedy (Hall), December 9, 1937, 7:47 A.M.

17. When St. Paul adopted a commission form of government in 1912, the department was officially renamed the Bureau of Police. Common usage, however, continued to be "St. Paul Police Department," and that name is used throughout this book.

Notes to Chapter 2: Complicating Circumstances

1. Virginia Brainard Kunz, *St. Paul: Saga of an American City* (Woodland Hills, CA: Windsor Publications, 1977), 41.

2. US Department of the Interior, National Park Service, National Register of Historic Places Inventory—Nomination Form, Historic Hill District, Ramsey County, Minnesota, Date Received: August 13, 1976, 39; hereafter: Historic Hill Nomination.

3. Historic Hill Nomination, 41.

4. History of Aberdeen taken from Paul Clifford Larson, *Minnesota Architect: The Life and Work of Clarence H. Johnston* (Afton, MN: Afton Historical Society Press, 1996), 62–64, 171, and Larry Millett, *Lost Twin Cities* (St. Paul: Minnesota Historical Society Press, 1992), 201–11.

5. Historic Hill Nomination, 40; Kunz, *Saga of an American City*, 69.

6. Annual Report of the Commissioner of Public Works of the City of St. Paul for the year ending December 31, 1933, 1934, 1935, Milton Rosen (Commissioner of Public Works), 33, 48.

7. Historic Hill Nomination, 44–45.

8. Annual Report of Public Works, 1933–35, 33; MR, Jakobsen, December 15, 1937.

9. MR, Jakobsen, December 15, 1937.

10. *Saint Paul Police Department: A Historical Review 1854–2000* (Paducah, KY: Turner Publishing Company, 2000). This book is extremely rare. Its text is excerpted as a fifteen-page essay titled "In the Beginning," available at https://www.spphs.org/history/2000/index.php.

11. Paul Maccabee, *John Dillinger Slept Here: A Crooks' Tour of Crime and Corruption in St. Paul, 1920–1936* (St. Paul: Minnesota Historical Society Press, 1995), 35.

12. Maccabee, *John Dillinger Slept Here*, 30.

13. *St. Paul Daily News*, March 16, 1934, 1; *St. Paul Daily News*, March 31, 1934, 1, 2.

14. *St. Paul Daily News*, March 31, 1934, 1, 2.

15. *St. Paul Daily News*, March 31, 1934, 1, 2; Maccabee, *John Dillinger Slept Here*, 254.

16. *St. Paul Daily News*, June 24, 1935, 1.

17. *St. Paul Daily News*, June 24, 1935, 1.

18. Maccabee, *John Dillinger Slept Here*, 256.

19. *St. Paul Dispatch*, September 15, 1936, 1; *St. Paul Daily News*, June 24, 1935, 1.

20. Edward J. "Ed" Steenberg, "John Joseph O'Connor and the 'Layover Agreement' (One Person's Observations)," St. Paul Police Historical Society, https://www.spphs.org/history/oconnor/index.php; Maccabee, *John Dillinger Slept Here*, 256. For a complete account of Brown's career, see Timothy Mahoney, *Secret Partners: Big Tom Brown and the Barker Gang* (St. Paul: Minnesota Historical Society Press, 2013).

21. St. Paul Police Annual Report 1937, 11; *St. Paul Dispatch*, April 16, 1937, 1.

22. St. Paul Police Annual Report 1937, 11; Edward J. Steenberg, "St. Paul Police Department Reform, 1933–1940," mnopedia.org.

23. St. Paul Police Annual Report 1937, 11.

24. *St. Paul Dispatch*, February 15, 1937, 1.

25. *St. Paul Dispatch*, February 13, 1937, 3.

26. *St. Paul Dispatch*, February 16, 1937, 1.

27. *St. Paul Dispatch*, February 15, 1937, 2.

28. *St. Paul Dispatch*, February 18, 1937, 3.

Notes to Chapter 3: The Key to Identification

1. MR, Carrier and Kennedy, December 9, 1937, 7:47 A.M.

2. Personnel info cards, St. Paul Police Department, Human Resources Unit. Charles J. Tierney's brother John J. Tierney was also on the force. A third brother, Patrolman Lawrence Tierney, had been shot and killed in 1934 by a burglar he was chasing. See St. Paul Police Historical Society, "Annual Report of the Bureau of Police, Department of Public Safety of the City of Saint Paul, Minnesota for the Year 1930," http://www.spphs.org/history/1930/roster.php, and "Honor Roll: Officers Killed in the Line of Duty," http://www.spphs.org/honor_roll/index.php.

3. MR, Lt. Talbot, Jakobson, and Merrill, December 9, 1937, 10:00 A.M.

4. MR, Merrill, December 9, 1937, 4:25 P.M.

5. In many of the addresses given in this book, the numbers are paired: 286–288 Dayton, for example. The buildings share a roof but have two numbers, one for east and one for west halves. Addresses provided in the text follow the numbers given in the reports.

6. MR, Kampmann and R. Schmidt, December 9, 1937, 7:50 A.M.

7. MR, Kampmann and R. Schmidt, December 9, 1937, 7:50 A.M.

8. MR, Kampmann and R. Schmidt, December 9, 1937.

9. MR, Lt. R. McCarthy, December 9, 1937.

10. Ruth Munson's diary, Offense File 33436, St. Paul Police Department.

11. Ruth Munson's address book, Offense File 33436, St. Paul Police Department.

12. MR, V. Michel and A. Curran, December 9, 1937.

13. MR, Kennedy and Carrier, December 9, 1937.

14. MR, Carrier and Kennedy, December 9, 1937.

15. MR, Lt. Talbot and Jakobson, December 9, 1937, 2:45 P.M.

16. MR, Kampmann and Schmidt, December 9, 1937, 7:50 A.M.

17. Ruth Munson's diary; Ruth Munson's address book.

18. In 1937, law enforcement officers were not required to warn witnesses and suspects that what they say could be used against them in legal proceedings. The "Miranda warning," as it is now popularly called, was established by the US Supreme Court in *Miranda v. Arizona* (1966).

19. Statement, Joan Pivoran, December 9, 1937, 2:15 P.M.

20. Statement, Bertha Hopland, December 9, 1937, 2:20 P.M.

21. MR, Schlichting and Harkness, December 9, 1937, 2:30 P.M.

22. Statement, Mrs. Raymond Nelson, December 9, 1937, 4:27 P.M.

23. For a map of the streetcar lines, see "Minneapolis–St. Paul Streetcar System 1933," old.trolleyride.org/History/PDFs/Streetcar_colored_map.pdf.

24. Statement, Derrick Das, December 9, 1937, 3:45 P.M.

25. MR, Kampmann and R. Schmidt, December 9, 1937, 7:50 A.M.; MR, Merrill, December 9, 1937, 4:25 P.M.; Letters, Ruth Munson to Derrick (Dick) Das, November 3 and November 5, 1937.

26. *St. Paul Dispatch*, December 9, 1937, 1, 4.

27. *St. Paul Dispatch*, December 9, 1937, 1, 4.

28. *St. Paul Dispatch*, December 9, 1937, 1, 4.

29. *St. Paul Dispatch*, December 9, 1937, 1.

30. *Minneapolis Journal*, December 9, 1937, 1.

31. Statement, Belle Luke, December 9, 1937, 8:05 P.M.

32. MR, Carrier, Kennedy, and Murnane, December 9, 1937, 8:30 P.M.

33. Statement, Alma Hill, December 9, 1937, 8:40 P.M.

34. Statement, Sue Schaffer, December 9, 1937, 8:55 P.M.

35. Statement, Marie Miller, December 9, 1937, 9:15 P.M.

36. Statement, Marion Gavin, December 9, 1937, 9:30 P.M.

37. Statement, Olaf Anderson, December 9, 1937, 9:35 P.M.

38. MR, Talbot and Jakobson, December 9, 1937, 10:00 P.M.

39. Statement, Theodore Thompson, December 9, 1937, 10:20 P.M.

40. Statement, Carl Gash, December 9, 1937, 10:45 P.M.

Notes to Chapter 4: Gathering Facts

1. *St. Paul Daily News*, December 10, 1937, 1.

2. *St. Paul Dispatch*, December 10, 1937, 1; *Minneapolis Journal*, December 10, 1937, 1, 4.

3. *St. Paul Dispatch*, December 10, 1937, 1; *Minneapolis Journal*, December 10, 1937, 1, 4.

4. *St. Paul Daily News*, December 10, 1937, 1. Neither the Ramsey County coroner's official autopsy report nor anything more detailed than a Janu-

ary 6, 1938, summary report by Dr. John B. Dalton, police criminologist, has survived, leaving the issue of whether Ruth Munson was sexually assaulted something of a mystery.

5. *St. Paul Pioneer Press*, December 10, 1937, 1.

6. MR, Enebak and Soderberg, December 10, 1937, 9:30 A.M.

7. MR, Talbot and Jakobson, December 10, 1937, 1:30 P.M.

8. *St. Paul Daily News*, December 10, 1937, 1.

9. MR, Hanft and Jansen, December 10, 1937.

10. MR, Kampmann and R. Schmidt, December 10, 1937.

11. *St. Paul Daily News*, December 11, 1937, 1. In 2024, the structure housed the Caffe Biaggio.

12. MR, Carrier and Kennedy, December 10, 1937, morning.

13. *St. Paul Daily News*, December 10, 1937, 1.

14. MR, Harrington and Grun, December 10, 1937, 12:00 P.M.

15. Statement, Oscar Loberg, December 10, 1937, 12:45 P.M.

16. Statement, Clarence Loberg, December 10, 1937, 12:45 P.M.

17. MR, Lt. R. McCarthy, December 10, 1937, 1:30 P.M.

18. Statement, Bertha M. Wormley, December 10, 1937, 3:00 P.M. Wormley used "Ella" as her given name.

19. MR, Carrier and Kennedy, December 10, 1937, P.M.

20. MR, Carrier and Kennedy, December 10, 1937, P.M.

21. Statement, William Nelson, December 10, 1937, 7:40 P.M.

22. MR, Carrier and Kennedy, December 10, 1937, 9:00 P.M.

23. MR, Carrier and Kennedy, December 10, 1937.

24. Statement, Vincent Nels Sorg, December 10, 1937, 10:15 P.M.

25. MR, Stockton, December 10, 1937, 3:40 P.M.

26. Walter S. Ryder, "The Negro in St. Paul," *Opportunity: Journal of Negro Life* (June 1931): 170–73.

27. Calvin F. Schmid, *Social Saga of Two Cities: An Ecological and Statistical Study of Social Trends in Minneapolis and Saint Paul* (Minneapolis: Minneapolis Council of Social Agencies, Bureau of Social Research, 1937), 181; Ryder, "The Negro in St. Paul." Because the area was older, mixed use, and racially diverse, New Deal inspectors working for the Home Owners' Loan Corporation in the 1930s graded the neighborhood as "D, hazardous," and marked it red—redlined it. Suddenly, banks would not provide residents with home mortgages. (Ruth Munson's neighborhood was tagged "C, definitely declining.") See Bill Lindeke, *St. Paul: An Urban Biography* (St. Paul: Minnesota Historical Society Press, 2021), 106. The sources cited in this book generally did not make a distinction between porters, who worked on the trains, and red caps, who stayed in St. Paul and worked in the depot.

Notes to Chapter 5: "Mighty Near the Perfect Murder"

1. *Minneapolis Star*, December 11, 1937, 1, 2; MR, Schlichting, December 28, 1937, 9:30 A.M.

2. *St. Paul Dispatch*, December 11, 1937, 1.

3. *St. Paul Pioneer Press*, December 11, 1937, 1.

4. *St. Paul Daily News*, December 10, 1937, 10.

5. *St. Paul Pioneer Press*, December 11, 1937, 1, 4.

6. *St. Paul Pioneer Press*, December 11, 1937, 1; *Minneapolis Star*, December 11, 1937, 1.

7. MR, Lt. Talbot and Jakobson, December 12, 1937, 9:00 A.M.

8. Statement, Walter Lucci, December 11, 1937, 8:35 A.M.

9. Statement, Darrell Wilber, December 11, 1937, 10:00 A.M.

10. MR, Heaton and Merrill, December 11, 1937, 1:00 P.M.

11. Statement, August "Gus" Gavanda, December 11, 1937, 11:00 A.M.

12. Statement, H. A. Nielsen, December 11, 1937, 1:15 P.M.

13. MR, O'Keefe, December 11, 1937, P.M.; MR, McCarthy, December 11, 1937, 1:10 P.M.

14. MR, Frank R. Cullen, December 11, 1937, 3:15 P.M.

15. Statement, Dorothy Lolly, December 11, 1937, 5:38 P.M.

16. Statement, A. F. Meyer, December 11, 1937, 6:00–7:00 P.M.

17. MR, Lt. McCarthy, December 11, 1937.

18. MR, Stutzman and Nielsen, December 11, 1937, 6:45 P.M.

19. MR, H. Schlichting, December 11, 1937, 9:45 P.M.

20. MR, McGowan and Lannon, December 11, 1937, 9:40 P.M.

Notes to Chapter 6: Contrasts

1. The Friendship Club was started by Bob Kenny, who "figured that there were lots of people who couldn't afford a $3, $4, or $6 evening, but would still like to have a place to dance at a reasonable price. He also felt for lonely people who had nobody to dance with or felt that they were too old to dance with the youngsters." Dances were broadcast on various radio stations over the years. It closed in 1961. See Twin Cities Music Highlights, "Mr. Lucky's," https://twincitiesmusichighlights.net/venues/mr-luckys/, which includes the grand opening display advertisement for the Friendship Club.

2. MR, Enebak, Kampmann, R. Schmidt, and Soderberg, December 12, 1937, 8:30 A.M.–1:00 A.M. The report incorrectly lists their starting time as A.M. rather than P.M.

3. MR, Woodhouse and R. Schmidt, December 12, 1937, 2:00 A.M.

4. *St. Paul Pioneer Press*, December 12, 1937, 1.

5. MR, Kampmann and R. Schmidt, December 12, 1937, 8:30 A.M.; MR, Talbot and Jakobson, December 9, 1937, 10:00 P.M. This report includes a handwritten note added at a later date that Lyttle had stepped out with Ruth Munson.

6. Statement, Joseph J. Rhiner, December 12, 1937, 11:00 A.M.; Statement, James Chapman Lyttle, December 13, 1937, 8:30 A.M.

7. MR, Vick and Woodhouse, December 12, 1937, 10:15 A.M.; Letter, H. H. Elmquist to members of Union Lodge No. 82 of the Scandinavian American

Fraternity, December 1, 1937; Letter, Helen C. Munson to Assistant Chief of Police Charles Tierney, December 13, 1937.

8. MR, Woodhouse and R. Schmidt, December 12, 1937.

9. MR, Harrington and Grun, December 12, 1937, 12:00 P.M.; Statement, Hiram Miller, December 12, 1937.

10. *St. Paul Daily News*, December 13, 1937, 2; *Journal of Burnett County*, December 16, 1937, 1, 10.

11. *St. Paul Daily News*, December 13, 1937, 2; *St. Paul Daily News*, December 14, 1937, 1; *St. Paul Dispatch*, December 14, 1937, 1.

12. MR, Heaton and Merrill, December 12, 1937, 1:30 P.M.

13. MR, Jakobson and Schlichting, December 12, 1937; MR, Jakobson, December 12, 1937.

14. MR, Jakobson, December 12, 1937.

15. MR, Jakobson, December 12, 1937.

16. MR, Jakobson, December 12, 1937.

17. MR, Joe McDonnell and Schimmel, December 12, 1937, 7:02 P.M.; MR, Sargent and Knyphausen, December 12, 1937, 2:30 P.M.; MR, Burg, Jr. 288 and A. Pagel 494, December 12, 1937, 4:30 P.M.

18. MR, Baum and Jahnke, December 12, 1937, 11:00 P.M.

19. Statement, Bernard E. Boerger, December 12, 1937, 11:15 P.M.

20. MR, Lt. Heaton and J. Cook, December 18, 1937.

21. MR, Kennedy, Carrier, and Harkness, December 12, 1937. Ruth noted in her diary that her sister Helen accompanied her to the Friendship Club on occasion. Patrons of the Ace uniformly described one of the two women who accompanied Ruth to that nightspot as a redhead, raising the question of whether Ruth had two sets of two women friends.

22. MR, Kennedy, Carrier, and Harkness, December 12, 1937.

23. MR, Kennedy, Carrier, and Harkness, December 12, 1937.

Notes to Chapter 7: Sensational Clues

1. *St. Paul Pioneer Press*, December 13, 1937, 1.

2. *St. Paul Dispatch*, December 13, 1937, 1.

3. *St. Paul Dispatch*, December 13, 1937, 1.

4. *St. Paul Daily News*, December 13, 1937, 1.

5. Letter, Oran Stutzman to Assistant Chief Tierney, December 12, 1937.

6. MR, Carrier and Kennedy, December 13, 1937, A.M.

7. MR, Schroeder and R. Schmidt, December 13, 1937, 8:20 A.M.

8. MR, Schroeder and R. Schmidt, December 13, 1937, 8:20 A.M.

9. Classified ad in *St. Paul Recorder*, December 24, 1937, 6.

10. MR, Murnane and Soderberg, December 13, 1937, 10:00 A.M.

11. Statement, Herman Hasse, December 13, 1937, 10:30 A.M.

12. MR, Sauro and Johnson, December 12, 1937, 11:30 A.M.

13. Statement, Elvin Gordon Garrison, December 13, 1937, 1:50 P.M.

14. Statement, Mrs. Clara Broughton, December 13, 1937, 2:30 A.M.

15. MR, Jakobson, December 13, 1937.

16. MR, Martin and Olson, December 13, 1937, 8:00 P.M.; includes post-script by Schroeder and Woodhouse, December 14, 1937.

17. MR, Coates, December 13, 1937, 9:58 P.M.

Notes to Chapter 8: Intriguing Leads

1. Ruth Munson's diary; Ruth Munson's address book.

2. MR, N. Smith and L. Schultz, December 14, 1937, 1:00 A.M.

3. MR, L. Schultz and N. Smith, December 14, 1937, 2:00 A.M.

4. MR, Vick and R. Murnane, December 14, 1937, 9:00 A.M.

5. MR, Vick and Murnane, December 14, 1937, 9:00 A.M.

6. *Minneapolis Journal*, December 14, 1937, 1; *Minneapolis Sunday Tribune*, March 31, 1937, 1, 4; *Minneapolis Tribune*, July 25, 2021, B4.

7. *St. Paul Pioneer Press*, December 14, 1937, 1.

8. *St. Paul Pioneer Press*, December 14, 1937, 1; *Minneapolis Tribune*, December 14, 1937, 2.

9. *Minneapolis Tribune*, December 14, 1937, 2; *St. Paul Pioneer Press*, December 14, 1937, 1, 4.

10. *St. Paul Daily News*, December 14, 1937, 1; MR, Ra Murnane, December 14, 1937, 11:00 A.M.

11. White-Slave Traffic Act, Pub. L. 61–277; *Literary Digest* 122, no. 26 (August 29, 1936): 26–28; List of persons who have been arrested for various sex crimes for the year 1937, in Offense File 33436, St. Paul Police Department. For a comprehensive study of the FBI's campaign against so-called "white slavery," see Jessica R. Pliley, *Policing Sexuality: The Mann Act and the Making of the FBI* (Cambridge, MA: Harvard University Press, 2014).

12. MR, Carrier and Kennedy, December 14, 1937, A.M. Kenneth Dahlberg would later gain infamy for turning over a donation check for $25,000 to Richard Nixon's 1972 reelection campaign that eventually made its way into the account of a Watergate burglar.

13. MR, Carrier and Kennedy, December 14, 1937, 12:00 noon.

14. *St. Paul Daily News*, December 14, 1937, 1.

15. *St. Paul Dispatch*, December 14, 1937, 1, 2.

16. Statement, Robert Brown, December 14, 1937, 2:40 P.M.

17. Statement, Guadalupe Yniguez, December 14, 1937, 3:05 P.M.

18. Statement, Aylene Stivers, December 14, 1937, 4:40 P.M.; Statement, Dorothy Yniguez, December 14, 1937, 4:50 P.M.; Statement, Dorothy Mondar, December 14, 1937, 5:00 P.M.; MR, Carrier and Kennedy, December 17, 1937, 11:00 A.M.

19. MR, R. Murnane and Nielsen, December 14, 1937, 3:45 P.M.

20. MR, Johnson and Sauro, December 14, 1937, 12:30 P.M.

21. Letter, C. A. Hackert, chief of police, to Leo Utecht, warden, Minnesota State Prison, December 14, 1937.

22. MR, Jakobson, December 14, 1937.

23. MR, C. Olinger and Carrier, December 15, 1937, P.M.

Notes to Chapter 9: New Clues, New Theories

1. *St. Paul Pioneer Press*, December 15, 1937, 1; *Minneapolis Tribune*, December 15, 1927, 11.

2. *St. Paul Daily* News, December 15, 1937, 1.

3. *Minneapolis Journal*, December 15, 1937, 17.

4. *Minneapolis Journal*, December 15, 1937, 17; MR, Vick and Murnane, December 10, 1937, 8:30 P.M.

5. *Minneapolis Journal*, December 14, 1937, 1; MR, R. Schmidt, December 14, 1937, 11:40 A.M.

6. *St. Paul Daily News*, December 15, 1937, 1; *St. Paul Dispatch*, December 15, 1937, 1.

7. *St. Paul Dispatch*, December 15, 1937, 1.

8. *St. Paul Daily News*, December 15, 1937, 1.

9. MR, R. Schmidt, December 14, 1937, 11:40 A.M.; MR., Schroeder and R. Schmidt, December 15, 1937, 2:35 P.M.

10. MR, Jakobson, December 15, 1937.

11. MR, T. F. Franckowiak, December 15, 1937, 10:55 A.M.

12. MR, Jakobson and Schlichting, December 15, 1937, 12:30 P.M.

13. MR, E. J. Kane, December 15, 1937.

14. MR, Lt. Talbot, December 15, 1937, 2:30 P.M.

15. Minnesota House of Representatives, HF 82, January 15, 1913; *National Advocate*, October 17, 1918, 1. Alaska and Hawaii, not yet states at this time, also never enacted a miscegenation law: https://sharetngov .tnsosfiles.com/tsla/exhibits/blackhistory/pdfs/Miscegenation%20laws.pdf.

16. *Twin City Star*, August 7, 1915, 2.

17. *Northwestern Bulletin*, January 31, 1925, 1.

18. *Minneapolis Spokesman*, June 19, 1936, 2.

19. Letter, Ruth Munson to Elmer Unglamb, aka "Whitey," December 7, 1937.

20. Statement, Elmer Unglamb, December 15, 1937, 3:00 P.M.

21. MR, Schroeder and R. Schmidt, December 15, 1937, 11:50 A.M.

22. Statement, Adolph W. Hultgren, December 15, 1937, 4:15 P.M.

23. MR, Carrier and Kennedy, December 15, 1937, 9:00 P.M.

24. MR, Vick and Welander, December 15, 1937, 11:00 P.M.

Notes to Chapter 10: Witnesses and Suspects

1. MR, J. Schmitz, Salaba, Vick, and Welander, December 16, 1937, 1:29 A.M.

2. *St. Paul Pioneer Press*, December 16, 1937, 1.

3. *St. Paul Daily News*, December 15, 1937, 8.

4. *St. Paul Dispatch*, December 16, 1937, 1; *St. Paul Daily News*, December 16, 1937, 1.

5. *Minneapolis Journal*, December 16, 1937, 17.

6. *St. Paul Daily News*, December 16, 1937, 1.

7. MR, Murnane, December 16, 1937.

8. *Minneapolis Journal*, December 15, 1937, 17; *St. Paul Pioneer Press*, December 16, 1937, 1.

9. Statement, Mr. and Mrs. Peter Gustafson, December 16, 1937, 11:00 A.M.

10. MR, Kennedy and Carrier, December 16, 1937. Bohan is spelled Bohen in other reports.

11. MR, Lt. Coffey and L. Schultz, December 16, 1937, 11:00 A.M.; MR, Lt. Coffey and L. Schultz, December 16, 1937.

12. MR, Lt. Coffey and L. Schultz, December 16, 1937.

13. MR, F. R. Cullen, December 16, 1937, 12:30 P.M.

14. *St. Paul Pioneer Press*, December 13, 1937, 1.

15. Statement, Robert Gatzke, December 16, 1938, 1:15 P.M. The 1938 date was probably a typographical error missed by the stenographer. Based on other sources, the author has dated this document as December 16, 1937.

16. Statement, Earl Carl Gussman, December 16, 1937, 2:30 P.M.

17. Statement, Helen Laska, December 16, 1937, 3:00 P.M.

18. Postcard, Anonymous to Chief of Police, undated, attached to MR, Schlichting and Jakobson, December 16, 1937, 4:30 P.M.

19. MR, Schlichting and Jakobson, December 16, 1937, 4:30 P.M.

20. MR, Lt. R. McCarthy, December 16, 1937, 8:00 P.M.

21. Statement, George W. Nado, December 16, 1937, 9:30 P.M.

22. MR, O. Enebak, December 16, 1937, 9:30 P.M.

23. Statement, Walter Couture, December 16, 1937, 11:00 P.M.

Notes to Chapter 11: "A Long Hard Drag"

1. *St. Paul Pioneer Press*, December 17, 1937, 2:13.

2. *Minneapolis Tribune*, December 17, 1937, 6; *Minneapolis Journal*, December 17, 1937, 2.

3. MR, Carrier and Kennedy, December 17, 1937.

4. Letter, undated, unsigned, attached to MR, Coffey and L. Schultz, December 17, 1937, 10:00 A.M.; MR, Coffey and L. Schultz, December 17, 1937, 10:00 A.M.

5. MR, Martin and Olson, December 16, 1937, 7:00 P.M.; Statement, Mrs. Valentine Marie Wiegand, December 16, 1937, 9:50 P.M.

6. Statement, Weston Hill, December 17, 1937, 10:55 A.M.

7. *St. Paul Daily News*, December 17, 1937, 1.

8. *St. Paul Daily News*, December 17, 1937, 1; *Minneapolis Journal*, December 18, 1937, 3.

9. *St. Paul Dispatch*, December 18, 1937, 1.

10. MR, Robert Williams, December 17, 1937, 10:05 P.M.

11. *Minneapolis Star*, December 18, 1937, 11; *St. Paul Dispatch*, December 18, 1937, 1.

12. *St. Paul Pioneer Press*, December 18, 1937, 1.

13. MR, H. Schlichting, December 18, 1937, 10:30 A.M.

14. MR, H. Schlichting, December 18, 1937, 10:30 A.M.

15. MR, Lt. Heaton and J. Cook, December 18, 1937.

16. *St. Paul Dispatch*, December 18, 1937, 1.

17. MR, F. Nielsen, December 18, 1937.

18. MR, Talbot and Williams, December 18, 1937, 8:00 P.M.

19. MR, Kampmann and Stow, December 19, 1937, 12:20 A.M.

20. MR, Morse and L. Tynan, December 19, 1937, 12:45 A.M.

21. *St. Paul Pioneer Press*, December 19, 1937, 1.

22. MR, Kennedy and Carrier, December 19, 1937.

Notes to Chapter 12: Dead Ends

1. *St. Paul Pioneer Press*, December 20, 1937, 1.

2. *St. Paul Pioneer Press*, December 20, 1937, 1.

3. *St. Paul Pioneer Press*, December 20, 1937, 1.

4. *St. Paul Dispatch*, December 20, 1937, 1.

5. MR, Carrier and Kennedy, December 20, 1937, 2:05 P.M.

6. *St. Paul Dispatch*, December 20, 1937, 1; *St. Paul Daily News*, December 20, 1937, 1.

7. *St. Paul Daily News*, December 20, 1937, 1.

8. MR, Jakobson and Schlichting, December 20, 1937, 11:30 A.M.

9. MR, B. Carrier, December 20, 1937.

10. MR, Baum and Stow, December 20, 1937, 6:30 P.M.

11. *St. Paul Daily News*, December 20, 1937, 1.

12. MR, Arndt and Doth, December 21, 1937.

13. MR, Kennedy and Carrier, December 21, 1937; MR, Kennedy and Carrier, December 21, 1937. They filed separate reports for each trip, but it is unclear which man was picked up first.

14. Statement, James E. McGinley, December 21, 1937, 12:20 P.M.

15. Statement, Willard E. Wolf, December 21, 1937, 2:05 P.M.

16. Ruth Munson's diary, June 28 and June 29, 1937.

17. Statement, Horace Dupont, December 21, 1937, 2:45 P.M.

18. Statement, Adolph Hultgren, December 15, 1937, 4:15 P.M.

19. MR, J. Conroy and Joe McDonnell, December 21, 1937, 6:11 P.M.

20. MR, H. Schlichting, December 22, 1937, 10:00 A.M.

21. MR, H. Schlichting, December 22, 1937, 11:00 A.M.

22. MR, H. Schlichting, December 22, 1937, 10:30 A.M.

23. MR, H. Schlichting, December 22, 1937, 11:45 A.M.

24. MR, Soderberg and Harken, December 22, 1937, 2:44 P.M.

25. Statement, Merton Ewing, December 22, 1937, 4:00 P.M.

26. MR, Carrier and Kennedy, December 22, 1937, 3:45 P.M.

27. MR, Jakobson, December 23, 1937; MR, Merrill, December 23, 1937, 9:00 A.M.

28. MR, Kennedy and Carrier, December 23, 1937, 11:30 A.M.; List of persons who have been arrested for various sex crimes for year 1937.

29. *St. Paul Daily News*, December 24, 1937, 3.

30. MR, H. Schlichting, December 24, 1937, 9:00 A.M.; MR, H. Jakobson, December 24, 1937.

31. MR, J. Axness, December 26, 1937.

32. MR, Lt. Heaton and J. Cook, December 27, 1937, 1:00 P.M.

Notes to Chapter 13: Focus Areas

1. *St. Paul Pioneer Press*, December 13, 1937, 1; Statement, Robert Gatzke, December 16, 1938, 1:15 P.M. The 1938 date is probably a typo not caught by the stenographer. Based on other sources, the author has dated the document as December 16, 1937.

2. MR, Lt. Talbot, December 27, 1937, 3:00 P.M.

3. MR, Lt. Heaton and J. Cook, December 27, 1937, 3:00 P.M.

4. MR, Johnson and Sauro, December 28, 1937; List of persons who have been arrested for various sex crimes for the year 1937.

5. MR, Jakobson, December 28, 1937; MR, H. Schlichting, December 28, 1937, 9:00 A.M.; MR, Jakobson and Schlichting, December 28, 1937, 9:00 A.M.; MR, Schlichting, December 28, 1937, 9:30 A.M.

6. MR, Kennedy and Carrier, December 28, 1937, P.M.

7. MR, Carrier and Kennedy, December 28, 1937, 5:30 P.M.

8. MR, R. Costello, December 29, 1937; MR, Lt. Coffey and L. Schultz, December 31, 1937, A.M.

9. MR, Lt. N. Smith, December 30, 1937.

10. MR, Grace, Cullen, and N. Smith, December 31, 1937, 9:00 A.M.

11. MR, Kampmann and Stow, December 30, 1937, 9:30 P.M.

12. Statement, Robert Brown, December 14, 1937, 2:40 P.M.

13. MR, Kennedy and Carrier, December 31, 1937, morning.

14. MR, Lt. Coffey and L. Schultz, December 31, 1937. The suspect is listed as Robert Bloom in other reports.

15. St. Paul Police Annual Report 1937, 16–17.

16. *St. Paul Pioneer Press*, January 3, 1938, 1.

17. MR, Lt. T. Jansen, January 3, 1937 (really 1938), 1:30 P.M.

18. MR, Lt. Heaton and J. Cook, January 3, 1938.

19. MR, Kennedy and Carrier, January 3, 1938, 4:00 P.M.

20. MR, T. Jansen, January 3, 1938, 6:00 P.M.–11:00 P.M.

21. Letter, Henry N. Stream, sheriff of Chisago County, to C. A. Hackert, chief of police, St. Paul, January 3, 1938.

22. MR, Lannon, McGowan, and Courtney, January 4, 1938, 4:00 P.M.

23. MR, Lannon, McGowan, and Courtney, January 4, 1938, 4:00 P.M.

24. MR, Williams and Turpin, January 5, 1938, 1:30 P.M.
25. MR, Dr. John H. Dalton, January 6, 1938, 9:00 A.M.; *St. Paul Daily News*, December 10, 1937, 1.
26. MR, Dr. John B. Dalton, January 6, 1938, 9:00 A.M.
27. MR, Chief Hackert and Insp. McMullin, January 7, 1938.
28. MR, McGowan, Lannon, and Courtney, January 7, 1938.
29. MR, Merrill, L. Schultz, and T. Shanley, January 7, 1938.
30. MR, Merrill, L. Schultz, and T. Shanley, January 7, 1938.
31. Ruth Munson's diary, July 17, 1937.

Notes to Chapter 14: Suspects and Theories
1. Letter, C. A. Hackert, chief of police, to Albert M. Pett, January 8, 1938.
2. MR, Kennedy, Carrier, and Cook, January 8, 1938.
3. MR, Vick, Stutzman, and Lt. Jansen, January 8, 1938, 5:00 P.M.
4. MR, Cook, Carrier, and Kennedy, January 8, 1938, 6:00 P.M.
5. *St. Paul Dispatch*, January 13, 1938, 1.
6. *St. Paul Pioneer Press*, December 16, 1937, 1.
7. Statement, Charles B. Moore, January 13, 1938, 1:30 P.M.
8. *St. Paul Pioneer Press*, January 14, 1938, 1.
9. *St. Paul Dispatch*, January 14, 1938, 2:17; *St. Paul Pioneer Press*, January 15, 1938, 5.
10. Letter, Anonymous to Chief of Police, Minneapolis, January 4, 1938, attached to Chief Tierney's copy of MR, R. Schmidt and Schroeder, January 14, 1938, 4:00 P.M. The term "mulatto," referring to a biracial person with a Black parent and a white parent, is now considered offensive.
11. MR, R. Schmidt and Schroeder, January 14, 1938, 4:00 P.M.
12. MR, Cook, Kennedy, and Carrier, January 14, 1938, 10:15 P.M.
13. MR, Cook, Kennedy, and Carrier, January 15, 1938.
14. Statement, Mrs. Arthur Stevenson, January 15, 1938, 12:05 P.M.
15. *St. Paul Pioneer Press*, January 15, 1938, 5.
16. *St. Paul Dispatch*, January 18, 1938, 13.
17. *St. Paul Pioneer Press*, January 16, 1938, 4:5.
18. Statement, Arthur Stevenson, January 17, 1938, 10:30 A.M.
19. *St. Paul Dispatch*, January 17, 1938, 1.
20. *St. Paul Pioneer Press*, January 18, 1938, 7; *Minneapolis Tribune*, January 18, 1938, 2.
21. *St. Paul Dispatch*, January 18, 1938, 13.
22. MR, O'Heron, January 18, 1938, 11:35 A.M.
23. MR, O'Heron, January 18, 1938, 11:35 A.M.
24. MR, Harken, January 19, 1938, includes manuscript note by Olson and Murnane, dated January 19, 1938.
25. MR, Harken, January 19, 1938, includes manuscript note by Olson and Murnane, dated January 19, 1938.
26. MR, Merrill, L. Schultz, and Shanley, January 7, 1938.

27. MR, Cook, Kennedy, and Carrier, January 19, 1938, A.M.

28. MR, Cook, Kennedy, and Carrier, January 19, 1938, A.M.

Notes to Chapter 15: Ransom Notes and Truth Serum

1. *Minneapolis Tribune*, January 24, 1938, 12; *Minneapolis Star*, January 24, 1938, 5.

2. *Minneapolis Tribune*, January 20, 1938, 2.

3. MR, Dr. J. B. Dalton and H. H. Goetzinger, January 21, 1938; MR, Dr. J. B. Dalton and H. H. Goetzinger, January 22, 1938.

4. Anonymous note, undated, attached to MR, Insp. Wm. McMullin, January 22, 1938, 11:15 P.M.

5. MR, Insp. Wm. McMullin, January 22, 1938, 11:15 P.M.

6. MR, to Lt. Nate Smith from Ray McCarthy, January 24, 1938, includes handwritten addendum dated January 26, 1938, from Kennedy, Carrier, and Cook.

7. MR, to Lt. Nate Smith from Ray McCarthy, January 24, 1938, includes handwritten addendum dated January 26, 1938, from Kennedy, Carrier, and Cook.

8. MR, Cook, Carrier, and Kennedy, January 24, 1938, 9:00 A.M.

9. MR, Robert Williams, December 17, 1937, 10:05 P.M.; MR, Williams and Turpin, January 31, 1938, 9:40 P.M.

10. *St. Paul Dispatch*, February 5, 1938, 3.

11. Statement, William Wesley Lawrence, February 7, 1938, 10:10 A.M.

12. MR, Supt. Hetznecker, February 10, 1938, 5:15 A.M.

13. MR, L. Schultz, February 14, 1938.

14. Statement taken at Bethesda Hospital, William Wolf, February 12, 1938, 5:00 P.M. All of the dialogue between Kamman and Wolf and Tierney and Wolf in this account is taken from this source.

Notes to Chapter 16: Pimps, Shear Pins, and Possible Suspects

1. MR, Nate Smith, Dr. Dalton, Mitchell, and Goetzinger, February 18, 1938.

2. MR, Nate Smith, Dr. Dalton, Mitchell, and Goetzinger, February 18, 1938. For background on prostitution in Minneapolis, see Penny A. Petersen, *Minneapolis Madams: The Lost History of Prostitution on the Riverfront* (Minneapolis: University of Minnesota Press, 2013).

3. MR, Nate Smith, Dr. Dalton, Mitchell, and Goetzinger, February 18, 1938.

4. MR, Mitchell, February 23, 1938.

5. Statement, Charles Moore, January 13, 1938, 1:30 P.M.

6. Letter, Anonymous to Dear Sirs, February 17, 1938, attached to MR, Carrier, Cook, and Kennedy, February 25, 1938.

7. MR, Carrier, Cook, and Kennedy, February 25, 1938; MR, Carrier, Cook, and Kennedy, February 26, 1938.

8. Letter, Thomas J. Gibbons, sheriff, to Chas. J. Tierney, ass't chief, February 27, 1938, includes memo, February 26, 1938.

9. *Minneapolis Tribune*, March 2, 1938, 2.

10. Statement, Frank Andreff [*sic*], March 2, 1938, 12:00 noon.

11. *Minneapolis Tribune*, March 3, 1938, 13.

12. Note, Offense File 33436, St. Paul Police Department, with accompanying handwritten notes.

13. MR, H. F. Jansen, February 28, 1938, 9:31 P.M.; MR, L. Schultz and Merrill, March 1, 1938, 5:30 P.M.; MR, Cook, Kennedy, and Carrier, March 1, 1938; MR, T. Lee and Vick, March 6, 1938, 2:00 P.M.; MR, Lt. N. Smith, March 8, 1938; MR, Shanley and Courtney, March 10, 1938.

14. Letter, C. A. Hackert to Albert N. Pett, January 8, 1938.

15. Letter, C. A. Hackert to Albert N. Pett, January 8, 1938; MR, John B. Dalton, March 12, 1938, 9:30 A.M.

16. MR, John B. Dalton, March 12, 1938, 9:30 A.M.

17. MR, Martin and Harkness, March 22, 1938, 8:19 P.M.

18. MR, John B. Dalton, March 23, 1938, 11:30 A.M.

19. *Minneapolis Tribune*, April 7, 1938, 12.

20. Interoffice communication, C. A. Hackert to Charles J. Tierney, April 8, 1938. In the note, Hackert spelled the first name "Thorwood."

21. Interoffice communication, C. A. Hackert to Charles J. Tierney, April 8, 1938.

22. Note by Det. Lt. Ray McCarthy, in MR, Baum and Schroeder, April 7, 1938, 4:00 P.M. The date of this report is inaccurate, as the call to Hackert that launched this investigation occurred on April 8, 1938.

23. MR, Baum and Schroeder, April 7, 1938, 4:00 P.M.

24. MR, Baum and Schroeder, April 28, 1938.

25. MR, C. H. Hoffman, April 29, 1938, 11:00 A.M., includes attached handwritten note, May 5, 1938, 4:30 P.M.—Whalen—Jakobson.

26. MR, Kennedy, Carrier, and Merrill, December 9, 1937, 8:30 P.M.

27. MR, C. H. Hoffman, April 29, 1938, 11:00 A.M., includes attached handwritten note, May 5, 1938, 4:30 P.M.—Whalen—Jakobson.

Notes to Chapter 17: "Known Only to the Police"

1. MR, Carrier and Kennedy, December 17, 1937, 11:00 A.M.

2. Statement, Mrs. Leo Gifford, July 7, 1938, 11:10 A.M.

3. Statement, Margaret Yost, July 8, 1938, 10:40 A.M.

4. Statement, Llyod Johnson, July 8, 1938, 11:00 A.M.

5. MR, Lt. Nate Smith, July 7 or 8, 1938. A strikeover by the typewriter makes it impossible to tell which date was intended.

6. MR, Lannon and McGowan, July 22, 1938, 8:00 P.M.; MR, Whalen and Merrill, July 24, 1938, 12:24 A.M.

7. MR, Nielsen and Jakobson, July 23, 1938, 11:33 A.M.

8. MR, Schimmel and McDonnell, July 23, 1938, 11:26 A.M.

9. MR, Schimmel and McDonnell, July 24, 1938, 10:25 A.M.; *Polk's St. Paul City Directory, 1936* (St. Paul, MN: R. R. Polk and Company, 1936), 815.

10. Statement, Margaret Yost, August 13, 1938, 10:15 A.M.

11. Letter, J. Edgar Hoover, director, FBI, to Clinton Hackert, chief of police, September 8, 1938.

12. Note, A Friend to Chief [Clinton Hackert], September 14, 1938; MR, Kennedy and Cook, September 22, 1938, 6:00 P.M.

13. MR, Robt Williams, September 21, 1938, 8:50 A.M.

14. MR, Failes and Williams, September 23, 1938, 9:30 A.M.

15. MR, Jakobson, December 29, 1937.

Notes to Chapter 18: "The Cat Out of the Water"

1. Statement, Wilfred Van Danacker, October 13, 1938, 11:30 A.M.

2. MR, Blade and Jakobson, October 29, 1938, 7:10 P.M.; *Minneapolis Tribune*, October 31, 1938, 8.

3. MR, Mitchell, November 23, 1938, 5:00 P.M.; MR, Cook and Kennedy, November 25, 1938, 2:30 P.M.

4. Statement, Charles Williams, November 26, 1938, 8:35 A.M.

5. Statement, William Fields, November 26, 1938, 9:05 A.M. In this statement the stenographer spelled the name Charley; other stenographers spelled the name Charlie.

6. Statement, John Warren, November 26, 1938, 9:30 A.M.

7. Statement, Mrs. Charles Williams, November 26, 1938, 11:45 A.M.

8. Statement, Mrs. William Fields, November 26, 1938, 12:15 P.M.

9. Statement, Henry Williams, November 28, 1938, 9:50 A.M.

10. MR, Zerahn and Fahey, November 27, 1938, 5:45 P.M.; MR, Baum and Morse, November 28, 1938, 4:30 P.M.

11. Postcard, Anonymous to Police Department, postmarked December 15, 1938.

Notes to Chapter 19: Death Threats and Silverware

1. *Minneapolis Tribune*, January 3, 1939, 11.

2. Typed version of original letter from Mary Connelly to Saint Paul Chief of Police, February 15, 1939, attached to MR, O'Keefe, Shanley, Sauro, and A. Johnson, February 16, 1939.

3. MR, O'Keefe, Shanley, Sauro, and A. Johnson, February 16, 1939.

4. MR, Tynan and Enebak, April 10, 1939, 5:30 A.M.

5. MR, Goodrow and Soderberg, June 8, 1939, 11:00 A.M.

6. MR, Lt. Nate Smith, Dr. Dalton, Mitchell, and Goetzinger, February 18, 1939; MR, Mitchell, February 23, 1938; MR, Mitchell, November 23, 1938, 5:00 P.M.

7. St. Paul Police Historical Society, database listing police employees from the territorial days to present, used by permission. Ranks of offi-

cers and police department staff appearing in this text are taken from this source.

8. MR, R. Halvorson and Pehoski, undated, written late October 1939.

9. MR, R. Halvorson and Pehoski, undated, written late October 1939.

10. MR, Pehoski and R. Halvarson, undated, dated by author as October 25, 1939.

11. MR, Pehoski and R. Halvarson, undated, dated by author as about October 27, 1936.

12. MR, Pehoski and R. Halvarson, undated, dated by author as October 26 or October 27, 1939.

13. MR, R. Halvorson and Pehoski, October 27, 1939.

14. MR, R. Halvorson and Pehoski, October 27, 1939.

15. MR, R. Halvorson and Pehoski, undated, dated by author as just before October 30, 1939.

16. MR, Kennedy and Carrier, January 3, 1938, 4:00 P.M.

Notes to Chapter 20: Taking Failure Personally

1. Typed note, Art. Stattman to Asst. Chief Chas. Tierney, February 15, 1940.

2. MR, Mathiesen and Nielsen, March 22, 1940, 2:00 P.M.; MR, L. Schultz and Nielsen, March 18, 1940, 10 A.M.; Nielsen and Mathiesen, March 29, 1940, 1:50 P.M.; Nielsen and Mathiesen, March 29, 1940, 2:00 P.M.

3. *St. Paul Pioneer Press*, December 29, 1940, 11.

4. *St. Paul Dispatch*, April 2, 1941, 1.

5. *St. Paul Pioneer Press*, May 15, 1941, 1.

6. *Minneapolis Star-Journal*, May 16, 1941, 30.

7. *St. Paul Pioneer Press*, November 26, 1941. The suspect is unnamed in newspaper accounts, and there are no copies of relevant interviews or reports in the Munson file.

8. *Minneapolis Star-Journal*, November 26, 1941, 8; *Minneapolis Morning Tribune*, November 27, 1941, 20.

9. *Minneapolis Star-Journal*, October 9, 1942, 6.

10. *St. Paul Pioneer Press*, July 31, 1943, 1.

11. *Minneapolis Morning Tribune*, February 1, 1944, 9.

12. *Minneapolis Star-Journal*, August 18, 1944, 9; *Minneapolis Morning Tribune*, August 18, 1944, 9.

13. *St. Paul Pioneer Press*, March 22, 1945, 11; *St. Paul Pioneer Press*, October 8, 1945, 11.

14. Letter, Milton C. Anderson, county attorney, Richland Co., Montana, to Chief of Police, Minneapolis Police Department, December 2, 1946 (typed copy of the original).

15. Letter attributed to Chief of Police Charles J. Tierney to Milton C. Anderson, county attorney, Sidney, Montana, December 10, 1946.

16. *Minneapolis Star*, August 13, 1948, 10; *St. Paul Pioneer Press*, August 12, 1948, 1.

17. *St. Paul Pioneer Press*, May 27, 1949, 26. St. Paul Police Historical Society, database listing police employees from the territorial days to present. Ranks of officers and police department staff appearing in this text are taken from this source.

18. *Minneapolis Morning Tribune*, May 31, 1952, 1; *St. Paul Pioneer Press*, May 31, 1952, 1.

19. MR, Biagi, Stutzman, and Plummer, September 2, 1953, 4:45 P.M.

20. MR, Leo O. Burr, MD, September 4, 1953, 4:30 P.M.; with MR, Biagi, Stutzman, and Plummer, September 2, 1953, 4:45 P.M.

Notes to Chapter 21: A Lack of Evidence and a Number of Theories

1. MR, Vick and Murnane, December 14, 1937, 9:00 A.M.; *Minneapolis Journal*, December 15, 1937, 1.

2. MR, L. Schultz and Lt. Nate Smith, December 14, 1937, 2:00 A.M.; Statement, Elvin Gordon Garrison, December 13, 1937, 1:50 P.M.

3. MR, Heaton and Merrill, December 12, 1937, 1:30 P.M.

4. MR, Merrill, L. Schultz, and T. Shanley, January 7, 1938.

5. Statement, Oscar Loberg, December 10, 1937, 12:45 P.M.; MR, McGowan and Lannon, December 11, 1937, 9:40 P.M.

6. MR, McGowan and Lannon, December 11, 1937, 9:40 P.M.; *St. Paul Daily News*, December 15, 1938, 1; *St. Paul Dispatch*, December 15, 1937, 1.

7. Statement, Stephen Waugh Westbrook, December 12, 1937, 10:00 A.M.; MR, Schroeder and Woodhouse, December 10, 1937, 9:45 P.M.

8. MR, Goodrow and Soderberg, June 8, 1939, 11:00 A.M.; Statement, Charles Williams, November 26, 1938, 8:55 A.M.

9. MR, Dr. John B. Dalton, January 6, 1938, 9:00 A.M.

10. MR, Dr. John B. Dalton, January 6, 1938, 9:00 A.M.

11. *Minneapolis Journal*, December 15, 1937, 1; MR, Kampmann and Stow, December 30, 1937, 9:30 P.M.

12. *St. Paul Pioneer Press*, December 13, 1937, 1.

13. MR, Harken, January 19, 1938; MR, O'Heron, January 18, 1938, 11:35 A.M.

14. MR, Lt. Nate Smith, Dr. Dalton, Mitchell, and Goetzinger, February 18, 1938; Statement, Charles Moore, January 13, 1938, 1:30 P.M.

Notes to Chapter 22: A Secret Life

1. MR, Hanft and Jansen, December 10, 1937; Statement, Clara Broughton, December 13, 1937, 2:50 P.M.; MR, Morse and Yost, December 20, 1937.

2. MR, Harkness, Kennedy, and Carrier, December 12, 1937; MR, Jakobson, December 14, 1927.

3. *St. Paul Pioneer Press*, December 13, 1937, 1; MR, Woodhouse and R. Schmidt, December 12, 1937.

4. US Bureau of the Census, www.census.gov. In 1930, the median age for a first marriage of a US female was 21.3 years. In 1940, it was 21.5 years. Statement, William Nelson, December 10, 1937, 7:40 P.M.; Statement, Olaf Anderson, December 9, 1937, 9:35 P.M.

5. Statement, Mrs. Valentine Marie Wiegand, December 16, 1937, 9:30 P.M.

6. Letter, Ruth Munson to Derrick (Dick) Das, November 3, 1937; Ruth Munson's diary, November 4 and November 5, 1937.

7. Statement, Adolph W. Hultgren, December 15, 1937, 4:15 P.M.

8. Letter, Ruth Munson to Derrick (Dick) Das, November 3, 1937; Letter, Ruth Munson to Elmer "Whitey" Unglamb, December 7, 1937.

9. MR, Kennedy and Carrier, December 10, 1937.

10. Statement, Walter Lucci, December 11, 1937, 8:35 A.M.; MR, Kennedy and Carrier, December 31, 1937, morning; MR, R. Schmidt and Schroeder, December 13, 1937.

11. MR, Lt. Nate Smith, Dr. Dalton, Mitchell, and Goetzinger, February 18, 1938.

12. *St. Paul Recorder*, December 31, 1937, 1; *Twin Cities Star*, January 18, 1919, 3; Michael Fedo, *The Lynchings in Duluth* (1979; repr., St. Paul: Minnesota Historical Society Press, 2000). This is an excellent, detailed account of the events leading up to the brutal lynching of three Black carnival workers and the tragedy's aftermath. *Northwestern Bulletin*, April 8, 1922, 2; Postcard, Anonymous to Chief of Police, undated, attached in author's copy of files to MR, Jakobson and Schlichting, December 16, 1937, 4:30 P.M.

Notes to Chapter 23: Rife with Racism

1. Statement, Walter Lucci, December 11, 1937, 8:35 A.M.

2. MR, Jakobson, December 12, 1937; MR, Cook, Carrier, and Kennedy, January 24, 1938, 9:00 A.M.

3. MR, Talbot and Williams, December 23, 1937; Postcard, Anonymous to Chief of Police, undated, attached in author's copy of files to MR, Jakobson and Schlichting, December 16, 1937, 4:30 P.M.

4. *Northwestern Bulletin*, April 8, 1922, 2; Statement, Charles B. Moore, January 13, 1938, 1:30 P.M.

5. St. Paul Police Annual Report 1937, 19.

6. Statement, Bernard E. Boerger, December 12, 1937, 11:15 P.M.; MR, Lt. Heaton and Cook, December 18, 1937.

7. MR, Soderberg and Harken, December 22, 1937, 2:41 P.M.; Statement, Merton Ewing, December 22, 1937, 4:00 P.M.; *Minneapolis Spokesman*, August 13, 1943.

8. MR, Lt. Heaton and Cook, December 16, 1937.

9. MR, Williams and Turpin, January 5, 1938, 1:30 P.M.

10. Statement, Charles B. Moore, January 13, 1938, 1:30 P.M.

11. *St. Paul Recorder*, January 29, 1937, 1.

12. List of persons who have been arrested for various sex crimes for the year 1937; Field notes of detectives investigating the possible purchase of silverware for Ruth Munson by a Black man.

13. MR, Ed. Kane, December 15, 1937; MR, Merrill, L. Schultz, and T. Shanley, January 7, 1938.

14. *St. Paul Recorder*, June 4, 1937, 1.

15. James S. Griffin, *Blacks in the St. Paul Police and Fire Departments 1885–1976* (St. Paul, MN: E & J Inc., 1978), 10.

16. Griffin, *Blacks in the St. Paul Police and Fire Departments*, 10.

17. MR, Mitchell, November 23, 1938, 5:00 P.M.; MR, Goodrow and Soderberg, June 8, 1939, 11:00 A.M.

18. MR, Robert Williams, December 17, 1937, 10:05 P.M.; MR, Williams, September 21, 1938, 8:50 A.M.; MR, Kennedy and Carrier, December 16, 1937; MR, Failes and Williams, September 23, 1938, 9:30 A.M.

19. MR, Williams and Turpin, January 31, 1938, 9:40 P.M.

20. Statement, Charles Moore, January 13, 1938, 1:30 P.M.; MR, Talbot and Williams, December 18, 1937, 8:00 P.M.

21. James S. Griffin with Kwame JC McDonald, *Jimmy Griffin: A Son of Rondo* (St. Paul, MN: Ramsey County Historical Society, 2001) 39; Griffin, *Blacks in the St. Paul Police and Fire Departments*, 10, 15, 39.

22. Griffin, *Blacks in the St. Paul Police and Fire Departments*, 15.

Notes to Chapter 24: Missed Opportunities

1. MR, Carrier and Kennedy, December 31, 1937; MR, Pehoski and Halvorson, October 27, 1939.

2. Statement, Margaret Yost, August 13, 1938, 10:15 A.M.

3. MR, Carrier and Kennedy, December 17, 1937, 11:00 A.M.

4. MR, Kampmann and Stow, December 30, 1937, 9:30 P.M.; Statement, Robert Brown, December 14, 1937, 2:40 P.M.

5. MR, Robt. Williams, September 21, 1938, 8:50 A.M.

6. MR, Kennedy and Carrier, December 16, 1937.

7. MR, Pehoski and R. Halvorson, October 27, 1939.

8. Statement, Charles Williams, November 26, 1938, 8:55 A.M.; MR, Goodrow and Soderberg, June 8, 1939, 11:00 A.M.

Notes to Chapter 25: Can the Ruth Munson Case Ever Be Solved?

1. MR, O'Heron, January 18, 1938, 11:35 A.M.; *St. Paul Pioneer Press*, January 9, 1938, 1.

2. MR, Merrill, L. Schlutz, and T. Stanley, January 6, 1938, 8:00 P.M.

3. Letter, J. Edgar Hoover to Chief of Police Clinton Hackert, September 8, 1938.

4. Email, Christina Jones, archivist, Special Access and FOIA Programs RF, National Archives and Records Administration, to author, September 14, 2021.

Notes to Afterword

1. Federal-Aid Highway Act of 1956, Pub. L. 84–627.

2. *St. Paul Daily News*, December 10, 1937, 1; Jesse Van Berkel, "Minnesota Poll: Majority of Women Have Experienced Sexual Harassment," *Star Tribune*, January 17, 2018; Minnesota Bureau of Criminal Apprehension, "2021 Uniform Crime Report," 10, 12, 14–17.

3. "2022 Status of Women and Girls in Minnesota," prepared by the Women's Foundation of Minnesota, Center on Women, Gender, and Public Policy, Humphrey School of Public Affairs, University of Minnesota, 5, 13.

Index

Page numbers in *italics* refer to illustrations.

Hoenhouse, Mrs. Otto, 72–73
Hoffman, C. H., 192–93
Holly Avenue, 141, 144
Hoover, J. Edgar, 92, 171, 201, 266
Hopkins, MN, 71
Hopland, Bertha, 33–35
Howard, Mozelle, 175
Hugo, MN, 51, 53, 125
Hull, Chester, 173
Hultgren, Adolph (Ade), 98, 105–6, 249
Hunters Club, 88, 112–13
Huntsberger, Willis, 229–30

ice melting effort, 122–29
identification of Ruth, 13, 26, 29, 39, 46, 110
Iglehart Avenue, 74, 224–25
Igo, Arnold, 79–80
informant theory, 169, 266
Ingerson, Dr. C. A., 26, 39, 47, 77, 125, 152
inner city transportation, 15
interracial marriage, 103–4, 251
Ironwood, MN, 226
Iverson, George, 145

Jackson, Dorothy, 103
Jahnke, Erwin, 74
Jakobson, Alfred: Aberdeen search, 27, 33; canvassing work, 44, 79, 86, 97–98, 102, 140–41, 143–44, 203; citizen tips, 193; Gertrude Were report, 252; Ivor Shelby, 131; Lee Len arrest, 48, 206; Miller Hospital, 72; Mrs. Otto Hoenhouse, 72–73; note bearing a disturbing message, 116; Phil Lukenheimer, 59; portraits of Ruth, 247; scavengers and adventurers at the Aberdeen, 198–99
Jamie, Wallace Ness, 20
Jansen, Thomas, 48–49, 50–51, 53, 148–50, 152, 157, 247

Jeffers, Clarence, 198
Jefferson, Clifford, 174–76
Jessie (waitress), 147
Jew Ethel, 184–85
Jim Williams's bar, 88, 120
John (from Chicago), 52
Johnson, Alvin, 82, 97, 143, 221
Johnson, Florence, 174
Johnson, J. H., 169–70
Johnson, John A., 15
Johnson, Kenneth, 131–32
Johnson, Lloyd, 195–97, 200
Johnson, Marie and Irene, 151
Johnson, Nellie, 37
Johnson, Paul, 24–25
Johnston, Clarence H. Sr., 15

Kahn, Howard, 19–20
Kamman, Dr. Gordon, 177, 181–82
Kampmann, Donald: Ace Box Lunch, 55; anonymous letter sent to the Minneapolis police chief, 162; Bertha Hopland and Joan Pivoran interviews, 33–35; Clara Broughton, 28–30; Dorothy Wagner interview, 146; Friendship Club, 67; James Lyttle, 69; light in the Aberdeen, 126; Mrs. McKernan, 27; Ninth Street South, 37–38; William Harris home, 49
Kane, Edmond, 103, 256
Katz, Joe (Sixty), 266
Kaufman, Louis, 218–19
Kellogg Boulevard, 116, 198
Kennedy, Frank: Aberdeen crime scene, 9–13; Ace Box Lunch, 54–55; Ancker Hospital, 78; Ann Noren and Ella (Bertha) Wormley, 106–7; Arthur Conlin interview, 144; Bernice Berglund, 226; Carl Gash, 45; Charles B. (Big Slim) Moore, 174; Charles Sands interview, 169; Chester Hull, 173; Chisago City, MN, tip, 186;

Rice, Henry M., 14
Rice Lake, MN, 43, 233
Rice Lake, WI, 233
Rice Street, 56, 209
Richardson, Dehlia, 184–86
Richland County, MT, 233–34
Riverside Cemetery, 71
Riverview Hotel, 48
robbery motive, 244–45
Roberts, Bea, 120
Robert Street, 103, 174
Rogers & Company, 150
Rondo Avenue, 7, 56, 123, 202, 206,
    207–18, 257
Rondo neighborhood, 56–57, 80,
    125–26, 131, 147, 174, 207–18,
    253–55, 256–58, 269–70
Room 825 of the Aberdeen, 27
Ross, Charles S., 171
Rossini, Benny and Dan, 87
Rossini, Harry, 117
Rossini's, 86–87, 116–17, 206
Roundup Bar, 235–36
Roxy Café, 117–18
Russell, A., 63–64
Russell, Genevieve, 64
Ryan, Catherine, 98
Ryan Hotel, 63

Sabo, Knute, 221
St. Albans Street, 7
St. Anthony Avenue, 88, 108, 207,
    211. See also 607 St. Anthony
    Avenue
St. Clair Avenue, 102
St. Cloud, MN, 130, 183–86
St. Cloud State Reformatory, 183–85,
    245–46, 257
St. Luke's Hospital, 108, 150, 159,
    226, 232
St. Paul Auditorium, 108, 116, 158–59
St. Paul Cathedral, 101, 123, 158
St. Paul Daily News: assaults on
    women, 48; bracelet, 93–94, 101;
cause of death, 152; editorial
    page, 58; focus on what was not
    known, 141; funeral, 71; Harold A.
    Creagan, 130; photo of Ruth, 46;
    police corruption, 19–20; reward,
    78, 132, 172; Selma Munson, 50;
    shear pins, 99–100; two women
    who accompanied Ruth, 91, 110;
    vulnerability of St. Paul women,
    109
St. Paul Dispatch: bracelet, 101;
    Charles B. (Big Slim) Moore,
    158, 161; dates with gentlemen
    friends, 124; next steps, 123;
    police department scandal, 23–24;
    questions about where Ruth was
    slain, 46–47; reward, 234; rumors
    of arrest, 109; screams reported
    to police, 94; sensational report-
    ing, 38–39; two women who
    accompanied Ruth, 78; veterans'
    records, 130
St. Paul Pioneer Press: autopsy
    report, 59; Charles B. (Big Slim)
    Moore, 108, 161, 164–67; coverage
    of the case to its second section,
    119; debris from the Aberdeen,
    129; dismemberment theory,
    77; front-page coverage, 99; on
    Hackert, 231; lack of helpful clues,
    58; Laura Kruse, 90; ownership of
    the bracelet, 110, 115; paperboy
    routes, 5–6; photo of Ruth, 49, 63,
    75; revenge theory, 245; reward,
    68, 234; sensational reporting, 77,
    91; shear pins, 148; sifting debris,
    127; Violet Thoreson, 77, 113,
    142–43
St. Paul Police Department: com-
    munication between FBI agents
    and, 169, 201, 266; letter from
    Minneapolis Police Department,
    234; new headquarters, 236;
    O'Connor layover agreement or

The interior text of *A Murder on the Hill* has been set in Chaparral, a typeface designed by Carol Twombly and released in 2000 through Adobe. Chaparral combines the slab serif designs of the nineteenth century with sixteenth-century roman type.

Interior text design by Wendy Holdman.